China and Its People
in Early Photographs

AN UNABRIDGED REPRINT OF THE CLASSIC 1873/4 WORK

BY

JOHN THOMSON
WITH A NEW FOREWORD BY JANET LEHR

D1613786

DOVER PUBLICATIONS, INC.
NEW YORK

Published in Canada by General Publishing Company, Ltd., 30 Lesmill Road, Don Mills, To-
ronto, Ontario.

Published in the United Kingdom by Constable and Company, Ltd., 10 Orange Street, London
WC2H 7EG.

This Dover edition, first published in 1982, is an unabridged republication of *Illustrations of
China and Its People,* as originally published in London by Sampson Low, Marston, Low, and
Searle (Vols. I & II, 1873; Vols. III & IV, 1874). The page sequence has been somewhat altered
from the original.

The Publisher is grateful to Janet Lehr, of Janet Lehr, Inc., 1411 Third Avenue, New York,
N.Y. 10028, for making her copy of the rare original available for direct offset photography, and
for writing a new Foreword specially for the present edition.

Manufactured in the United States of America
Dover Publications, Inc., 180 Varick Street, New York, N.Y. 10014

Library of Congress Cataloging in Publication Data

Thomson, John, F.R.G.S.
  China and its people in early photographs.

  Reprint. Originally published: Illustrations of China and its people. London: S. Low, Marston,
Low, and Searle, 1873-1874.
  Bibliography: p.
  1. China—Description and travel—To 1900—Views. 2. Thomson, John F.R.G.S. I. Title.
DS709.T475   1982   951′.03′0222   82-4587
ISBN 0-486-24393-1   AACR2

FOREWORD TO THE DOVER EDITION

Illustrations of China and Its People, published in 1873/4 after the return to England of its author, John Thomson (1837–1921), was the culmination of his efforts in photographing China from 1862 to 1872. Traveling with the specific goal of making a photographic record of the Orient, Thomson had also worked in Malacca, Cambodia, Siam and Formosa. With its 200 illustrations enhanced with text, *China and Its People* was a fairly comprehensive pictorial encyclopedia of the region.

John Thomson brought with him the photographic equipment of his day, the wet-plate outfit. Single plates had to be sensitized just before exposure, then quickly exposed while still wet or they would suffer loss of sensitivity. But even this cumbersome process, practiced under very primitive conditions, was relatively easy to master compared with controlling the dread in the minds of his subjects. "I was frequently looked upon as a forerunner of death," Thomson writes, "as a sort of Nemesis in fact; and I have seen unfortunates stricken with superstitious dread, fall down on bended knees and beseech me not to take their likeness or their life with the fatal lens of my camera." In his travel memoirs *Straits of Malacca, Indo-China, and China* he writes simply that his photographs were "of characteristic scenes and types."

Not allowing the complexities and wonders of Asia to awe or distract him, he honed his eye and exerted a harsh self-discipline. During the decade spent photographing in China, John Thomson produced several volumes: the *Antiquities of Cambodia*, which appeared in 1867; *Visit of His Royal Highness, the Duke of Edinburgh*, 1869; *Views of the North River*, 1870; and *Views on the River Min*. Thomson emerged as a great documentary photographer, always able to sublimate his personality and to allow the essence of his subject to register clearly.

In 1872 Thomson returned home with his wife, an English girl whom he met and wed in China. Six fruitful years followed which saw the completion of his work in China with the publication in 1873/4 of *Illustrations of China and Its People* in four volumes, as well as the development and completion of other important projects. In 1876 his translation of Gaston Tissandier's *History and Handbook of Photography* appeared in print. This last, a standard reference work, recognized today for its broad scope and clarity, is a credit to the directness and insight of John Thomson. A documentary of London street types, entitled *Street Life in London*, was published in 1877, as was his verbal record of the decade in China.

Having completed the tasks that had kept him in England, Thomson departed for Cyprus. In 1878 the product of this last adventure, *Through Cyprus with a Camera*, was published. Returning then to England, he ended a prolific career as a street photographer and settled into a comfortable life in London photographing on commission. His subsequent appointments as photographer to Her Imperial Majesty Queen Victoria and as a photographic adviser to the Royal Geographic Society were recognition of the regard in which his work was held.

JANET LEHR

VOLUME I

INTRODUCTION.

MY design in the accompanying work is to present a series of pictures of China and its people, such as shall convey an accurate impression of the country I traversed as well as of the arts, usages, and manners which prevail in different provinces of the Empire. With this intention I made the camera the constant companion of my wanderings, and to it I am indebted for the faithful reproduction of the scenes I visited, and of the types of race with which I came into contact.

Those familiar with the Chinese and their deeply-rooted superstitions will readily understand that the carrying out of my task involved both difficulty and danger. In some places there were many who had never yet set eyes upon a pale-faced stranger; and the literati, or educated classes, had fostered a notion amongst such as these, that, while evil spirits of every kind were carefully to be shunned, none ought to be so strictly avoided as the " Fan Qui " or " Foreign Devil," who assumed human shape, and appeared solely for the furtherance of his own interests, often owing the success of his undertakings to an ocular power, which enabled him to discover the hidden treasures of heaven and earth. I therefore frequently enjoyed the reputation of being a dangerous geomancer, and my camera was held to be a dark mysterious instrument, which, combined with my naturally, or supernaturally, intensified eyesight gave me power to see through rocks and mountains, to pierce the very souls of the natives, and to produce miraculous pictures by some black art, which at the same time bereft the individual depicted of so much of the principle of life as to render his death a certainty within a very short period of years.

Accounted, for these reasons, the forerunner of death, I found portraits of children difficult to obtain, while, strange as it may be thought in a land where filial piety is esteemed the highest of virtues, sons and daughters brought their aged parents to be placed before the foreigner's silent and mysterious instrument of destruction. The trifling sums that I paid for the privilege of taking such subjects would probably go to help in the purchase of a coffin, which, conveyed ceremoniously to the old man's house, would there be deposited to await the hour of dissolution, and the body of the parent whom his son had honoured with the gift. Let none of my readers suppose that I am speaking in jest. To such an extreme pitch has the notion of honouring ancestors with due mortuary rites been carried in China, that an affectionate parent would regard children who should present him with a cool and comfortable coffin as having begun in good time to display the duty and respect which every well-regulated son and daughter is expected to bestow.

The superstitious influences, such as I have described, rendered me a frequent object of mistrust, and led to my being stoned and roughly handled on more occasions than one. It is, however, in and about large cities that the wide-spread hatred of foreigners is most conspicuously displayed. In many of the country districts, and from officials who have been associated with Europeans, and who therefore appreciate the substantial benefits which foreign intercourse can confer, I have met with numerous tokens of kindness, and a hospitality as genuine as could be shown to a stranger in any part of the world.

It is a novel experiment to attempt to illustrate a book of travels with photographs, a few years back so perishable, and so difficult to reproduce. But the art is now so far advanced, that we can multiply the copies with the same facility, and print them with the same materials as in the case of woodcuts or engravings. I feel somewhat sanguine about the success of the undertaking, and I hope to see the process which I have thus applied adopted by other travellers; for the faithfulness of such pictures affords the nearest approach that can be made towards placing the reader actually before the scene which is represented.

The letter-press which accompanies the pictures, and which will render them, as I trust, more interesting and more intelligible, is compiled from information derived from the most trustworthy sources, as well as from notes either made by me at the time the subjects were taken, or gathered during a residence of nearly five years in China.

I have endeavoured to arrange these notes and illustrations as far as possible in the natural order or sequence of my journeys, which extended over a distance, estimated roughly, of between 4,000 and 5,000 miles.

I shall start from the British colony of Hong-Kong, once said to be the grave of Europeans, but which now, with its city of Victoria, its splendid public buildings, parks and gardens, its docks, factories, telegraphs and fleets of steamers, may be fairly considered the birthplace of a new era in eastern civilization. I will next proceed by the Pearl river to Canton, the city above all others possessing the greatest historical interest to foreigners, as the scene of their early efforts to gain a footing in the country. Thence I will cross to Formosa, an island which, by its tropical luxuriance and by the grandeur of its mountain scenery, deserves the name "Isla Formosa" which the early Portuguese voyagers conferred upon it. At Taiwan the ruin of the old fort Zelandia will be found both curious and interesting; it was the stronghold from which Koksinga, the famous Chinese adventurer, succeeded in driving the Dutch, some of whom are said to have sought shelter among the aborigines, who still possess old Dutch documents, and have traditions about the doings of their kind-hearted, red-haired brothers. This island is daily rising in importance, as the recent development of its resources is fostering a growing trade at the open ports, and it is destined to play a leading part in the future as one of the great coal-fields of China.

Crossing to the mainland, I will visit Swatow and Chow-chow-fu, noted for the quality of their sugar and rice, for their turbulent clans, and for village wars that remind one of the feudal times of Scotland.

I shall then pass northward to Amoy, one of the first ports visited by foreigners, remarkable in modern times as that part of the Fukien province from which a constant tide of emigration flows to the Straits of Malacca and to America, and noticeable also for the independent character of its people, as among the last who succumbed to the Tartar yoke. The river Min will here afford examples of the grand mountain scenery to be found in the Fukien province, and will form an attractive portion of the work, as the great artery which carries an annual supply of about seventy million pounds of tea to the Foochow market.

Following the route northward the reader will next be introduced to Shanghai, the greatest of the treaty ports of China, where, within a few years, a foreign settlement has sprung up, on the banks of the Woosang, of such vast proportions, as to lead a visitor to fancy that he has been suddenly transported to one of our great English ports; the crowd of shipping, the wharves, warehouses, and landing-stages, the stone embankment, the elegance and costliness of the buildings, the noise of constant traffic in the streets, the busy roads, smooth as a billiard-table, and the well-kept garden that skirts the river affording evidence of foreign taste and refinement, all tending to aid the illusion. One has only, however, to drive beyond the foreign settlement to dispel the dream, and to find the native dwellings huddled together, as if pressed back to make way for the higher civilization that has planted a city in their midst. Leaving Shanghai, I will proceed to Ningpo and Snowy Valley, the favourite spring resort of Shanghai residents, and justly celebrated for the beauty of its azaleas, its mountain scenery, its cascades and waterfalls; thence to the Yangtsze Kiang, visiting *en route* the treaty ports and the ancient capital, Nankin, passing through the weird scenery of the gorges of the Upper Yangtsze, and penetrating as far as Kwei-chow-fu. The concluding journey will embrace Chefoo, the Peiho, Tientsin and Peking. The remarkable antiquities, the palace, temples, and observatory; the different races in the great metropolis; the ruins of the Summer Palace and the Ming Tombs shall be presented to the reader: after which I will guide him through the Nankow Pass, and take my leave of him at the Great Wall.

VOL. I

LIST OF ILLUSTRATIONS.

LIST OF ILLUSTRATIONS.

Vol. I, Plate I

PRINCE KUNG.

RINCE KUNG, now about forty years of age, is the sixth son of the Emperor Tao Kwang, who reigned from A. D. 1820 to 1850. He is a younger brother of the late Emperor Hien-foong, and, consequently an uncle to the reigning Emperor Tung-che. Prior to 1860 he was little known beyond the precincts of the Court: but, when the Emperor fled from the summer palace, it was he who came forward to meet the Ministers of the Allied Powers, and negotiate the conditions of peace. He holds several high civil and military appointments, the most important that of member of the Supreme Council, a department of the Empire resembling most nearly the Cabinet with us. Quick of apprehension, open to advice, and comparatively liberal in his views, he is the acknowledged leader of that small division among Chinese politicians who are known as the party of progress.

Independently of his various offices, Prince Kung, as his title denotes, is a member of the highest order of Chinese nobility; an expression which, to prevent misconception, we must beg our readers' permission to explain. There have been from the most ancient times in China five degrees of honour, to which men whose services have been eminent may attain; the titles vesting, as we should say, in remainder to their heirs male. The latter, however, cannot succeed without revival of their patent, and even then, as a rule, the title they succeed to is one degree less honourable than that of their predecessor; so that were the usage in vogue with us a dukedom would dwindle to a baronetcy in five generations.

The Manchu family, which rules the country, or to speak more correctly those of the stock who are within a certain degree of the Imperial line, have no less than eighteen orders of nobility, liable, however, like the old system spoken of above, to gradual extinction, except in a few particular instances where the patent ensures the title in perpetuity.

Prince Kung received such a patent in 1865.

HONG-KONG.

HONG-KONG is one of a group of islands situated a little north of the mouth of the Canton or Pearl river. It is about ten miles long, by four and a-half in breadth, and of igneous formation. From east to west, along its entire length, there runs a central rocky ridge or spine, chiefly composed of granite, and broken up into a series of jagged peaks, whose greatest elevation is 1,900 feet. Viewed from a distance, Hong-Kong may be readily distinguished from the islands which surround it by the bold outlines, and superior altitude, of its hills. The contrast in many cases being as striking as that between the islands of Arran and Bute. The granite in some parts of the island is in a state of disintegration; but great masses of the solid stone are to be found, and have proved of service in the construction of the forts, the docks, and the city of Victoria. The latter is to the north of the island, on the slope of the hill named Victoria Peak, and faces that portion of the mainland which is known as British Kowloon. The Kowloon coast here, and the northern shore of Hong-Kong, combine to form one of the finest harbours in the world, having a space of over six miles in length by two in breadth, available for the safe anchorage of the largest ships. The view which fronts this page is taken from the residence of Messrs. Jardine, Matheson and Co. at East Point. In the immediate foreground is shown the entrance to Wong-nei-chong or Happy Valley, noted for its picturesque hill scenery, its race-course, and its cemetery for Europeans. The eminence to the left is Morrison's Hill, crowned with a row of substantially built foreign residences, and commanding an extensive and imposing view of the city and ports.

Victoria, with its long line of wharves and warehouses, its public buildings, and its private residences in elegant rows, is seen resting on the slope of the hill; while characteristic masses of fleecy cloud are wrapped around the peak above. The masts of the shipping, which rise like a forest about the Victoria promontory, may give the reader some conception of the magnitude of our trade at Hong-Kong. By the treaty of Nankin, in 1842, the island was ceded to the British, and was erected into a colony on the 5th of April, 1843.

Previous to the above dates Hong-Kong was as barren and uninteresting as the islands around it at the present day, where one can find nothing more than a few fishing hamlets, enjoying, however, a degree of prosperity unknown before the advent of the British flag. There is only one ancient privilege the loss of which these villagers, it may be, deplore. Those among them who wore the peaceful garb of fishermen used to vary their pursuits, a little more than twenty-five years ago, by engaging in piracy when opportunities occurred. So confirmed is their relish for buccaneering, that, in spite of the heavy penalties now imposed upon the crime, it has not yet been completely rooted out; and, although much rarer, we still hear of piratical outrages in or near the very harbour of Hong-Kong. Such notices as the following, not unfrequent during the early history of the colony, are happily seldom met with in the present day: —" In March, 1846, a large body of pirates, some eighty in number, plundered the village of Shek-pai-wan,"[1] now known to foreigners as Aberdeen, and boasting an extensive dock. " On the 25th of April, 1854, a severe encounter took place between the police and a gang of hill robbers at Shek-pai-wan, in which several of the robbers were shot."[2] " Twenty-two piracies are noted in Hong-Kong waters between the 1st November, 1856, and 15th January, 1857."[3]

On the 15th January, 1857, an attempt was made to poison the entire foreign community by the Chinese bakers, who introduced arsenic into the bread. Had the drug been admixed in smaller quantities, an awful catastrophe might have taken place. But the presence of the poison was so easily detected, that public criers, promptly sent round, were in time to prevent many from taking the bread. These bakers had, no doubt, been bribed by more influential parties; but we believe few, if any, of the offenders were punished for the crime. When to the foregoing calendar of horrors we add the malignant fever, which swept off foreigners by the score, due, as was supposed, to the noxious gases exhaled from the surfaces of decomposed granite laid bare during the erection of the city, we must admit that the island fairly earned its reputation as the grave of Europeans.

---

[1] " Treaty Ports of China and Japan," p. 60.　　　[2] *Ibid.* p. 68.　　　[3] *Ibid.* p. 73.

Both it and the native inhabitants have undergone marvellous changes within the last twenty-five years. A splendid town has been built out of its barren rocks; and the hill-sides are covered with trees, which not only enhance the picturesqueness of the place, but are of great value in purifying the air, and improving the health of the population. In morality, too, it has undergone a change; though perhaps not quite so marked, as the organization of the police has become more perfect, while the good feeling and interest of the wealthy and respectable class of native residents have been enlisted in the suppression of crime.

The bands of desperate ruffians that used to infest the island are fast disappearing, although Hong-Kong still holds its own in crimes below piracy and assassination. The terrors of the law are insufficient to suppress pilfering and petty larceny, practised among domestic and other servants; and perjury constantly recurs, as the lower ranks of natives deem it fully as meritorious to benefit their friends by swearing to a lie as it would be criminal to injure them by telling the truth on oath. Under British rule, the population of Hong-Kong had increased from 7,450 in 1841, to 125,504, as returned by the census of 1865.[1] The resident foreign community is estimated at over 2,000, principally Europeans and Americans; few, if any, having been born at the place. The majority of these men are engaged in trade, and only reside in Hong-Kong long enough to obtain a competency with which they may retire to their native land. The facilities of transit now afforded by the various lines of steamers render a trip home so inexpensive and expeditious, that those who can afford it frequently avail themselves of a run to the old country; the more so as the increased commercial activity and competition of the present day have lengthened indefinitely the period of residence necessary for the accumulation of even a modest fortune.

---

[1] "Treaty Ports of China and Japan," p. 17.

Vol. I, Plate II

HONG-KONG HARBOUR.

IN this view, taken when H. R. H. the Duke of Edinburgh visited Hong-kong in 1869, H. M. S. Galatea is seen at anchor off Peddar's Wharf. Those familiar with the place will readily recognize the well-known range of hills that shelters the harbour on the Kowloon side; and few who were present when the Duke was landing will forget the scene that was then presented in the harbour. Ships of all nations vied in the splendour of their decorations; long lines of merchant boats guarded the approach to the wharf; and on a thousand native crafts, adorned with flags and shreds of gaudy cloth, appeared the dusky multitudes of the floating population, swarming over the decks, or clinging to the rigging of their vessels. The wharves too, and landing stages, were covered with a sea of yellow faces, all eager to catch a glimpse of the great English prince. Nor can I forget the regret expressed by some at finding that he was only a man after all, attired in the simple uniform of a captain; with no display of purple and fine linen, and with none of the mystic emblems of royalty to hedge his dignity around. A very different being this, surely, from the offspring of their own great Emperor, who is brother of the sun, and kinsman to the moon, on whose radiant countenance no common mortal can look and live.

The harbour, although sheltered by the hills of the mainland and Hong-kong, as well as by the islands round about, often suffers from the violence of the typhoons which are common during winter to the China seas.

During the typhoon months, the floating population, which numbers about 30,000 souls, carefully study the indications of the weather, and can calculate with great shrewdness the near approach of a storm. They usually, however, verify their own observations by ascertaining the barometrical changes from the foreign ship-captains in port. When they have settled in their own minds that a storm is coming on, the boats and fishing population cross the harbour "en masse," and shelter in the bays of Kowloon until the fury of the hurricane is spent. Round the harbour the scenery is remarkably picturesque, and picnic parties during the cold season find many a pleasant retreat among the islands, particularly Green Island and Wong-chuen-chow, or amid the woody hills and fertile valleys which diversify the mainland of Kowloon.

Vol. I, Plate III

A HONG-KONG SEDAN CHAIR.

THERE are no cabs in Hong-Kong; sedan chairs are the only public conveyances. The newly-arrived resident seldom takes kindly to this substitute for the wheeled vehicles of home, and is for a time affected with a sentiment of compassion towards the unfortunate men who bear him about on their shoulders. This, however, soon wears off: he feels the necessity of rest after a hard day's work in a hot, trying climate, and marks the happy, contented faces of the sturdy chair-bearers who clamour, all unconscious of degradation, for the favour of his regular patronage, and for the trifle which is to be paid for his fare. Chair-stands are to be found at all the hotels, at the corners of the chief thoroughfares, as well as on the wharves, where the eager chair-coolies pounce upon each freshly-arrived stranger as he lands at the port. These bearers vie with each other in keeping their chairs clean and attractive-looking, and in displaying to advantage the muscular proportions of their well-formed limbs, never weary of climbing the steep and tortuous streets, or the scorching pathways that wind about the hill. They address all sailors by the familiar cognomen of "Jack," while strangers in more costly attire come under the designation of "Captain." Simple are the habits of these chair-coolies! During the greater part of the year they have no settled dwelling, and sleep in the open air, at some spot where they will wake to find business early astir. They find their food cooked and ready at the street stalls, and they easily procure substitutes when they wish a few days' leisure and enjoyment.

Public chairs are licensed, and each carries a printed tariff of charges exposed in the chair, ranging from ten cents for the lowest fare to two dollars for the day. Sedan chairs have been in use in China from ancient times, and at the present day, in all parts of the country, they are looked upon as an important article in a civil officer's equipment, the rank of the owner being indicated by the number of bearers and followers attached to his sedan. Military officers are not permitted to employ chairs; if they do not care to walk, they are at liberty to use horses.

In some parts of the interior, as, for example, in the mountainous country above Ningpo, chairs of a lighter build are used for the ascent of the hills; these consist of a simple seat of ratan fixed to two bamboo poles, and having a narrow board slung from the chair by two cords for the purpose of resting the feet.

The chair of most importance is the Bridal chair. It is richly ornamented and gilded, and is hung with red silk curtains, which screen the blushing fair one, on the day of marriage, from the intrusive vulgar gaze. These Bridal chairs, as well as the gaudy paraphernalia suitable for the occasion, are hired from a contractor.

A CHINESE SCHOOL-BOY.

GOVERNMENT Schools for the education of native boys have long been established in different parts of Hong-Kong, and, in conjunction with the schools of the various Christian missions, contain about 2,000 boys, who receive an ordinary English education, such as fits them for useful employment as interpreters, compradores, treasurers, or clerks. The position these educated Chinamen fill in our official and commercial establishments could not well be undertaken by Europeans, for the Chinaman possesses a knowledge of the language and habits of his countrymen which a foreigner can never acquire, while his acquaintance with English is rarely sufficient to raise him above the status of a very careful painstaking copying clerk or accountant; although, versed as he is in our method of accounts, and quite at home in the equally perfect system of his own country, he proves in our mercantile offices a most valuable acquisition.

I have heard the industry and aptitude of the Chinese school-boy highly praised by those who have had experience in teaching European children and natives of the country side by side; and I am assured that, notwith-

Vol. I, Plate IV

Vol. I, Plate VI

standing the obvious disadvantages under which the native labours in having to acquire a foreign language and foreign habits of thought, his capacity for learning is so great that it will sustain him neck and neck in the race with his European rival.

There are a number of schools in different parts of the country, supported by the Chinese Government, in which foreign languages and sciences are taught by foreign and native professors. The most important, probably, is the College at Peking, under the supervision of Dr. Martin. There is also an extensive training-school at Foochow, where the pupils are taught naval architecture, engineering, mechanics, and the science of navigation. In this school the theoretical training is reduced to practice in the construction of steamers on the most approved foreign models, and by employment in actual navigation.

A CHINESE GIRL.

THE education of the girls of a Chinese family is conducted within the domestic circle. They are strictly secluded, and consequently Chinese history offers few examples of women who have been distinguished for their literary attainments. In the higher orders of society ladies here and there receive an education which enables them to form some slight acquaintance with the literature of their country, and to conduct and express themselves according to the strict and formal rules of etiquette which pertain to their position as the daughters or wives of men of learning and cultivation. In a few cases they are taught elegant accomplishments, playing on the lute, for example, that they may charm the leisure hours of their lords with song, but the science to which they devote themselves with most assiduity is the knowledge of the mysteries of cosmetics and the toilet; how to paint to the proper tint, finishing with the bright vermilion spot on the under lip; how to poise the quivering ornaments of kingfisher plumes or sprays of pearls about the coiffure; how to walk with grace on their tiny feet, and to sit down without furling or disarranging a fold of their silken attire. The women of the lower classes are seldom taught anything beyond the duties of the household, or the more arduous work of bearing burdens or labouring with the men of their family in the fields. Tea-picking, and the rearing of the silk-worm, are also female occupations. Such an education as this, however, is not unsuited for their lowly station in life, as they are trained to strict habits of industry and domestic economy.

A HONG-KONG ARTIST.

LUMQUA was a Chinese pupil of Chinnery, a noted foreign artist, who died at Macao in 1852. Lumqua produced a number of excellent works in oil, which are still copied by the painters in Hong-Kong and Canton. Had he lived in any other country he would have been the founder of a school of painting. In China his followers have failed to grasp the spirit of his art. They drudge with imitative servile toil, copying Lumqua's or Chinnery's pieces, or anything, no matter what, just because it has to be finished and paid for within a given time, and at so much a square foot. There are a number of painters established in Hong-Kong, but they all do the same class of work, and have about the same tariff of prices, regulated according to the dimensions of the canvas. The occupation of these limners consists mainly in making enlarged copies of photographs. Each house employs a touter, who scours the shipping in the harbour with samples of the work, and finds many ready customers among the foreign sailors. These bargain to have Mary or Susan painted on as large a scale and at as small a price as possible, the work to be delivered framed and ready for sea probably within twenty-four hours. The painters divide their labour on the following plan. The apprentice confines himself to bodies and hands, while the master executes the physiognomy, and thus the work is got through with wonderful speed. Attractive colours are freely used; so that Jack's fair ideal appears at times in a sky-blue dress, over which a massive gold chain and other articles of jewellery are liberally hung. These pictures would be fair works of art were the drawing good, and the brilliant colours properly arranged; but all the distortions of badly taken photographs are faithfully reproduced on an enlarged scale. The best works these painters do are pictures of native and foreign ships, which are wonderfully drawn. To enlarge a picture they draw squares over their canvas corresponding to the smaller squares into which they divide the picture to be copied. The miniature painters in Hong-Kong, and Canton do some work on ivory that is as fine as the best ivory painting to be found among the natives of India, and fit to bear comparison with the old miniature painting of our own country, which photography has, now-a-days, in a great measure superseded.

I shall have occasion to notice Chinese art and artists in a subsequent portion of this work.

THE CLOCK-TOWER, HONG-KONG.

THE clock-tower, designed by Mr. Rawlings in 1861, is a great ornament to the city, the clock too, when regulated properly, is of no inconsiderable service. It has, however, been a victim to the climate, and is liable to fits of indisposition, resting from its duties at the most inconvenient seasons, as if unable to contend against the heat. The tower is seen to advantage from the harbour, and the lighted dial of the clock forms a good landmark to guide the benighted steersman to the landing steps at Pedders wharf. In the street which conducts to the clock-tower from the wharf stand several of the oldest buildings in the Colony. On the right of this picture we see the residence lately occupied by Messrs. Hunt and Co.

In the foreground, to the left, is shown a part of the west wing of the palatial-looking building erected by Messrs. Dent, when commerce was most flourishing in the settlement; this edifice is now tenanted by three separate mercantile houses. On the left, and nearest to the tower, stands the Hong-Kong Hotel, constructed after the model of the large hotels in London. It has not proved to the shareholders a very profitable undertaking, being on a scale too vast for the requirements of the place. At present it is rented and conducted by a Chinaman, and none but Chinese cooks and waiters are employed. The management is good, and the hotel comfortable. To a visitor the large dining hall presents an animated and interesting scene, and he finds on further experience that the arrangements are perfect and the fare unexceptionable. The native waiters are remarkable no less for promptitude and politeness, than for the spotless purity of their light silk or linen robes, and for the fluency of " Pidgin " English, in which they converse; this is, however, a jargon intelligible only to the residents. The younger boy-servitors pronounce with a pure English accent; they can also read, write, and reckon in our language with facility, having most of them been trained at the Government School.

The turbaned figure on the right is an Indian policeman, of whom there were at one time about 300 in the force. They are now being gradually drafted off to India, and replaced by Europeans and West-Indian negroes. These tall Indian members of the constabulary were admitted on all hands to be highly ornamental, but proved comparatively useless for the maintenance of order among the Chinese, as, with one or two notable exceptions, they could neither converse in English nor in the language of China. One or two of the chair coolies are seen waiting for a fare; and as these men perform very important services for the native and foreign community, I propose to furnish the reader with a more detailed account of them on another page.

THE PRAYA, HONG-KONG.

HE Praya (for so the Portuguese term the broad stone-faced road along the harbour in front of the city) affords a pleasant drive some miles in extent, and joins the route to Show-ke-wan in the Ly-ee-moon Pass through which we approach the port from the East. This view is taken from the front of the Parade ground, and represents the principal business part of the Praya. The block of buildings facing the water on the left are the premises of the Hong-Kong and Shanghai and Chartered Mercantile Banks. The huge edifice in the centre was erected by Messrs. Dent. The merchants commonly have their offices on the ground-floor, and reside in the chambers above; there they command an extensive view of the harbour as they promenade in spacious verandahs " when the wind bloweth in from the sea."

The architecture is massive and strong, yet the designer has managed to impart an appearance of lightness to his work, insufficient, one would fancy, to resist the typhoons which sometimes blow with incredible violence. I remember during a typhoon, when the storm was at its height, a number of foreigners attempted to rescue two women from a small China boat. Their tiny vessel was as nearly as possible in the position now occupied by the yacht in the centre of the picture, and was kept there by the desperate efforts of the boatwomen, who strove to prevent it from being dashed against the Praya wall, which, having been entirely broken by the force of the sea, presented a front of jagged blocks of granite, interspersed with the wreck of boats that had been shattered to pieces on the stones. The strength of the wind was so great as to reduce the wild raging sea nearly to a level, catching up in its fury the tops of the waves, and hurling them in blinding spray into, and over the houses. We had to cling to the lamp-posts and iron-boat stanchions, and seek shelter against the walls and doorways. Advantage was taken of a lull in the storm to fire off rockets, but these were driven back like feathers against the houses. Two long-boats were dragged to the stone pier. The first was broken and disabled the moment it touched the water; the second met with a like fate, its gallant crew being thrown into the raging sea. Every effort proved abortive, and as darkness set in the boat and the unhappy women were abandoned to their fate. Next morning the whole length of the Praya presented a scene of wreck and devastation. Many of the natives had lost their lives; and many more, all that they possessed in the world, by the destruction of their boats; for these not only form their floating dwellings, but afford the means of gaining a subsistence. Much of the distress was at once relieved by the prompt liberality of the foreign and native community. This ready open-handed liberality is a characteristic of the foreign communities of Hong-Kong and the other ports of China. A kind of Christian charity is rife among them, requiring no efforts of pulpit oratory, no eloquent private appeals, no public dinners to wake it into action. A simple notification that there is a widow or an orphan to be aided, and the sympathy and funds are forthcoming to provide for them. I must not omit to mention the flagstaff shown on the Peak above the city; one of the early institutions of the Colony, and to which a resident signalman and code of signals are attached. It is an object of solicitous attention among the European community, for it proclaims the approach of every foreign vessel as she enters the Port.

Few who have made Hong-Kong for any time their home, have not watched with earnestness the bare post and spars of the signal staff, and experienced a sense of relief, or a quickened pulsation, as they noticed the little flag unfurled, and the flash from the Peak gun, that heralded the arrival of the mail in the harbour.

BOAT GIRLS.

HESE are the two daughters of a respectable boating family. They have been trained to the use of the oar, and the management of boats, from earliest childhood. Happy for them they are not slaves, purchased by some designing dame, and destined for a worse fate than the life of careful industry common to the labouring poor of Canton.

The hat worn by the elder sister is made of ratan, closely woven, and varnished so as to render it waterproof; it affords protection from the sun as well as the rain, and serves, indeed, all the purposes of an umbrella. It has, too, this advantage, that, while it shelters the body, it gives the wearer the free use of her arms.

Hundreds of the small passenger boats that ply for hire about the wharves of Canton, are managed by young girls, whose pride it is to keep them bright and attractive-looking. Each boat has a small cabin, open in front, having its floor covered with white matting, a broad, raised seat, covered with like material, on which the passenger will find a tobacco pipe, spills, and the apparatus for procuring a light. The walls of the little cabin are adorned with pictures and small mirrors. The girls propel the boat from behind, and are separated from the passenger by a partition of wood, or bulkhead. Viewed from without, the boat has an equally attractive appearance, every board of the deck has been scoured with sand, until it rivals in whiteness the matting within, while a stand fixed on the bamboo roof of the cabin supports a little garden of favourite flowers. The girls, dressed with modest simplicity, deck their glossy black hair with some bright-coloured flower that heightens the effect of their dark eyes, and olive skins.

A CANTON BOATWOMAN AND CHILD.

ANY thousands of the population of Canton pass their lives in their boats,—in them they are born, and from them they are carried to their graves. These floating dwellings afford many advantages to their poor owners, who, had they to live on land, would be crowded into miserable makeshift hovels in the unhealthiest quarters of the city. There they would have to inhale the polluted air of a neglected neighbourhood, as even in the most fashionable localities of a Chinese city all sanitary regulations are ignored. In a boat the owner finds profitable employment for himself and his family, and in many instances, a clean, comfortable, and attractive looking home, while he can shift his anchorage at pleasure, and move to where the society may be most congenial to his tastes, enjoying a degree of social intercourse by his nightly changes unknown even to the most favoured of those who dwell upon the land. When he visits his friends his house and family go with him. In time of sickness he moors close to his physicians, in some healthy country district, where an invalid can breathe purer air; or, it may be, hard by a favourite shrine, where he can solicit the aid of its healing spirit, the efficacy of whose powers has been handed down by tradition, and on whom he implicitly relies.

The old woman in the photograph is the grandmother living with her son's family in the boat; she still works cheerfully at the oar to help the domestic earnings; and nurses, all the while, one of the grandchildren. Probably this is the eldest son, the pride of the family, and the hope of her old age. The babe is carried in a cloth slung over the shoulders, after the manner of the Chinese race, and he presses his face against the back of his bearer during his hours of sleep. This custom is so common, as to account, to some extent, for the flat faces and broad noses of the boating and labouring classes in China.

MUSICIANS.

THE theory of music was understood by the Chinese at a very early period. It is recorded in their ancient Classics,[1] that 2000 years B.C., they used six tubes to produce the sharp notes, and six for producing the flat ones in the scale. These tubes were originally made out of reeds or bamboo. Subsequently, when they became the standard measures of the notes, they constructed them of some kind of gem.[2] These tubes, which seem to embody the first idea of the organ pipes, became in time the standards of lineal measure, as well as of sound. I have lately seen in China a small organ, said to be ancient, and in some respects resembling the description of the tubes which Dr. Legge has supplied. It has a small mouthpiece, and a series of orifices on the pipes for producing the different notes. The Laos people in the north of Siam construct a simple organ of reeds at the present day.

The Chinese have a number of plaintive and pleasing airs which they sing or perform on their string and wind instruments. They do not, however, appear to understand the principles of harmony, as a band of musicians either play in unison or produce discord; a strife seeming to exist among the respective players as to who will get through the greatest number of notes in the shortest period of time. Bands of music are hired to dispel malignant spirits and other evil influences, and with, I should think, decided success if these spirits are endowed with musical taste, and appreciate the harmony of sound that, in the tragedy of " Macbeth," appears to have afforded Hecate and her dark sisters a fiendish delight.

> " And now about the cauldron sing
> Like elves and furies in a ring,
> Enchanting all that you put in !"

The two illustrations represent the Chinese violin and guitar, with the performers, who are hired on festive occasions.

---

[1] Translation of " Shoo King," Part II. Book I. Dr. Legge.

[2] One would infer from the following note to " Lalla Rookh," that the ancient Chinese possessed, not only poetical but inventive genius of a rare order. " An old commentator of the Chou-King says, the ancients having remarked that a current of water made some of the stones near its banks send forth a sound, they detached some of them, and being charmed with the delightful sound they emitted, constructed *king* or musical instruments of them."—GROSIER.

> " Through the groves, round the islands, as if all the shores
> Like those of Kathay uttered music, and gave
> An answer in song to the kiss of each wave."
> *Lalla Rookh, The Light of the Harem*, p. 301.

Vol. I, Plate VII

A CANTON JUNK.

HE term junk, applied by Europeans to all Chinese craft, whether trading vessels or ships of war, is probably derived from "jung" the Javanese word for a large boat or vessel. Chinese ships vary in dimensions, model, and appearance, in the different parts of the Empire as much as do the sailing craft of Europe. The vessel under sail on the left of the photograph is a coasting trader of Kwang-tung build, and may be regarded as one of the clipper fleet of Southern China. It looks heavy and unhandy, but it will make good sailing with a fair wind. The hull consists of a double planking or shell of wood, having the seams carefully caulked with oakum and gum damar; the latter article is largely imported from the forests of the Malayan Archipelago, Siam and Cambodia. The hull of the vessel is strengthened and held together by massive hard-wood beams or girders, sweeping in a triple row from stem to stern. The hold is divided into watertight compartments, so that were an injury sustained, and one or more compartments filled with water, the vessel might still have buoyancy left to float ashore or into dock. This junk is a fine type of its class, and has in her model something of the foreign ship, though retaining quite enough of the old Chinese build to soothe the prejudices of the nation. We can still notice the huge unwieldy rudder perforated to break the force of the sea, for the Chinese have not yet got the length of perceiving that a very much smaller rudder, fully immersed, would be quite as serviceable and infinitely less exposed to the risk of disaster. There, too, are the great eyes, and the configuration about the stem resembling the head and features of a fierce sea-monster, and intended to scare away the deep sea-demons, or huge fish, that might at any time impede the voyage. The mat sails, with their ribs of bamboo, still look like the spread wings of a huge bat, or the fiery dragon of the Celestial Mythology. Her rig, however, is not so unmanageable as appearances would imply; with a fair and willing crew the sails can be set with care and speed, while they will fall if the ropes be unfastened, and furl, without an effort, of themselves. The anchor is of hard wood that has a greater specific gravity than water. The ropes and cables are of ratan, bamboo, or palm fibre, and are so strong that they will stand as great, if not a greater strain than anything in use with us. They have the disadvantage, however, of being less flexible and not so easily stowed. These trading junks are usually well-armed, carrying, at least, half-a-dozen smooth-bore guns of foreign make for six or eight-pound shot, a number of matchlocks, and a quantity of ammunition.

These vessels are frequently owned and sailed by a party of small traders, a number of the better class of sailors having a venture in the cargo as well. This complication of petty interests and the absence of a recognized commander, or indeed of anyone scientifically trained in navigation, leads to constant disputes, and to a total disregard of discipline on the part of the crew, for these are men of the lowest social order, the more respectable and industrious of the labouring classes preferring a shore-life to the hardships and risks of the sea.

In a case of emergency, such as a storm, a consultation takes place as to the fittest mode of handling the vessel, and the decision is frequently referred for final settlement to "Machu"[1] the sailor's goddess, who has a shrine set apart for her on board. Each sailor carries about his person a small bag containing the ashes from some favourite altar of this goddess, and holds them as an infallible charm to ward off shipwreck and the diverse perils of the deep.

[1] "Social Life of the Chinese," Doolittle, vol. I. p. 262.

Vol. I, Plate VIII

It is customary before proceeding on a voyage to offer sacrifice to " Machu." A cock is decapitated, and its blood, together with some of its feathers, are stuck to the bow and foremast, a small cup of wine is at the same time cast over the bow into the sea. This ceremony of decapitating a cock is also used by the Malays, as well as the Chinese, in taking an oath. I have met with instances of this with both races when a person has been accused of uttering a falsehood, his reply being that he was prepared to take his oath over the head of a cock.

Sailing, as I have above observed, is managed, not by the study of the compass, barometer, or by astronomical observations, but by a knowledge of the currents, and headlands, and the prevailing winds of the season. The compass is used, but it is an instrument of primitive construction, having a very small tremulous needle in the centre of a disc of wood, covered with a formidable array of Chinese symbols, astrological and others. It seems strange that the reputed inventors of the mariner's compass should have left to other nations the merit of applying it to its proper scientific use.

These remarks on Chinese vessels, it must be understood, apply only to trading craft, as it will be hereafter shown that the Chinese have made much more progress in constructing vessels of war.

FRONT OF KWAN-YIN TEMPLE, HONG-KONG.

THIS is a small temple on the hill-side, to the east of the city of Victoria. It is dedicated to Kwan-yin, the goddess of mercy, and is liberally supported by the Chinese of Hong-kong. Like the majority of Chinese temples, it has been erected in a position naturally picturesque, and is surrounded by fine old trees and shady walks, commanding an extensive view of the harbour. A never-ceasing crowd of beggars infest the broad granite steps by which the temple is approached, and prey upon the charitably-disposed Buddhists, who make visits to the shrine. These beggars trade upon the knowledge that in the Buddhist it is a meritorious act to help the poor and needy. The temple front is a good specimen of the elaborate ornamentation with which these places of worship are adorned. The direct entrance to the sacred interior is barred by a heavy screen of wood, which stands about six feet within the central door. This screen is a very common piece of furniture in Chinese dwellings, as well as in temples. It serves the double purpose of securing additional privacy to the inmates, while it wards off malignant spirits, which are popularly supposed to travel in direct lines, and not by circuitous routes. Within the threshold, on the right, is a dispensing department, where an apothecary makes up the numerous prescriptions of the goddess; on the left, an aged priest disposes of the paper counterfeits for money, which are bought by the worshippers, and burned as offerings at the shrine. Kwan-yin, a female figure draped in flowing robes and wearing a benign expression of countenance, is observed in the centre of the apartment, seated in a dim recess behind the altar, on which are an array of brazen bowls, vases, lighted candles, and smouldering incense sticks. On the floor, there are a number of straw mats, for the use of the kneeling worshippers, on one of which an aged woman is bent, supplicating the goddess in behalf of a sick son. She is muttering some incoherent prayer, and from time to time looks for a favourable omen, not from the clay lips of the painted goddess,—no, poor soul! her tearful eyes are bent down with solicitude upon two plano-convex bits of bamboo, which, tossed in the air, have fallen on the floor, recording by the sides which lie uppermost a good or bad omen. She pleads with the touching fervour of a fond mother : persistently tossing the sticks of fate, she will take no denial. At length, after many turns of disappointment, she secures a good omen, and proceeds to spend her mite in offerings to Kwan-yin.

A MENDICANT PRIEST.

THIS priest is attached to the Kwan-yin Temple ; his duty is to beg for the benefit of the establishment, and to perform unimportant offices for the visitors to the shrine, lighting incense-sticks, and teaching short forms of prayer. I paid him half-a-dollar to stand for his portrait. He was very wroth, declaring the sum quite inadequate, as the picture had bereft him of a portion of his good luck, which he would require to work up again with offerings. He further informed me that a good run of praying visitors would have paid him much better for his time. He was undoubtedly of an avaricious disposition, and well up in his profession of begging. I would judge, however, from his starved miserable appearance that he was a faithful disciple of Buddha, and that a very small portion of his gains was devoted to his dress or sustenance. He is a type of thousands of the miserable, half-starved hangers-on of monastic establishments in China. Equally indispensable are tribes of loathsome beggars infesting the gates of the temples, and herds of hungry, howling dogs, that live, or die rather, on temple garbage and beggars' refuse.

A STREET IN HONG-KONG.

IN the street shown in the picture Hong-kong residents will readily recognize the semi-Chinese, semi-European roadway which leads to Wanchi, Wong-nei chong, or Happy Valley.

It is chiefly occupied by native shopkeepers, who supply the wants of the soldiers and their families, residing in the extensive barracks of the neighbourhood. Among others, there is a Chinaman who has been some years in California, where he learned the art of foreign shoe-making. He imports the leather from America, and has taught a number of workmen, whom he has in his employ, to make boots and shoes, which for general appearance, for durability, and price, will bear comparison with the best work of foreign manufacture. A number of cane-chair makers reside in the street, and drive a thriving trade with Europeans, furnishing a variety of light easy-chairs for the open verandahs of foreign houses.

In passing along the street at any hour, from sunrise to nearly midnight, one has many opportunities of observing the constant industry of the Chinese. They appear to have no set hours of labour, but work day and night until their tasks are done.

OPIUM-SMOKING IN A RESTAURANT.

THE opium pipe has become an indispensable Chinese luxury, in which the poorest find time and money to indulge. Many of the worst class of beggars are confirmed opium-smokers,—men who have been dragged down from positions of comfort or affluence by the vice. Long lost to all sense of honour and self-respect, and sunk so low as to become the begging pests of their former friends and associates, they would give the last rag that covers them to gratify their passion for the drug that has consumed their reputation, their substance, and their flesh ; such men are a prey to morbid fits of melancholy and depression, leading to frequent suicide. The mode of destroying life, most commonly resorted to by such men, Dr. Young, of Hong-kong, tells me, is by taking a dose of opium refuse or ash. This is carefully gathered, and kept by the opium-shop, or restaurant-keeper, so that it may be procured in quantity sufficient to destroy life. It is usually taken in water, after which the unfortunate will stretch himself out, to die like a dog, in a lane or dust-heap. The narcotic taken in this form is always fatal, as it adheres so tenaciously to the coating of the stomach as to prevent its removal.

The drug sold in the low public opium-shops is of inferior quality, being mixed with opium ash in its preparation. These shops or dens have a noxious atmosphere, heavy with the fumes of opium, which, added to the livid and death-like appearance of the smokers stretched upon the benches, recalls the horrors of a nightmare.

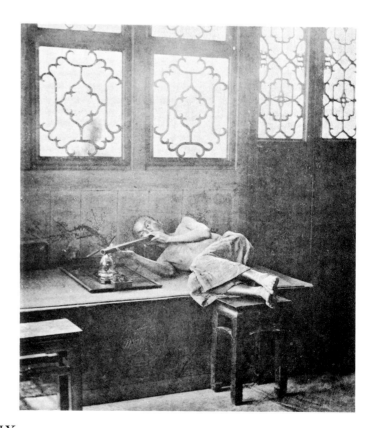

Vol. I, Plate IX

VOL. I, PLATE X

A WHIFF OF OPIUM AT HOME.

THIS picture shows the method in which opium is smoked by the wealthier classes among the Chinese. The smoker here has leisure and money at his command, so that he is able to indulge freely in the use of the drug. His opium pipe is a formidable-looking instrument, not at all resembling the "hookah" of India, or the light tobacco pipe in use with us. It consists of a metal or bamboo tube, having at one end a wide mouthpiece, and closed at the other. The bowl, of metal, or sometimes porcelain, is usually very ornamental, and has a small aperture on the top into which it receives the drug, which is prepared by the Chinese in the form of an aqueous extract, by boiling the crude opium into the consistency of thick syrup. The smoker when he takes to his pipe must literally lay himself out for his work, and this he does by stretching himself on a bed or couch of polished wood, propping his head with a pillow of the same unyielding material. Near at hand he has a small opium lamp, over which, either he or his attendant, if he can afford one, roasts the tiny pellet of opium on a needle's point before placing it in the bowl of the pipe. All being now ready, the smoker brings his opium-charged bowl once more in contact with the flame and inhales the fume into his lungs, expelling the vapour by his mouth and nostrils when it has been retained for a short time in his body. He must now abandon himself to the influences of the drug, giving up all thought of business or occupation till the effects of the narcotic have passed away.

Opium-smoking is one of the most enslaving vices, which, when it has secured its victim, gradually poisons and destroys the finer feelings of his nature, causing him to neglect his business, dispose of his property, and even sever the sacred ties of kindred by selling his wife and children into slavery so that he may gratify his ruling passion. When once indulged in it is difficult, and sometimes dangerous, to throw off the habit. Were the pipe suddenly withdrawn a painful physical re-action would set in, and death itself has been known to ensue. The smoker may wean himself from the use of opium by taking gradually diminishing inward doses of the drug, which allay the craving for the pipe; added to this, he must have nutritious food and tonics to restore the tone of his stomach. After a time his desire for the drug will pass off.

The charms of opium must at first be irresistible, as is shown by the multitude of its votaries: but when the habit has been ingrained these exhilarating influences dwindle, and a fearful craving succeeds, which the victim must satisfy at any cost. I know a remarkably clever painter of miniatures, a Hong-Kong Chinaman, who was ruined by opium-smoking at last. Five years ago I recollect him a handsome, fashionably-dressed youth; his tail a model of perfect plaiting, and his head shaven as smooth as a billiard ball. No silks were more beautiful or richer than his; while his finger nails, long as vultures' claws, were the envy of his companions and his own secret pride. This good-looking dandy was at that time in full work as a portrait-painter. Some years afterwards I fell in with him again—a shrunken, hollow-eyed, sallow-faced old man. He was still working at his craft, but only on two days a week, the rest of his time being uninterruptedly devoted to the demands of his opium pipe. This instance gives some notion as to the completeness with which the habit may master even young, successful and vigorous men. There are, I am told, many examples of temperate opium-smokers who adhere steadily to a moderate quantity of the narcotic—say a mace a day. I have no reason to doubt the statement; but, as the practice among men of this class is kept as secret as possible, it is difficult to be certain on the matter.

AFTER DINNER.

THIS is an after-dinner gathering on the verandah of a Chinaman's house. The entire domestic circle smoke tobacco, but their pipes differ from our own. The old woman and her daughter use a pipe which resembles the "hookah," having a small compartment filled with water, for cooling and purifying the smoke. Paterfamilias is fondling and sucking the end of what appears to be a very formidable walking stick; but it is in reality his favourite pipe, having a cherished history attached to it, and invested with a degree of individuality that appeals to the tenderest feelings of its proprietor. In this we have a trait that reminds us of the regard, bordering sometimes on insanity, which smokers in our own country bestow upon the blackened bowl of an ancient meerschaum. And here let me ask my reader's sympathy for a devoted husband, whom his wife's misguided behaviour drove to the verge of despair. This unfortunate woman, rejoicing, in the unselfishness of a loving nature, to see her husband delighting in a smoke, took advantage of his absence from home to prepare a little surprise ; and so his nasty black pipe was, with a world of trouble, carefully scraped, cleaned, and varnished with furniture oil. Alas! this pipe was a relic of bachelor days, a masterpiece of colouring, and mellowed by age, till its fumes were as delicate as the ripened tones of an old violin.

There is then among the Chinese the same after-dinner companionship in smoking which in our own country strengthens the social ties ; but with this important difference, that in China the ladies smoke. Among people of higher rank the water-pipe is filled and brought in by a servant, who, waiting till a pause occurs in conversation, adroitly inserts the stem into her mistress's mouth. This custom, to an "outer barbarian," may at first seem strange, and doubly so, perhaps, when he perceives with dismay the swallowed smoke issuing during animated talk from the ladies' nostrils and mouth, belched forth in jets, as if to add force and piquancy to the conversation.

READING FOR HONOURS.

THE rule in China, from the earliest times, has been to confer rank and honours of the highest grade only on men distinguished for rare genius or exceptional literary attainments. By the system of periodical literary examinations established in the chief cities of the Empire, even the poorest student may win his way to a proud position in the government of his country. Who can tell how much the stability of an empire, that for countless generations has remained entire, may owe to such a system as this! Through its agency a healthy influence is diffused among the poorest of the people, binding them more closely to the governing classes, and giving all a common interest in the maintenance of order and peace. Of course, in so large a community many unsuccessful candidates for literary distinction are to be found. Such men as these support themselves by teaching ; perhaps they may have passed the lower degrees, and from failing health, incapacity, or old age, can get no further in their career. They, however, meet with universal respect, and are enabled to earn a livelihood by training others for the race. This has been the lot of the venerable scholar in the photograph. He is convinced that there must have been some mistake, or some underhand influences operating in the examinations to which he has been subjected from time to time. He still studies, however, and hopes against hope, that even yet, in his declining years, he will pass with credit to himself and his family, and hold his head with the best. This end attained, he proposes to institute new and improved regulations to suppress corruption in the examinations, and to give men such as he a fair chance of rising to the level, from which nothing but an iniquitous combination has hitherto barred his approach. We rarely find a Chinaman who has not some knowledge of reading, and few parents neglect to devote a portion of their earnings to their son's education, in the hope that his capacities may be so developed as one day to elevate him from obscurity to renown.

THE TOILET.

THE ladies of China are skilled in the use of cosmetics ; but their ways are not as our ways. No well regulated Chinese beauty would be guilty of washing her face ; it must be polished with a hot damp cloth ; when this process is over, the surface is ready to receive its coating of finely prepared white powder. This powder is made up in the solid form of a small disc, neatly fitted into an ornamental paper box, a slight pressure reducing it to a condition fit for use, when it is carefully rubbed into the cheeks, after which the smooth whitened skin is tinted with carmine. The carmine is a Chinese manufacture, and is sold in small books, each page of which is covered with a coating of the dye, and wears a glistening brown-like surface. The lady has only to moisten her finger, and apply it to this pigment, to obtain a beautiful flesh tint, resembling that produced by the coal-dye sold in crystals in this country and designed for a similar use. This she lays artistically over her powdered cheeks. Their mode of removing hair from the face is ingenious. With two fine silken cords arranged upon the fingers so as to yield to the form of the face, and at the same time act as pincers, the lady trims her eyebrows to the proper breadth, and uproots stray hairs from the cheeks, the neck, and even the forehead, if she wishes the latter to appear large and full.

The coiffure presents a variety of styles differing in the different provinces. Hereafter I shall supply some examples of these, which in every instance are most elaborate, and achieved by painstaking manipulation. Many of the patterns of the female headdress are very picturesque and might furnish our own countrywomen with hints. Before the hair is built up into shape it is stiffened with a vegetable gum contained in wooden shavings of a resinous tree, and which exudes therefrom on soaking them in water. The powder, carmine, comb, hairbrush, tooth-brush, tongue scraper, gum, hairpins, and all the other appliances of the feminine toilet, are preserved in a small brass or silver bound dressing-case carrying a mirror within the lid. I must not omit to inform my reader that false hair and even wigs are in common use among Chinese ladies. When the long black tresses have become thin and short, an artificial chignon can be had for a trifle from the barber close by ; or, if required for a lady of taste, she will have it made to order by a professional artist of her own sex.

Vol. I, Plate X

FOUR HEADS, TYPES OF THE LABOURING CLASS.

F the four heads shown in these pictures, the two upper ones are fair types of the aged labourers of China. Darby and Joan have for many years been associated together, and their life has been a uniform scene of hardships and toil. Two generations have now grown up around them, and their sons and grandsons have succeeded them as the bread-winners of the family. The old woman still busies herself in the lighter domestic duties; she is skilful with her needle, and invaluable as a nurse in time of sickness. Her hair has grown thin and white, but she still dresses it with neatness and care.

The old man, who is venerated as the head of the family, gratifies his taste for information by spelling through the cheap literature of the day. This commonly consists of what to us would appear tedious and uninteresting tales, which appeal greatly to the credulity of the reader. The popular books are printed in the more simple and elementary characters of the language, to suit the capacities of the unlettered class. The old man's eyes failed him years ago, and the use of spectacles was reluctantly forced upon him. These spectacles are of native manufacture, having larger and heavier frames than those which our great-grandfathers wore. The lenses, like our own, are double convex or double concave, to suit peculiarities of vision; and being made of the finest rock crystal, they possess advantages only appreciated by us at a comparatively recent date. It seems that the Chinese have not so extended this knowledge as to construct microscopes and telescopes. But this branch of optics is now being taught by foreigners in the Foochow Training School.

The two lower heads are those of a son and daughter belonging to the same class. The male is stripped to the waist, as is his wont during the hours of toil. His plaited queue is at such times coiled up out of the way and fixed with a bamboo bodkin at the back of the head. When work is over he will put on his jacket, and betake himself to the nearest barber's, that the front of his head may be shaved. He is a type of the coolies who used to be kidnapped and sent to South America to labour in plantations or mines. Thousands of these men have emigrated to the United States, and have there left a lasting monument to their industry in the great embankments of the Pacific Railroad.

The female head is that of an unmarried woman, engaged with her family in the management of a cargo boat, used in the loading and unloading of ships. The cloth on her head is worn as a protection from the sun. The hair of unmarried women of this class, combed back and plaited into a queue behind, is then coiled up and fastened with a silver pin. In front it is allowed to fall over the forehead, like a silken fringe. After marriage, it is dressed in the form of the old woman's coiffure shown above.

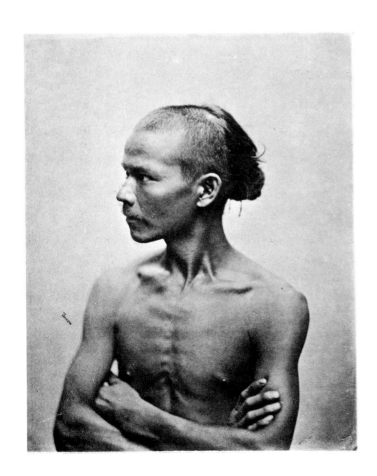

Vol. I, Plate XI

VOL. I, PLATE XII

HOI-HOW, THE PROPOSED NEW TREATY PORT, ISLAND OF HAINAN.

HAINAN is an island off the southern coast of China, and forms part of the province of Kwang-tung. Hoi-how, the chief port there, was first thrown open to foreign trade during the middle of 1872, and an English consul was thereupon appointed to reside at the post. According to the Chinese annals of the Kwang-tung province, Hainan was first occupied by the Chinese A. D. 654.[1] It was celebrated at an early period for its pearl fisheries, and is the place to which Su-Tang-po, a distinguished statesman and scholar of the eleventh century, was banished. Here, too, as in Formosa, the Chinese authorities have been put to trouble in keeping the independent tribes in check, and in both cases the aborigines have been driven back from the sea-board, to find shelter in the mountain fastnesses of the interior.

Hoi-how is situated on the north-west of the island, and the two forts shown in the photograph protect the approach to it from the river. The distance from Hong-kong is about one-and-a-half or two days' steam. The channel at the mouth of the river is a shallow and dangerous one, owing to numerous sand-bars, which are said frequently to shift. The anchorage for trading vessels is at present four miles from the city, to reach which place one must resort to small passenger-boats, which flock to provision the vessels, or to convey their passengers to Hoi-how.

The town is well-built, and, in common with many other cities of China, is surrounded by a massive wall. Its streets also appear cleaner and better kept than those on the mainland. The country, for about twenty miles inland, is flat, diversified here and there with insignificant hills. Beyond these low hill-ranges a chain of mountains appears, presenting a number of irregular peaks. Mr. Swinhoe has estimated the loftiest of them to be 7,000 feet above the sea-level.[2] " The hills we traversed were very lovely—green, chequered by lines of trees crossing one another, like a park at home in a hilly country."

The plain is well-cultivated with rice, millet, sweet potatoes, ground-nuts, and sugar, all of which are grown with great success, having every advantage of soil and climate to assist them. Rice, however, may be regarded as the chief article of produce. The island being further south, is naturally more tropical than any other part of the Kwang-tung province. The cocoa and areca-palms here grow to great perfection, and the oil of the former supplies an important article of exportation. The fruits, with the addition of the Lichee, are similar in kind and variety to those of Singapore or Malacca. The trade of the island has hitherto been entirely in the hands of native merchants.

From what little we know of the Li, or aborigines of Hainan, they appear to resemble the hill-tribes of Formosa and the " Miau-tzu " of the mountains of the mainland of China; but our information as to their habits and language is too slender to form the basis of any definite conclusions. I had two Hainau Chinamen in my employment for upwards of six years, and from them I have heard many stories of the wild mountain-tribes of their native land; but these were evidently too untrustworthy to be seriously taken into account, if we may judge by the persistence with which they affirmed that the wild mountaineers were closely allied to apes, and carried short, stumpy tails appended to their persons.

---

[1] " A History of the Kwang-tung Province, Bowra," p. 19.   [2] " Shanghai Courier," paper by Mr. Swinhoe.

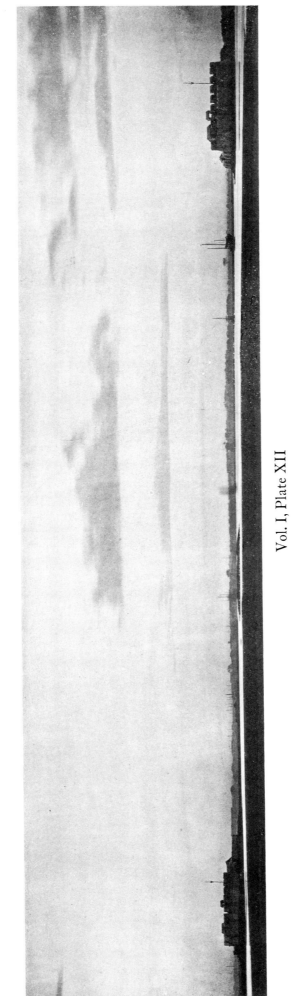

Vol. I, Plate XII

JUI-LIN, GOVERNOR-GENERAL OF THE TWO KWANG PROVINCES.

THE governor-general (Jui-Lin) of the provinces of Kwang-tung and Kwang-si, familiarly called the viceroy of Canton, from the locality in which his residence is situated, is one of the highest dignitaries in the Chinese empire, and at the same time is, perhaps, of all Chinese officials the most widely known by Europeans. A Manchu by birth, he became at an early age employed in public functions at the capital; and, having gained the favour of the Emperor Tao Kwang, he rose to high employ, reaching at length the dignity of cabinet minister, when about forty-five years of age. After occupying this post for several years, he was degraded from his rank and honours in consequence of the defeat which befell the Chinese forces at the battle of Pa-li Chiao, in October, 1860, on the advance of the British and French forces against Peking. At this engagement Jui-lin officiated as second in command, and narrowly escaped being taken prisoner. Having served subsequently to this period in the operations conducted against the Nien Fei banditti, Jui-lin was re-admitted to favour, and in 1864 was appointed to fill the important office of general commanding the Tartar garrison of Canton. In the following year he took charge of the governor-generalship or viceroyalty of the two provinces on the occurrence of a vacancy, and shortly afterwards was confirmed in this distinguished post, which he has held without intermission until the present day. The importance of his position, and the proximity of the British Colony of Hong-Kong to his seat of government, combine to bring the governor-general into frequent personal relations with European officials, with whom his intercourse has invariably been marked by perfect courtesy, and an obvious desire to cultivate friendly relations. Under his administration the provincial revenue has prospered, a degree of public tranquillity unknown for many years previously has been attained, and .ameliorations have been introduced in several departments of the public service, including the organization of a squadron of steam gunboats commanded by European officers, through which piracy, once rampant on the coast, has been almost wholly extinguished. The governor-general was restored in 1869 to the rank of cabinet minister; and in July, 1872, he was promoted to one of the highest posts in the ministry of state. He is at present about sixty-five years of age.[1]

---

[1] The above information was kindly supplied by W. F. Mayers, Esq.

Vol. I, Plate XIII

TARTAR SOLDIERS.

THE Manchus, commonly called Tartars, conquered China in 1644, but the subjugation at that date was by no means complete, and it was not until the 24th of November 1650, that Canton was taken, or rather delivered into the hands of the besiegers, by the treachery of its governor.[1] The Dutch ambassadors, who were in the city shortly after its capture, thus describe the scene:—

"It was upon the 25th of November, 1650, when the Tartars, upon this advantage, rushed with their whole army into the city, which was soon subdued by them. The besieged not being in a condition to make any resistance.

"The whole Tartar army being got into the city, the place was soon turned to a map of misery; for every one began to tear, break, and carry away whatever he could lay hands on. The cry of women, children, and aged people was so great that it exceeded all noise of such loud distraction, so that, from the 26th of November to the 15th December, there was heard no cry in the streets but, Strike, kill, and destroy the rebellious barbarians. All places were full of woful lamentations, murder, and rapine."

After the overthrow of Canton, the Tartars, following the plan which they had adopted in Peking and other cities of the Empire, established a permanant garrison composed of Tartars and of the Chinese and Mongols that had sided with them. Their encampment remains to this day, occupying about one-fourth of the entire area of the city, and still retaining a few of its original characteristics, although the descendants of the warlike conquerors have lost much of their martial bearing, by adopting the luxuries, and taking up the more objectional characteristics, of the conquered race. "In establishing an encampment there were in equal portions men of the three nations who had accompanied the conqueror from Manchurian Tartary," Manchus, Mongols and Chinese. These were divided under eight banners distinguished by colours, red, blue, yellow, and so forth. In the quarters of the Tartar city occupied by the different banner-men at Peking there is a paper lantern of the banner of the occupant placed on a stand before each door-way.

The banner-men of Canton number 1,800, many of them being extremely poor; for although their nominal pay is good, it never reaches the recipient in full. The government pittance is thus insufficient to support them, and, while during the past two centuries they have been steadily losing their national characteristics, they have scorned to imitate the patient industry of the Chinese, or to adopt their trades and occupations. Hence the great poverty and destitution in many of the mud hovels of the Tartar quarter.

Thoroughly drilled and disciplined, and with a commissariat that would provide effectively for their wants, they would still make good soldiers. Under Jui-lin, the present able governor-general of the two Kwang provinces, a number of Tartar and Chinese soldiers have been instructed in the system of European drill, and in the use of foreign arms.

The reader cannot fail to be struck with the fine manly build and soldierly appearance of the Tartar artillery-men shown in the photograph. These men formed the native guard of Sir D. B. Robertson, our consul at Canton.

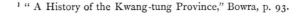

[1] "A History of the Kwang-tung Province," Bowra, p. 93.

Vol. I, Plate XIV

A CANTON LADY.

A LADY in China passes her life in strict seclusion. Her little world is her home, her companions the ladies of her own household, or relatives of her own sex. If married, she has a separate suite of apartments for herself, children, and maid servants. If she pays a visit, a sedan chair conveys her from her own door; silken curtains screen her from the public gaze; and thus protected, she is borne to the ladies' quarter in her friend's home, with jealous privacy and concealment. When seated among her friends she partakes of tea and a pipe, and displays in her conversation a far greater knowledge of the outer world than one might at first have expected. In passing through the streets her eyes have been busy between the spaces of her blinds, and she has formed her own impressions of the faces and figures as they went by. However contented she may be, her lot must at least appear monotonous to the ladies of western lands. Her life is hedged round with so many restrictions; she is not even permitted to monopolize the privilege of wearing false hair, for the gentlemen use it extensively, to add to the length and attractiveness of their queues. Neither are they free to dress as they may choose, for there is an Imperial edict which regulates her attire. I question, however, whether this law, which thus hampers the Chinese lady, is a more rigorous despot than fashion, which in our own country sways the gentler sex.

I shall have occasion to notice the Chinese ladies in a future part of the work, and I shall then show the costumes which prevail in different quarters of the Empire.

THE LADY'S MAID.

THIS maid is a slave girl, bought in childhood for a trifling sum from her poor parents, as female children are at a sad discount in many parts of China, where infanticide is still practised. This girl has been reared in the bosom of the family, and trained to wait on the ladies of the household, to attend to the children, and to make herself generally useful. In this picture she is represented on her way to market, the slave enjoying more freedom in going abroad than does her mistress. In her left hand she holds a small lacquered-ware case for cakes and confections, and in her right a huge fan to screen her from the sun. It is wonderful to notice how careful the poorest women in China are of their complexions, how they dread being tanned by the sun, and how universally the fan is employed as a sunshade, as well as for keeping down the temperature of the body; excessive heat and cold being considered two of the leading causes of disease. Even the men delight in a pale skin, and may be seen during summer wearing the fan spread out to shade the face, and fixed to the head by means of the tail.

A BRIDE AND BRIDEGROOM.

MY fair readers will gather from what has gone before that women's life in China is by no means an enviable lot. The monotony of creation with them is enlivened by none of the entertainments which ladies find indispensable in our own quarter of the globe. No balls, no concerts, conversaziones or picnics, no private theatricals, no—not even a lecture—save from a venerated husband's lips, who jealously keeps watch over their actions, and, with careful mistrustfulness, confines them within doors. It has been suggested that the custom of pinching their feet, now regarded as an essential element of female beauty in China, originated in the selfish jealousy of man. For as ladies could not be trusted to go about alone, it was considered necessary to make them cripples, so that they might never appear abroad without attendants to assist them. Be that

Vol. I, Plate XV

as it may, unmarried women have very little freedom. To choose future husbands for themselves is a foreign and barbarous custom, and never to be even dreamt of among them : and when the marriage is over they are more slaves than their bondwomen.

Before the wedding takes place, the parties most interested in the contract have little or nothing to do with the arrangements ; all is settled for them by their respective parents or guardians.

There is no period of courtship to distract a lover from his business. It is the Astrologer who has to be consulted. He, for a small consideration, pronounces that the couple are suitable, investigates their horoscopes, and fixes the wedding day. Then the blushing bride (alas, she paints !) is arrayed for the ceremony, and carried from her father's house to the bridal sedan. At the threshold she is held over the flames of a fire, to dispel, as they explained to us, any lurking devilry that might mar her future happiness. The marriage presents are paraded through the street, a band of music accompanies the litter, and away goes the bride to wed some one, no matter whom, selected by the taste of her parents. Dreary and uninteresting from beginning to end is a Chinese marriage ceremony, and in too many cases it must lead to a lifetime of disappointment and tears. In China, as in other parts of the world, ladies prefer, if they can, to get a glimpse of their intended partners. This may be done if circumstances are favourable, but frequently they never see their lord and master, until the day when they are united to him for ever. One can readily fancy that, at such times, the first sight of an ill-favoured face will create a sad feeling of disgust and disappointment.

Filial piety has a strong hold upon the people, and it is esteemed a high virtue to bear in dutiful silence such bitter crosses as these. Let us hope that the time is not distant when these women will be allowed the free use of their natural feet to aid them in the search for husbands. I can fancy I hear some lady saying, " What of their dress ? " The photograph only wants colour to answer the question. The prevailing colour of the dress is red. A bride would as soon do without paint as wed in blue. Blue is the hue of mourning in China—true, it might betoken her mood before the ceremony is over, when her blighted hopes are buried in her bosom. Still, the fair interrogant will say, " Do the creatures never dress in white ? " No, sad to relate ; they would as soon think of breakfasting on the dust of their ancestors as dressing in graveclothes for their wedding ; it is only when bereft of their husbands that they wear white robes.

I will now briefly dispose of the bridegroom by saying, that for the marriage ceremony he is at liberty to wear the robes of a mandarin, thus showing the high esteem in which the relationship imposed by marriage is held by the State, or, it may be, to denote the absolute power which from the day of marriage is vested in the husband as head of the household. He, too, wears red, in the form of a bridal scarf thrown over the shoulder. I must not omit to notice the bride's cap, with its sprays of pearls that veil her face.

It is customary for the poorer members of society to hire their bridal dresses from a costumer, whose business it is to furnish the paraphernalia for wedding and other ceremonies.

CANTON.

CANTON is the capital of Kwang-tung, the most southerly of the maritime provinces of China, and the province which, above all others, has engrossed the attention of foreign nations. The first authentic notice of Kwang-tung occurs in the native writings of the Chow dynasty, B. C. 1122.[1] The name Kwang-tung was not applied till the fifth century, when the Sung family were in possession of the imperial throne. The Buddhist bonzes, who arrived towards the close of the first century with their religious classics from India, besides being the pioneers of a new faith which has taken deep root in the empire, appear also to have led to the opening of commercial relations between their native country and China. Foreign intercourse with China is supposed to have begun with the reign of the Han emperor Hwan, A. D. 147.[2] It is recorded, however, that a practice of bringing tribute of spices from India commenced some seventy years before this. The intercourse which China has from that time held with outer nations has been subject to periodical interruptions, and its history has been one of endless strife and contention—the Chinese, on the one hand, adhering steadfastly to their policy of exclusiveness, and throwing all kinds of barriers in the way of foreign trade, while nations outside have with equal persistence applied a pressure to which the Chinese have gradually given way, and thus the mutually advantageous treaty-relations have by tardy steps been established.

Canton is situated on the north bank of the "Chu-kiang," or Pearl River, about ninety miles inland, and is accessible at all seasons to vessels of the largest size. Communication between the capital and the other parts of the province is afforded by the three branches which feed the Pearl River, and by a network of canals. A line of fine steamers plies daily between the city and Hong-Kong, and the submarine telegraph at the latter place has thus brought the once distant Kathay into daily correspondence with the Western World. It is a pleasant trip from Hong-Kong up the broad Pearl River. From the deck of the steamer one may view with comfort the ruins of the Bogue forts, and think of the time and feelings of Captain Weddell, who, in 1637, anchored the first English fleet of merchant vessels between what the Chinese, in their ignorance of the outer barbarians, regarded as the jaws of death. From this point the gallant captain, through the jealousy, misrepresentation, and slander of the Portuguese, had to fight his way up to Canton, where he was ultimately supplied with cargoes for his ships, but at such unprofitable rates that the trade was abandoned for more than twenty-five years.

The Portuguese of the Kwang-tung province had done much by their own duplicity to damage the reputation of foreigners, and to confirm the Chinese maxim, that "The barbarians are like beasts, and not to be ruled on the same principle as citizens. Were any one to attempt to control them by the great maxims of reason, it would tend to nothing but confusion. The ancient kings well understood this, and accordingly ruled barbarians by misrule. Therefore, to rule barbarians by misrule is the true and the best way of ruling them."[3] If the Chinese tried our patience by the application of the above maxim, we have returned the compliment with interest by our hard blows, and by a persevering determination which has forced them to throw open their country to the benefits of foreign trade and intercourse—benefits now beginning to show themselves in the gradual development of the natural resources of the country, and in the various branches of native industry which supply our wants. Japan has recently abandoned its long-cherished principle of isolation, courts the friendship of Western nations, adopts their arts, studies their sciences, and even remodels its religion. As the Chinese will find it inconvenient, before the lapse of many years, to have a nation so accomplished so contiguous to their shores, one is almost safe in predicting a like change in the Chinese policy, and that before the end of this century the "Great Middle Kingdom" will have been brought within the pale of that higher civilization whose existence it has so sedulously ignored.

---

[1] Bowra's "Kwang-tung Province," p. 3.　　　[2] *Ibid.* p. 8.　　　[3] "The Chinese," Davis, p. 28.

THE OLD FACTORY SITE, CANTON.

IN 1684 a small patch of land on the bank of the river at Canton was granted to the East India Company, with permission to erect a factory there, provided all their traders and trading operations were strictly confined within its circuit. This site, with its present boundary-wall and buildings, surrounded by the miserable makeshift huts of the poorest class of the population, is shown in the photograph annexed. It now forms the American Concession Ground, and its buildings are occupied by Messrs. Russel, and by Messrs. Smith Archer, two of the oldest American houses in China. The appearance of this site in 1751 is well described in Osbeck's "Voyage," where some account may be found of the many dangers and disadvantages to which the merchants of a century ago were constantly exposed. They were restricted from entering the city, and were also held responsible for the payment of the heavy duties on merchandise. Their profits, however, in those days were so enormous as to enable them to retire in affluence after effecting one or two successful shipments. Time has wrought great changes since. While the city of Canton and its people have remained *in statu quo*, a vast foreign trade has sprung up, and multitudes of pale-faced merchants now transact their business with all the facilities which steamboats, telegraphs, and a thoroughly organized system of imperial Customs afford. But rapid fortunes are much more rarely accumulated now than when the factories were flourishing in years gone by. Sha-mien, the British Concession Ground, has taken the place of the "Factory Site;" and its green sward, its rows of trees, its flower-garden and promenade fronting the river, its elegant stone residences, and well-built church, would not disgrace a fashionable suburb in London.

The repellent policy of the Chinese Government subjected foreigners to much humiliation, and ended in a declaration of war in 1839. Canton was ransomed when on the point of being captured by the British forces in 1841, and peace was thereupon re-established by the treaty of Nankin. Notwithstanding the terms of the treaty, the Chinese persisted in closing Canton against foreigners, and their obstinacy culminated in fresh hostilities in 1856. On the 15th of December in that year, the houses on the "Factory Site" were pillaged and burned—on the 29th December the city was captured by the allied forces of England and France, and occupied till 1861.

Canton, although boasting of a great antiquity, has few ancient monuments to show, owing to the perishable nature of the material out of which the houses and public buildings have been constructed. Its wall is about six miles in circuit and thirty feet in height, built of brick on a basement of granite, and backed by an embankment of earth. An inner wall, running east and west, divides the enclosure into the old and new city, the former being approached by four gates, and the latter by twelve. The present population of Canton is estimated at one million.

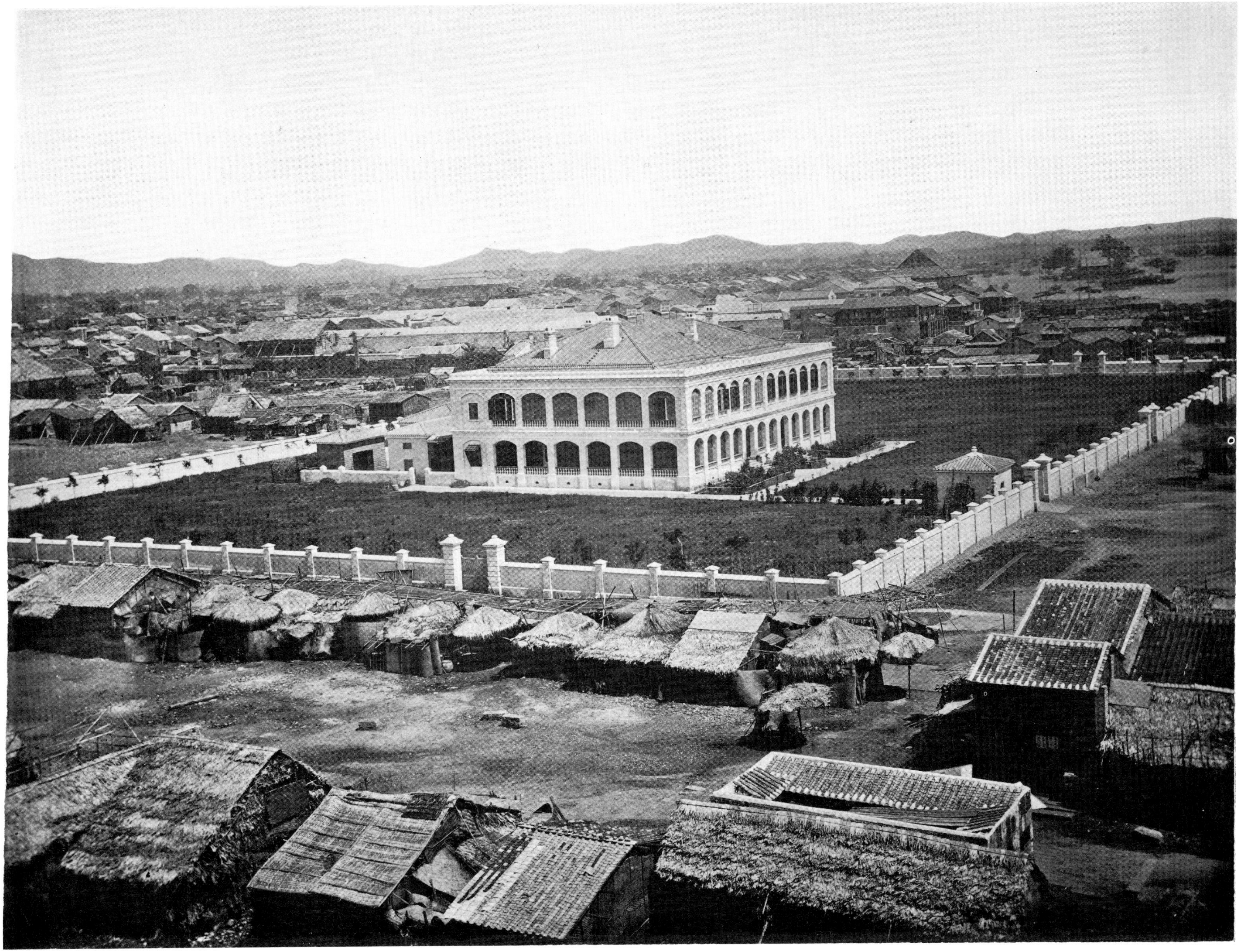

Vol. I, Plate XVI

THE BRITISH CONSULAR YAMUN, CANTON.

THE yamuns, or residences of the governor-general and other high officers of the province, are situated in the Tartar quarter of the city. The area covered by each of these yamuns is considerable, for it includes, besides the private dwelling of the mandarin, the courts and offices of his departments in the administration.

We enter the governor-general's yamun by a triple gateway, and pass through a series of paved and highly ornamental courts, overshadowed by the rich foliage of venerable trees, by groves of bamboo, and the huge leaves of the banana. These courts conduct us straight to the official reception hall; beyond this, and approached by a succession of passages adorned with quaint vase-shaped doorways, and a profusion of wood panels carved in the most exquisite designs, are the private gardens and apartments of His Excellency's household. These gardens are embowered in trees, beneath which are pleasant shady walks, winding now round lotus pools, now between strange porcelain walls mantled with a variety of flowering shrubs. Here and there we come upon a little rocky retreat, covered with moss, fern, and lichen; the whole representing the perfection of Chinese landscape gardening; though to a foreigner more attractive for the novelty and beauty of its detail than for the general effect of the whole.

The British Consulate is formed by the rear-half of the Tartar general's yamun. A wall encloses a space of six or seven acres, laid out, for the most part, as a garden or park. In this park are arbours of fine old trees, which afford shade to a herd of deer, so tame that they will feed from their keeper's or the consul's hands.

The consular residence is entered by a round opening in the wall, through which we catch a glimpse, as we approach, of a court adorned with rockeries, of gold fish in vases, and of pots of rare shrubs set in ornamental china stands. The house itself consists of two flats, and is purely Chinese in its construction. The only other buildings of importance in the enclosure are a suite of apartments built in a row, and approached by granite steps, frequently used for the accommodation of visitors. The consular offices and residences of the junior members of the consulate are situated on the British concession of Shamien.

This photograph is taken from the steps of the row of buildings just noticed, showing a portion of the garden; and, in the centre, the ruined gable of a palace, occupied about two centuries ago by the son-in-law of the Manchu conqueror. The pagoda is known to the Chinese as the " Flowery ornate" Pagoda. It is one of the oldest in the south of China, and is said to have been erected during the reign of Wu-Ti, A. D. 537. Its shape is octagonal, it has nine stories, and is 170 feet high. It was scaled in 1859 by some British sailors, but the natives are not allowed to run the risk of an ascent.

A CANTONESE PAWN-SHOP.

THE Pawnbroker establishments of the Kwang-tung Province recalled the high square towers I have seen in Scotland, and which, in ancient times, were used as strongholds and places of defence. The square tower in the illustration is a specimen of the pawn-shops throughout the South of China, which lift their heads above the houses, and mark the site of the villages that are scattered over the plains of Kwang-tung. The tower stands close to the side of the old Canton factories, uprearing its bare sides from a plot of ground which is encircled by a lofty wall; while the door by which it is entered is strong as some castle gate. Within, on the ground floor, is the office for the transaction of business, and thence a square wooden scaffolding, standing free of the inner walls, runs right up to the roof. This scaffolding is divided into a series of flats, having ladders as their means of approach. On the ground flat are stowed pledges of the greatest bulk, such as furniture or produce. The smaller and lighter articles occupy the upper flats, while one nearest the roof is exclusively for jewellery or other property of great intrinsic value. Every pledge from floor to ceiling is catalogued, and carries a ticket denoting the number of the article, and the date on which it was deposited. Thus everything can be found and redeemed at a moment's notice. An iron railing and a narrow footpath run round the outside of the roof, and a store of heavy stones is piled up there, to be hurled upon the head of a robber, should he attempt to scale the wall. Valuable property is insecure in this part of the country. This tower is consequently a place of safe repose for the costly jewels and robes of the wealthy classes of the community; besides which, as a licensed pawnbroking establishment, it advances money temporarily to the poor who may have security to lodge. In such establishments three per cent. interest per month is charged on sums under ten taels, save in the last month of the year, when the rate is reduced to two per cent. When over ten taels, the rate is two per cent. per month. Pledges are kept for three years in the better class of pawnshops.

HONAM TEMPLE, CANTON.

HONAM TEMPLE, one of the largest Buddhist establishments in the south of China, stands on the southern bank of the Pearl River at Canton. Passing along the broad granite pavement which conducts from the water-side, and entering the outer porch, beneath the shade of venerable trees, the visitor finds himself within a spacious outer compartment, having gigantic gateways in front and to the rear. Two colossal statues, deities of Indian mythology, and armed and equipped as warriors, present themselves next to his gaze. These are the adopted guardians of Buddha, and in temples even greater than that of Honam these panoptical champions are increased to four. We next ascend by a flight of broad steps to an inner causeway, and the vista shown in the photograph comes thereupon into view. Beyond, in a central court, is the adytum, or inmost shrine, where three images of Buddha glisten with a coating of polished gold. Here the air is laden heavily with the fumes of incense, rising in spiral columns from the altar in front of the gods. A priest tends the burning tapers that from generation to generation have been kept alight; and all round are bowls of bronze, and vases filled with ashes, embers of incense sticks, and the relics of a thousand votive gifts. The candles which burn upon the altar cast a lurid flare over the mystic images and amid the silken hangings of the roof. The constant tinkling of a bell, or the solemn monotonous chant of some aged priest, the surrounding darkness of the dim interior, combined with the worship of a strange god, induce a sense of depression, which is speedily dissipated by a stroll in the wonderful garden beyond. Here the priests delight to tend and rear rare and beautiful plants, dwarf trees, growing marvels in the form of tiny boats and bird-cages, and plants, whose stems are trained into a hundred curious devices. Here, too, is a pen full of fortunate pigs, guaranteed immunity from slaughter, as under the protecting roof of Buddha, the mighty saviour of life.

THE TEMPLE OF THE FIVE HUNDRED GODS.

HIS celebrated shrine, which the Chinese call " Hua-lin-szu," " Magnificent Forest Temple," is situated in the western suburbs of Canton, and was erected by Bodhidharama, a Buddhist missionary from India, who landed in Canton about the year 520 A. D.[1] and who is frequently pictured on Chinese tea-cups ascending the Yangtsze on his bamboo raft. The temple was rebuilt in 1755, under the auspices of the Emperor Kien-lung, and with its courts, halls, and dwellings for the priests, covers a very large space of ground. It is the Lo-Han-T'ang, or Hall of Saints, partly shown in the photograph, that forms the chief attraction of the place.

This Hall contains 500 gilded effigies of saints out of the Buddhist calendar, representing men of different Eastern nationalities. Colonel Yule, in his new edition of " Marco Polo," says that one of these is an image of the Venetian traveller; but careful inquiry proves this statement incorrect, as there is no statue presenting the European type of face, and all the records connected with them are of prior antiquity. The aged figure shown in the next picture is that of

THE ABBOT,

R Chief Priest of this temple. About three years ago, when I paid my first visit to this establishment, in company with a native gentleman from the Canton Customs Office, I was introduced to this Abbot· He received us with great courtesy, conducted us to his private apartments, and there refreshed us with tea-cakes and fruit. The rooms he occupied were enclosed by a high wall, and approached through a granite-paved inner quadrangle, adorned with a variety of rare and beautiful flowers. Conspicuous among the latter was a splendid specimen of the Sacred Lotus, in full bloom, and growing in an ornamental tank, on whose surface floated many other brilliantly green aquatic plants. The old gentleman had spent half his lifetime in this secluded place, and was greatly devoted to his flowers, discoursing on their beauty with an eloquent fondness, and expressing his delight to discover in a foreigner kindred sentiments of admiration. The furniture of the apartments consisted of chairs of skilfully carved black wood, one or two tables, and a shrine of the same material; while a number of well-executed drawings, hung about the white walls, displayed a simple taste and refinement in keeping with the surroundings of their proprietor's secluded life. Two years afterwards I visited the temple again, and executed the photograph here represented. On the second occasion I met with the same kind hospitality at the hands of the Abbot and the priests in his care—a hospitality which, with one exception, I enjoyed in all the Buddhist establishments I visited throughout my travels in China.

---

[1] " A History of the Kwan-tung Province," p. 12, Bowra.

Vol. I, Plate XVIII

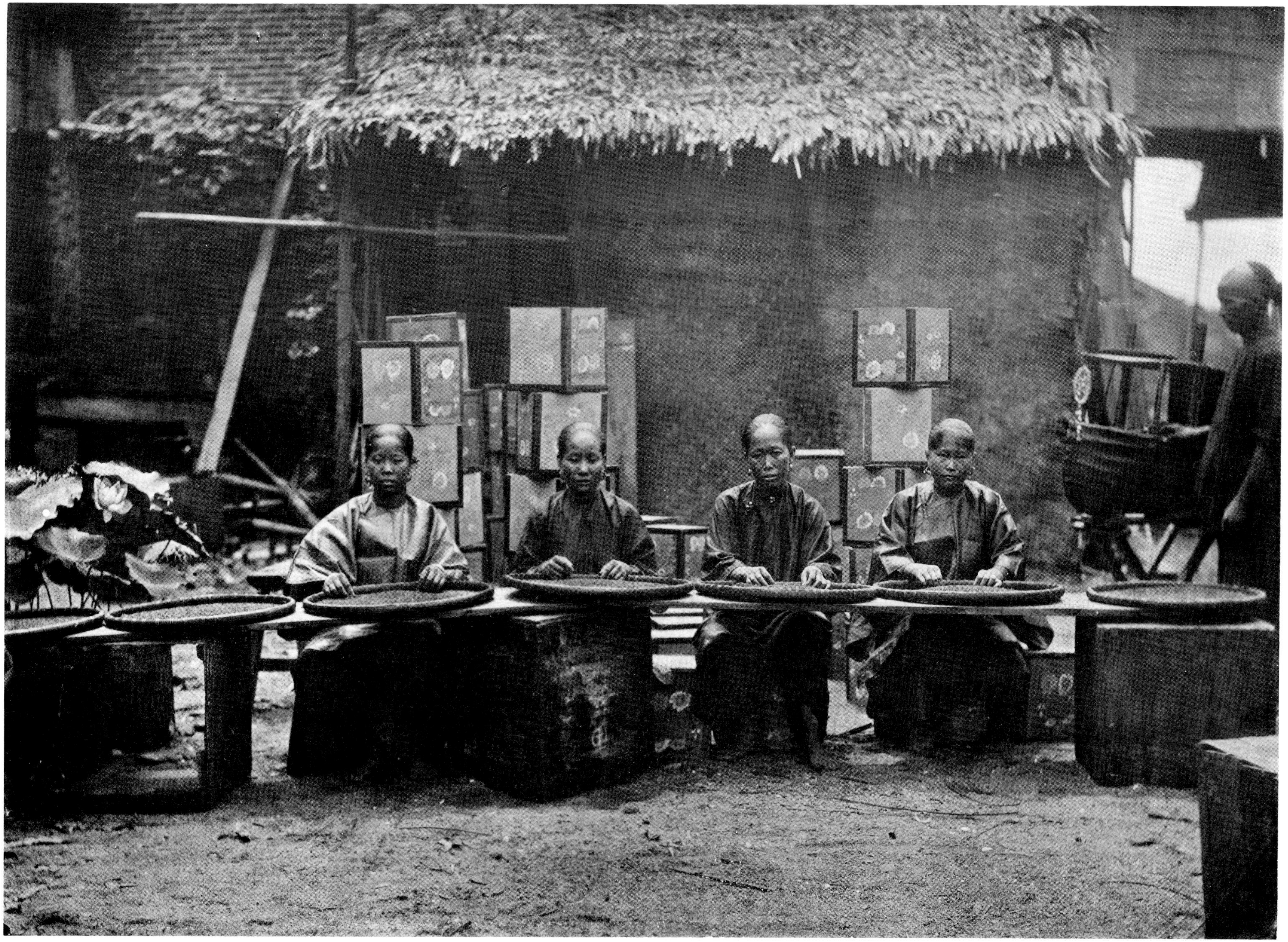

Vol. I, Plate XIX

TEA PICKING IN CANTON.

IN former times, before Hankow or the Yangtsze River was thrown open to foreign trade, all the tea from the great Tung-ting Lake district was brought to Canton for exportation. The bulk of the tea shipped now-a-days from Canton is grown in Kwang-tung, of which province that city is the capital.

From the leaf of the Tai-shan plantations, which are the most noted in that neighbourhood, the "Canton District Congou," and the "Long Leaf-Scented Orange Pekoe," are manufactured. These teas are prepared by twisting the leaf in the hand; when so twisted it frequently shows a small white feathery tip at the end of the leaf, known as the "Pekoe tip."

Lo-ting leaf makes "Scented Caper" and Gunpowder teas. These teas are rolled in a bag with the feet until the leaf is twisted into round pellets.

Macao is the port from which the bulk of District Congous are exported, and Canton is famous for its Scented Capers and Scented Orange Pekoe. The green tea trade from Canton is of secondary importance, this tea being chiefly exported to the continental countries of Europe. The cultivation of tea in Kwang-tung, and the consequent export trade from Canton, are on the increase. The business fell off during the war between Germany and France; but this has turned out to be nothing but a temporary check. As the reader will have inferred, the preparation of tea for the foreign markets is carried on extensively at Canton. The Congou and Pekoe teas are brought down from the plantations, rolled by hand, dried in the sun, and then they are in a condition suitable for subsequent firing and preparation for the market. As I shall hereafter have occasion to describe the planting and packing of tea, I will confine my remarks here to a brief notice of the process by which the leaf at Canton is prepared for exportation.

Black teas, after being partially dried in the sun, and slightly fired, are rolled either by the palm of the hand on a flat tray, or by the foot in a hempen bag. They are scorched in iron pans over a slow charcoal fire, and after this spread out on bamboo trays, that the broken stems and refuse leaves may be picked out. It is this operation, which is performed by women or children, that is shown in the photograph. The teas are then separated by passing them through sieves, so as to form different sizes and qualities of tea. The greatest care and economy are observed in carrying all these processes on, the tea-dust being sedulously gathered up and used in forming a very inferior and cheap quality of spurious tea.

PHYSIC STREET, CANTON.

THE streets of a Chinese city differ greatly from those of Europe, and are always extremely narrow, except at Nankin and Peking. They are paved crosswise with slabs of stone, usually worn down by the traffic to a hollow in the centre of the path, and this disagreeable substitute for the gutters of European thoroughfares forms the only means by which the rain-water is carried off. The shops in good streets are all nearly uniform in size; a brick party-wall divides each building from its neighbour; all have one apartment, which opens upon the street, and a granite or brick counter for the purpose of displaying their wares. A granite base also supports the upright sign-board, which, as with us in former days, is the indispensable characteristic of every shop in China.

Opposite to the sign-board stands a small altar or shrine dedicated to the God who presides over the tradesman and his craft. This Deity is honoured regularly when the shop is opened, and a small incense stick is lit and kept burning in a bronze cup of ashes placed in front of the shrine.

The shops within are frequently fitted with a counter of polished wood and finely carved shelves, while at the back is an accountant's room. screened off with an openwork wooden partition, so carved as to resemble a climbing plant.

In some conspicuous place stand the brazen scales and weights, ever brightly polished, and adorned with red cloth, which is wound in strips around the beam. These scales are used for weighing the silver currency of the place, for chopped money is but too common among the Chinese. When goods are sold by weight, the purchaser generally brings his own balance, so as to secure his correct portion of the article which he has come to buy.

Physic Street, or, more correctly, Tsiang-Lan-Kiai (our Market Street), as the Chinese term it,—is one of the finest streets in Canton, and, with its varied array of brightly coloured sign-boards, presents an appearance no less interesting than picturesque.

But traversing it is by no means pleasant in wet weather, as the sloping roofs of the shops approach so near to each other that they rain a perpetual shower-bath on every passer by. The narrowness of the streets is intended to exclude the burning sun, and this object is assisted by covering the open space between the roofs with bamboo basket-work, sufficiently open in its construction to admit light and air, and yet an effective shelter from the heat. To each trade its special locality or street has been assigned, and each shop is a perfect counterpart of its neighbour. Here we find none of the display, none of those desperate efforts to secure the lion's share of custom, which competition has fostered in European towns; and nothing fills a foreigner with more surprise than the drowsy indifference among the shopkeepers of China with regard to the disposal of their wares. When a customer enters a shop the proprietor, a grey-headed man perhaps, but conveying by his well-dressed person a profound appearance of old-established honest trading, will slowly and calmly set down his pipe on the polished counter, or push aside his cup of tea, and then inquire politely the nature of his customer's demands. Should he have the article in stock, he will sell it at the price fixed by the members of the guild to which he belongs, or a higher one if he can obtain it; but, should he be discovered underselling his neighbour, he would be subjected to a heavy penalty.

The streets of the city of Canton are irregularly built and tortuous in their course; those of the poorer sort are much narrower than the one shown in the photograph; they are badly kept, filthy, and even more offensive than the most crowded alley in London, the right of way being contested between human beings, domestic pigs, and undomesticated mongrel curs. The shops and houses are built of light inflammable material, and a row of earthen pots of water disposed along the roof of each tenement is the sole precaution adopted to prevent the ravages of fire.

I am indebted to Mr. W. F. Mayers, the well-known Chinese scholar, for the translation of the sign-boards of Physic Street, and for the interesting note which follows on Schroffing dollars.

The signboards may be taken as fair examples of the street literature of China, showing the national tendency of the shopkeepers to introduce their commonest wares by some high-flown classical phrase, having, so far as I can see, no reference whatever to the contents of the shop. Tien Yih (Celestial Advantage), for example, offers a thoroughly terrestrial advantage to customers in the shape of covers and cushions; and why, one might be tempted to ask, should swallows' nests be a "Sign of the Eternal?"

These phrases are, however, simply intended as the signs, or names by which each shop is known, as with us in olden times, we used to have the "Golden Fleece," "The Anchor," and the quaint signs of our wayside inns.

Kien Ki Hao.—The sign of the symbol Kién (Heaven). Hwei-chow ink, pencils, and writing requisites.

Chang Tsi Tang (Chang of the family branch designated Tsi). Wax-cased pills of select manufacture.

Tien Yih (Celestial advantage). Table-covers, chair-covers, cushions for chairs, and divans for sale.

Tien Yih Shên (Celestial advantage combined with attention). Shop for the sale of cushions and rattan mats.

Yung Ki (sign of the Eternal) Swallows' Nests.

Money-schroffing taught here.[1]

K'ing Wēn T'ang.—The Hall of delight in Scholarship. Seals artistically engraved.

---

[1] The art of "schroffing," or of detecting spurious coin, and of ascertaining the difference between dollars of various issues, is very extensively practised in China, and is studied as a profession by hundreds of young men, who find employment in banks and merchants' offices. The establishments where "schroffing" is taught, are well-known to be in direct communication with the counterfeiters of Mexican dollars and other coin, and it has often been remarked that the existence of schroffs and of false money are mutually indispensable to each other. If the amount of counterfeit coin in circulation were less, the necessity for a multitude of schroffs would not be so severely felt as at present; and if the establishments where schroffage is taught did not exist, the counterfeiters would lose their principal means of passing false money into circulation.

Vol. I, Plate XX

ROLLING SCENTED CAPER AND GUNPOWDER TEAS.

THE manipulation required to produce Gunpowder Tea is one of the most curious and interesting of all the processes to which the leaf is submitted. The visitor, upon entering the Gunpowder department of a Tea House, is surprised to find a number of able-bodied coolies, each dressed in a short pair of cotton drawers, tucked up so as to give free action to the naked limbs. It is puzzling, at first, to conjecture what these men are about. Can they be at work, or is it only play? They rest their arms on a cross beam, or against the wall, and with their feet busily roll and toss balls, of perhaps a foot in diameter, up and down the floor of the room. One soon perceives, however, that it is work they are after, and hard work too. The balls beneath their feet consist of canvas bags, packed full of tea leaves, which, by the constant rolling motion, assume the pellet shape. As the leaves become more compact, the bag loosens, and requires to be twisted up tightly at the neck, and again rolled; the twisting and rolling being repeated until the leaf has become perfectly globose. It is afterwards divided through sieves into different sizes or qualities. The scent or bouquet of the tea is imparted after the final drying and scorching, and before the leaves have become quite cool, by intermixing them with the chloranthus, olea, aglaia, and other flowers. These flowers are left in the baskets of tea until it is ready for packing, and are then removed by passing the tea through a sieve.

WEIGHING TEA FOR EXPORTATION.

WHEN the market is about to open, the new teas are sorted out into qualities, or "chops," as they are usually termed. Samples of these assorted teas are then submitted to the foreign merchants, who carefully test the colour, size, make, taste and smell of the leaves, and their general appearance, wet and dry. When the professional tea-taster has settled all these points, a bargain is struck for so many thousand chests of the various descriptions of tea, and a day is appointed for examining and weighing the whole. The process of weighing is as follows:—The lead-lined chests (with which we are all familiar), soldered up and ready for exportation, are piled in symmetrical blocks in the weighing-room of the Chinese tea-house. Narrow passages are left between the rows to admit the foreign inspector, and he places his mark upon a score or more of chests, and directs them to be removed, opened and examined on the spot. This done, they are conveyed to the scales, and it is now that the caution of the inspector is called most prominently into play, for experience has taught the practised Chinese weigher how to poise his apparatus by placing his hands lightly upon the ropes of the balance, so that, by a slight effort on his part, the scale may be made to turn either way and confer an appearance of favour on a purchaser, whom in reality he is cheating out of his goods. Fair dealing, however, is as much a characteristic among Chinese merchants of repute as among the mercantile classes of our own community, and the tea chests selected, as described, from the bulk of the cargo, generally show that the transaction has been fulfilled with scrupulous honesty and exactitude.

Vol. I, Plate XXI

A TEA HOUSE, CANTON.

THE native tea-firing establishments of Canton adjoin the river, or the banks of a creek, and a granite or wooden wharf is one of their most indispensable accessories.

A number of men may be seen during the tea season in the front of the house, employed, as shown in the photograph, in picking, sampling, and sorting the tea, or in preparing the chests for its reception. Just within the entrance are one or two offices, where the partners, treasurer, and book-keeper pursue their various avocations ; while, out of doors, are a number of forms and chairs, and a small table bespread with hot tea and cups, set in readiness for the accommodation of visitors. Beyond is a large apartment for storing the tea ; it is here also it is weighed and prepared for exportation. After this we enter an open court, and pass into a firing, picking, sorting, and packing department. Above this chamber there is usually a loft where women and children are engaged in removing the stalks and refuse from the bamboo trays on which the tea is spread out. These trays are ranged in rows on long narrow tables, round which a closely packed throng of pickers and sorters ply unceasingly their busy occupation. This room presents the most animated scene in the house. Many of the women are pretty or attractive-looking, and move their small well-formed hands with a marvellous celerity, pouncing upon and tossing aside the smallest fragments of foreign matter which may chance to have become admixed with the tea, and which none but a thoroughly trained eye could ever have discovered at all. It is impossible to visit an establishment of this kind and not be impressed with the orderly habits and business-like atmosphere of the place, where a thoroughly organized system of divided labour has produced from the leaf of a single shrub so many varieties of one of the most delicate and salutary of the luxuries we possess.

A TEA-TASTING ROOM, CANTON.

THIS photograph represents two Chinese tea merchants in a foreign taster's room, awaiting an offer for their samples. Every foreign house in Canton that does any trade in tea has a room specially fitted up for the accommodation of the taster. The windows of the room have a northern aspect, and are screened off, so as to admit only a steady sky-light, which falls directly on the tea-board beneath. Upon this board the samples are spread in square wooden trays, and it is under the uniform light above described that the minute inspection of colour, make, and external appearance of the leaves takes place. On the shelves around the room stand rows of tin boxes, identical in size and shape, containing registered samples of the teas of former years. These are used for reference. Even the cups, uniform in pattern, and regularly ranged in rows along the numerous tables required, have been manufactured especially for the business of tasting tea. The samples are placed in these cups, and hot water of a given temperature is then poured upon them. The time the tea rests in the cups is measured by a sand-glass, and when this is accomplished all is ready for the tasting. All these tests are made by assistants who have gone through a special course of training, which fits them for the mysteries of their art. The knowledge which these experts thus acquire is of great importance to the merchants, as the profitable outcome of the crops selected for the home market depends, to a great extent, on the judgment and ability of the taster.

CANTONESE GENTLEMEN.

THE elder of the two gentlemen represented by the portraits before us is one who, in early life, devoted himself assiduously to the study of literature, and who, having obtained one or two degrees at the government civil examinations, and displayed a competent acquaintance with the classics, laws, and history of China, got his name enrolled as an unattached member of the Chinese civil service. In process of time he became a salaried official, and a mandarin of the sixth grade. When dressed in official costume, his rank is denoted by the style of his robes, and by the ornaments which adorn them, as well as by the colour and material of the button which surmounts his hat. The pay which he receives from government is small—probably not exceeding twenty pounds a year. This sum he is, however, at liberty to augment, by a system of bribery and extortion, to £1,000, or as much more as can be had in the ordinary course of his duties. Mr. Meadows[1] gives an instance of a mandarin whose annual legal income amounted to £22, and who complained bitterly that his supplemented revenue did not exceed £2,333.

The other portrait is that of a compradore, or treasurer in a foreign mercantile house—a man who, by his legitimate savings and private trading speculations, has accumulated a large fortune. It is the common practice of foreign merchants to employ a Chinaman of known repute and ability to act as treasurer to the firm. All the financial transactions of the house pass through this man's hands—he must therefore be one who merits the full confidence and support of his employers. He is a leading man among the native merchants, a member of their best clubs and guilds, and one whose intimate knowledge of foreign business diffuses a wide-spread influence among the wealthy traders who dwell at the Treaty Ports. This influence is unmistakeably one of the chief causes which induce Chinamen of means to become shareholders in foreign steam navigation companies, and in other commercial enterprises. The position of a Chinese compradore in a foreign house affords a striking example of the clannishness, or strong feeling of kinship, which binds the race together, and operates advantageously on the community at large. Thus the compradore is the head of his clan—all the native servants, and they are numerous in large foreign establishments, are engaged by him—and he it is who is held responsible for their honesty and good behaviour. The whole of the servants—from the coolie who carries the water, to the butler of the household—are members of the compradore's clan; and so thoroughly united are they, that they are careful to avoid disgracing their chief by any breach of good faith.

SCHROFFING DOLLARS.

SCHROFFING, or testing and examining dollars, is an operation conducted by the compradore's staff in receiving payment for cargoes, to ascertain that no counterfeit coin has been introduced. These tests are managed with dexterity and speed. In transferring the dollars from one sack to another, two are taken up at a time, poised upon the tips of the fingers, struck, and sounded, the tone of base metal being readily detected. The milling of the edge is also examined, as the Chinese show great cleverness in sawing the dollar asunder, scraping out and re-uniting the two halves, which they fill up with a hard solder made of a cheap metal, that when rung emits a clear silver tone. So deftly is the re-uniting done, that none but an expert can detect the junction of the two halves. When the dollars have all been schroffed, payment is made by weight.

REELING SILK.

THE superstitious dread with which the people regarded my photographic apparatus rendered it impossible for me to obtain more than this single picture in the silk-producing districts, although I had made a special journey thither, with the intention of securing a full series to illustrate the various operations connected with this branch of industry. The mulberry grows to perfection in the Kwang-tung province, and is used extensively in the rearing of the silkworm. This business gives profitable occupation to thousands of the families of small farmers, who set aside a portion of their gardens for the culture of the mulberry shrub. On the wives and daughters of the household falls the business of superintending the various delicate operations connected with the production of the silk—their duty it is to collect the eggs, to watch with care the process of hatching, which takes place in April, to nourish with the tender mulberry-leaves the tiny worm as he accomplishes his marvellous labours, and then, when he has finished his silken fabric, to arrest his career of industry, and wind off the cocoons for exportation to the looms of Europe. We owe much to China; and perhaps a knowledge of the rearing of the silkworm, and the introduction of silk are two of the greatest boons she has conferred upon Western nations. It was one of my most interesting experiences in the country to observe how modest were the aspects of this wide-spread industry, and how humble, yet sedulous, were the poor labourers whose lowly toil results at last in robes so magnificent and so dearly prized. In the village where the photograph was taken, all the women, as well as the children of sufficient age, were engaged in reeling silk. The machines are of a very primitive make, the most advanced and perfect being the one here shown. The labourers will not permit the introduction of anything more complex; and their guilds or trades' unions are so well organized that they can hold their own against their employers. This opposition offered by labourers in China to the introduction of new appliances that would tend to expedite labour is akin to what prevails in India. When extensive cuttings had to be made for railroads, the government furnished wheelbarrows to the coolies as a substitute for their small native baskets. The men used the wheelbarrows by placing a basketload in each, and marching off with the barrow mounted on the head. The Chinese workman is a very independent character, who, if he conceives he is wronged by his employer, has effectual means of redress. An English merchant in Hong-Kong gave me a striking example of the combined power of Chinese operatives. My friend had been in the habit of furnishing yellow metal in sheets of a certain thickness, to a coppersmith in Fatshan, the Birmingham of southern China. Some metal a shade thinner was offered —the smith said it would suit admirably, and would save labour. The thin metal, however, was submitted to the men, who at once decided to strike work were it introduced, as it would rob them of the time and labour consumed in beating metal of the old kind and shape, and thus give the master an undue advantage. The metal was accordingly rejected.

Vol. I, Plate XXII

MACAO.

MACAO, in ancient times a small island off the mainland of Hiang-shan in the Kwang-tung Province, has since been united to the coast by a sand-bar. This occurrence so disgusted the Chinese, that in 1573, shortly after the troubles which the settlement of a few Portuguese at Macao involved, they built a barrier across the bar, with a view to exclude the foreigners from intruding into the interior of the country. The Chinese account of the early Macao Portuguese, and of the manner in which the colony was established, differs materially from that supplied by the Portuguese writers. It appears that, about the beginning of the sixteenth century, the Portuguese had attempted to form trading factories at Ningpo, and near Swatow. These they were compelled to abandon. In 1552 they are said to have obtained permission from the Chinese Government to erect mat-sheds for storing goods at Macao. This, then, seems to have been the germ from which the city has grown to its present proportions.[1] " Fortifications and a church were among the first building works undertaken. Ground-rent was not demanded by the Chinese Government until long after the settlement was formed—not, in fact, until 1582." "About 1580 Macao was erected into an episcopal see by Gregory III., and thirteen bishops have been consecrated in succession to this port." Macao was in its most flourishing condition shortly before the conclusion of the war with Great Britain and the establishment of our colony at Hong-Kong.

It was just prior to these events that the best houses were erected, and the place gradually assumed its present picturesque appearance. The principal residences front the bay, round which runs a broad carriage-drive, known as the Praya Grande, shown in the illustration. This picture was taken from the hill above Bishop's Bay, at the southern extremity of the Praya. The inner harbour is on the north-west side of the peninsula, and here the oldest part of the town is to be found. A number of narrow dingy lanes lead from the Praya to the main streets in the upper part of the town; and here the houses wear an interesting, antique appearance, greatly marred, however, by a variety of bright colours with which the owners daub their dwellings, alike regardless of symmetry and harmony of combination. To a European the effect is as distasteful as a glowing patch of carmine on the shrunken cheeks of a faded beauty. There is now hardly a sign of trade in these once busy streets—or, indeed, of active life in any form—save at noon when tawny worshippers hasten in crowds to the cathedral, or during the evening promenade on the Praya, when the band is playing in the gardens. Influences—local, social, climatic—and fusion of races have dealt unkindly with these descendants of the early Portuguese. They suffer greatly by comparison with the more recent arrivals from the parent land, being smaller in stature, and darker in complexion, than either the Portuguese of Europe or the native Chinese. There are, of course, rare and notable exceptions, but one seldom meets with a moderately well-formed and attractive countenance. This, it must be understood, applies to the lower orders of the population, and to those only among them who are of mixed blood.

The same result may be noticed among the Portuguese in Malacca, where it would often be hard to perceive the faintest trace of Western origin, but for the presence of some article of European apparel—a beaver hat for example—passed down in succession from father to son, and still held an indispensable element in a costume

[1] " Treaty Ports of China and Japan," p. 204.

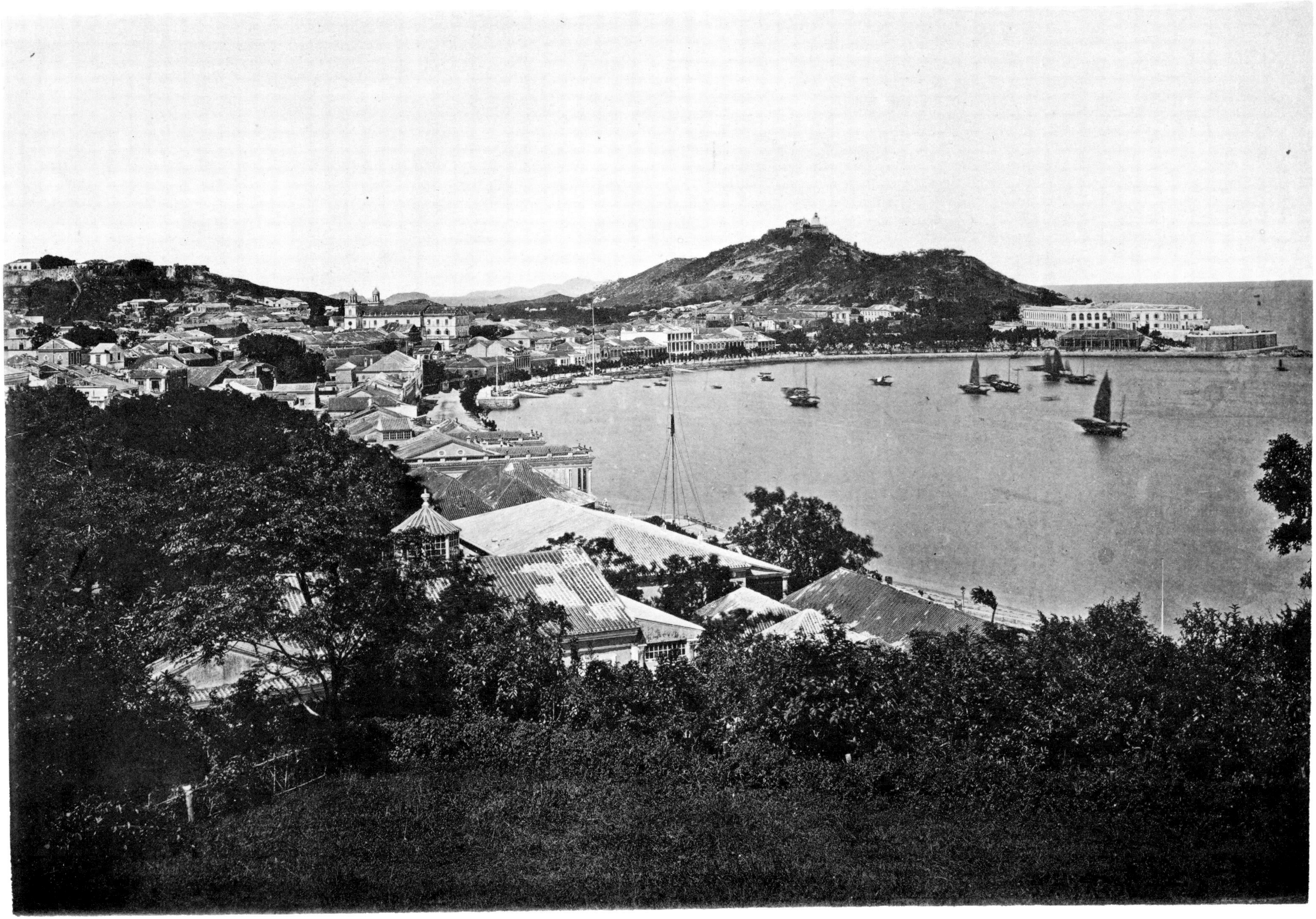

Vol. I, Plate XXIII

displaying a ludicrous compromise between native and foreign attire. Macao forms a pleasant resort during summer for the residents of Hong-Kong. A steamer plies daily between the two ports, and occupies about four hours in accomplishing the run. A good hotel stands on the Praya Grande, and from its verandah one may enjoy the sea-breeze and the view of the bay, where fleets of fishing-boats lie at anchor, or sail to and fro among the islands. Three times a week travellers may take steamer to Canton, and make the tour of that ancient and most interesting city. There are many picturesque walks in and around Macao, and retired sandy bays invite the wanderer to taste the luxury of a sea-bath. In the garden, now included in the grounds of a private residence, stands the grotto of Camöens, who is said to have resided there when he composed the greater part of Lusiadas, or the Epic of Commerce, as it has been termed. The career of Camöens, both before and after his residence in Macao, was one of strange adventure. " As a soldier, he fought in the empire of Morocco, at the foot of Mount Atlas, in the Red Sea, and in the Persian Gulf. Twice he doubled the Cape, and was led by a deep love of nature to spend sixteen years in watching the phenomena of the ocean in the Indian and China seas. Camöens was banished to Macao in 1556, on account of certain satires which he wrote against the Government "[1]—a summary treatment adopted for the suppression of poets and men of genius in other countries as well as Portugal, and not wholly unknown even in modern times. Macao since 1848 has earned an unenviable notoriety for its traffic in coolies. These unfortunate men were shipped to Cuba, Peru, and other ports on the South American Coast, and were, many of them, kidnapped in the province of Kwang-tung or the islands round about. Shut up first in Macao barracoons, they were thence packed off in crowded ships—inhuman treatment frequently leading to mutiny and massacre, or disease and death, perhaps, bringing to these poor bondsmen a last but grateful relief. That this is no exaggeration the following extract may show :—" The ship 'Dea del Mare' left Macao in October, 1865, bound to Callao. On touching at Tahiti she had only 162 emigrants alive out of 550."

The coolie trade of Macao is now under a strict surveillance, and is mainly indebted to the enlightened administration of the present governor for this urgently needed reformation.

---

[1] " A History of the Kwang-tung Province," Bowra, p. 84.

A MOUNTAIN PASS IN THE ISLAND OF FORMOSA.

THE island of Formosa stretches between 26° and 23° north latitude. It is about 250 miles long, and has an average breadth of 60 miles. A high mountain range bisects the island from north to south, and its peaks may be descried from the mainland when the weather is clear. The place is claimed by the Chinese, and is included as a dependency in the government of Fukien, off which province it lies. The central range of mountains, together with the lower ranges to the west, the spurs thrown off to the east, and a great portion of the eastern coast, are still inhabited by aboriginal and independent tribes. These, in configuration, colour, and language, resemble Malays of a superior type. Akin to them are the Pe-po-hoans, who dwell on the low hill lands and plateaux to the west of the central mountain chain. These Pe-po-hoan tribes are partially civilized, supporting themselves by agriculture, and being to some extent subject to the Chinese yoke. Outside of these districts, and occupying the fertile plains on the west, Chinese planters from the Fukien province are to be found : and intermingled with them are the Hak-kas, a hardy, industrious, and adventurous race, who emigrated from the north of the empire. The Hak-ka Chinese hold lands nearest to the savage hunting-grounds. They also make alliances with the mountain tribes, and carry on trade of barter, exchanging Chinese wares for camphor-wood, horns, hides, ratan, etc.

The present population of Formosa is probably 3,000,000. The island is growing rapidly in commercial importance in consequence of the remarkable fertility of its soil. The cultivation of tea has recently been introduced in the northern districts of the island, and is now carried on there with considerable success ; camphor, coal, and timber of many valuable kinds are plentiful, and enormous quantities of sugar and rice are exported to the mainland from the south. The great mineral wealth of the island is rather a matter of conjecture, as the central mountain ranges remain practically unexplored.

The Chinese claim to have found Formosa towards the beginning of the fifteenth century.[1] Probably the enterprising discoverer descried it from the mainland about that time. The island, however, did not become of much note until it was handed over, in 1614, to the Dutch, and they thereupon built fort Zelandia on an islet off the present capital Taiwanfu. This fort was intended to protect an inner harbour, but this has now totally disappeared, and an arid plain, uniting the islet to the mainland, is all that at present remains of the harbour. In 1661, Koksinga, that celebrated Chinese rover or sea-king, having brought his fleet past the fort into the inner harbour, succeeded ultimately in dislodging the Dutch, took possession of the island, and proclaimed himself king of Taiwan (Formosa). The island was afterwards surrendered to the imperial government by Koksinga's successor, and it is only within the past few years, since the opening of the treaty ports, that its real wealth and resources have become known.

The view of the mountain-pass, taken near La-ko-li, on one of the lower spurs of the central mountains, is intended to convey an idea of the grandeur of the scenery which is to be found in the interior of this " Isla Formosa."

See " Treaty Ports of China and Japan."

Vol. I, Plate XXIV

VOLUME II

VOL. II

LIST OF ILLUSTRATIONS.

LIST OF ILLUSTRATIONS.

NOTE.—*The numbers corresponding with the above list will be found marked in the lower left corner of each subject.*

Vol. II, Plate I

BAMBOOS OF BAKSA.

THE bamboo is one of the most serviceable plants of Southern China, for which reason I have assigned it an important place in this work. But its uses are not confined solely to the south, where it grows in greatest perfection. It figures extensively in the social economy of the people throughout the length and breadth of the Empire. Were every other means of support withdrawn, except bamboos and rice, these two plants would supply the necessaries for clothing, habitation, and food, indeed, the bamboo alone, as I propose to show, would bear the lion's share of the burden. No tending is needed for this hardy-natured plant, nor is it dainty in the choice of its locality, for it grows with equal vigour on the thin soil of rocky hill-sides, and in the well-tilled fields or gardens of the valleys below. It towers a stately clump of giant grass, one hundred feet or more in height, spreading out its leafy tops in graceful plumage and forming a thick, strong fence with its straight tough stems beneath, while its pale green foliage casts a grateful shade over the dwellings which it hedges around. The traveller, if he takes notice of the habitations of the Chinese, cannot fail to discover that both in the style of construction and ornamentation, much has originally been derived from the bamboo, as well as from the tent of nomadic life. Thus, in the rude homes of the villagers, the stout stems of the plant are still used for the main supports and frame-work. The slender stalks are split into laths, and the leaves furnish a covering for the walls and roof. In dwellings of greater pretensions, and in temples where brick and mortar have been employed, the painted and gilded hardwood beams have been fashioned to imitate the bamboo stems. The waterways along the roof partake of the same type, and the white plastered panels are embellished with spirited drawings of the much-loved bamboo. I will now glance at the duties which this plant is made to discharge in the domestic economy of the dwelling. Within, hanging from the rafters, are a number of hooks of prickly bamboo, and these support pieces of dried pork and such-like provision. There are rats about, but the prickles threaten with their *chevaux de frise*, and recall the motto of Scotland to the mind—"*Nemo me impune lacessit.*" In one corner are a waterproof coat and hat, each wrought out of leaves of bamboo which overlap like the plumage of a bird. Elsewhere we see agricultural implements, principally fashioned out of bamboo, and indeed, except the deal top of the table, the furniture of this simple abode is all of the same material. The fishing-net, the baskets of diverse shapes, the paper and pens (never absent, even from the humblest houses), the grain measures, the wine-cups, the water-ladles, the chop-sticks, and finally the tobacco-pipes, all are of bamboo. The man who dwells there is feasting on the tender shoots of the plant, and if you ask him, he will tell you that his earliest impressions came to him through the basket-work of his bamboo cradle, and that his latest hope will be to lie beneath some bamboo brake on a cool hill-side. The plant is also extensively used in the sacred offices of the Buddhist temples. Strangely contorted bits of bamboo root are set up in the shrine. The most ancient Buddhist classics were cut on strips of bamboo. The divination sticks, and the case which contains them, are manufactured out of its stem, while the courts outside the temple are fanned and sheltered by its nodding plumes.

It is impossible, in a volume such as this, to enumerate all the varied uses to which the bamboo is applied, or to form an estimate of its value to the inhabitants of China. Thus much, however, I may unhesitatingly affirm, that so multifarious are the duties which the bamboo is made to discharge, and so wide-spread are the benefits which it confers upon the Chinese, as to render it beyond all others the most useful plant in the empire.

THE NATIVES OF FORMOSA.

THOUGH the whole island of Formosa forms part of the Fukien province of China, the aborigines there still occupy, as independent territory, the mountain ranges that cover the central portion of the island, from its northern extremity to its southernmost point, as well as the spurs of their main chain, which, jutting in bold, rocky headlands into the sea, to the east present a wild, rugged coast-line, where neither harbour nor anchorage ground, as is alleged, can be discovered. Thus, while the savage tribes are effectually shut in, their more civilized neighbours, who have driven them from the fertile plains on the west to seek shelter in their mountain fastnesses and forests, have never yet succeeded in their furtive efforts to advance. There are still, however, several aboriginal tribes, who dwell in what we may properly term Chinese ground, who are controlled to a certain extent by Chinese jurisdiction, and who are known to the natives of Amoy as Pepohoan, or "foreigners of the plain." The settlements of these Pepohoan are scattered throughout the inland valleys and low hill-ranges at the western base of the central chain. The subjects of the illustration are taken from the Pepohoan of Baksa, a village about thirty miles inland from the capital, Taiwanfu, and they may be regarded as the most advanced types of those semi-civilized aborigines, who conform so far to Chinese customs as to have adopted the Amoy dialect, the language in use among the colonists from China. The men of Baksa wear the badge of Tartar conquest, the shaven head and the plaited queue, attributes of modern Chinese all over the world. The women, however, show a more independent spirit, and adhere to their ancestral attire, one that closely resembles in its style the dress of the Laos women whom I have seen in different parts of Cambodia and Siam. It will be readily perceived by those who have lived in China and in the Malayan Archipelago, that the features of the types here presented display a configuration more nearly akin to that of the Malay races who inhabit Borneo, the Straits settlements, and the islands of the Pacific, than to that of the Mongolian, and Tartar tribes of China. This affinity of race is indicated still further by the form and colour of the eyes, the costume, and by the aboriginal dialects of the people of Formosa. I am not aware that there is throughout the island any trace of the woolly-headed negro tribes found in the Philippines, on the mainland of Cochin China, in New Guinea, and elsewhere, and supposed by some to be the remnant of the stock from which the original inhabitants sprang. The Spanish traveller De Mas asserts that the negroes and the fairer races of the Polynesian Islands speak a common language, and that the Malays are the joint descendants of a pale-faced tribe, which at an early period overran the islands, drove the darker and weaker race to the hills, and retained the women for themselves. This theory would apply to all those islands where negro races exist; but there are many like Formosa, on which no trace of the negro can be found, and where the language affords clear proof of a Malayan origin. As already noticed, I have been much struck with the points of similarity between the Laos, the Pepohoan, and the Malays, as well as by the resemblance which all these races bear in common to the Miautse of China. My own observations on the last point find confirmation in illustrated Chinese books, and other evidence derived from Chinese sources. The Rev. Mr. Edkins is of opinion that the Burmese, the Laos, and the Shans are allied to the Lo Lo of China, as well as to the Li of Hainan. I believe that the Li are related to the Formosa aborigines, and the language of the latter leaves no doubt of their Malayan origin.[1] "Traces of the Malay language may be found extending over seventy degrees of latitude and 200 of longitude. In the table subjoined, I have contrasted the Formosa numerals with one or two examples taken from

---

[1] Crawfurd, "Ethnological Journal," 1848.

the languages spoken in the islands of the South Pacific, and I may add, that a more extended comparison of the vocabularies of Formosa and the Pacific Islands only tends to prove the common origin of the whole of the races who people them. The relationship of these islanders to the hill-tribes of Eastern Asia would seem to point to that part of the world as the early home of the fair, straight-haired races who inhabit the islands from Formosa to New Zealand, and from Madagascar to Easter Islands. This theory would account for the total extinction of the negro race in the islands nearest the coast of China, as well as for the circumstance that they are still found in abundance in the remoter islands, such as New Guinea, where the negroes have been enabled to hold their own against such small numbers of pale invaders as would have been able to reach their shores. In the intermediate islands the blacks have been driven to the mountains and forests, and in the north they have disappeared entirely, and given place to the fairer and stronger race. The illustrations Nos. 2, 3, 4 and 5 are female, while Nos. 6 and 7 are male heads of Pepohoan.

NUMERALS OF FORMOSA, MAGINDANO, AND ISLANDS OF THE SOUTH PACIFIC OCEAN.

ENGLISH.	MALAY.	SAMOBI TRIBE, FORMOSA.	BANGA TRIBE, FORMOSA.	NEW ZEALAND.[2]	PAPOUS DE WAIGIOU.[3]	PHILIPPINES. BISAYA.[4]	MAGINDANO.[5]
One	satu	itsa	lenga	tahi	sai	usa	isa
Two	dua	lusa[1]	noosa	rua	doui	duha	daua
Three	tigga	toroo	toro	toru	kioro	tolò	tulu
Four	ampat	sipat	pa'tu	wa	fiak	upat	apat
Five	lima	lima	lima	rima	rim	limà	lima
Six	anam	unam	neuma	ono	onem	uniem	anom
Seven	tugu	pito	pito	wtu	fik	pitò	petoo
Eight	d'lapan	aloo	nevaroo	waru	war	ualò	walu
Nine	sambilan	siva	bangato	iwa	siou	siàm	seaow
Ten	sa'pulo	poro	porooko	ngahuru	samfour	na'pulu	sampoolu

[1] In this example, *lusa* signifies "two," while in Malay the same word means "the second day." Throughout the above examples the numeral "five" is, with two exceptions, represented by *lima*. The late Mr. Crawfurd has, in one of his Essays, drawn attention to the fact that *lima*, in some African dialects, signifies "hand."

[2] Gaussin, "Du Dialecte de Tahiti," &c.

[3] "South Sea Vocabularies," D'Urville.

[4] Kennedy's "Ethnological and Linguistic Essays," page 74.

[5] Ibid. page 76.

Vol. II, Plate II

A PEPOHOAN DWELLING.

HE houses of the Pepohoans are tolerably clean, well-arranged, and comfortable, and present a striking uniformity of design in the different settlements throughout the island. The entire dwelling makes up three sides of a square, of which the portion in the rear is occupied by the family, while the two wings are invariably used for sheltering cattle, pigs, and poultry. In No. VIII. the rear and right wing of one of these Pepohoan village dwellings are shown, the left wing being exactly a counterpart of that on the right. The plot of ground thus enclosed is divided into two parts, the outer one, flanked with rough bamboo cattle-sheds, being employed for storing their simple farm implements, and for drying produce, while the inner one forms a raised clay platform for family use. On this space of hard level clay the most valuable produce is dried and prepared for the market. Here, also, the villagers meet in council or celebrate their festivals, and drink in company when the night has closed in. Whenever it has been decided to hold a feast, the firstborn son of the household, dressed in something like a bath towel, and tiara of fern-leaves, is sent to announce to the hamlet that his parents are to be at " home." Then merry guests troop in, the old and infirm to squat and cackle round the blazing logs that redden the copper-coloured group, crowning the sombre palms with golden crests, and shedding a weird reflection on the bamboo foliage around. The elders pile on reeds and wood, and the young men and women dance in the firelight to the time of a wild song, until the night is far advanced. The inner raised platform serves, however, for other purposes than these, and one of the most important is to keep the house dry during the wet season, when the surrounding fields are flooded. A number of domestic shrubs and trees are planted about the enclosure, as, for example, the papaya, shown in the right of the picture. This plant yields abundant fruit, is easily grown, and, like the cocoa-palm, reaches greater perfection, and affords more food, as well as ampler shelter, when near a dwelling, than if cultivated with the greatest care, in the centre of some pleasure-garden apart. The low, broad-leaved shrub growing against the house, above the two small baskets, is tobacco, and this they dry for smoking themselves. Their pipes, I may add, are also cut out of the roots and stems of their own bamboo. This tobacco is of a fine quality, but they frequently use it when still rather green. Another shrub, indigenous, I believe, to the island, is a description of trailing vine, known to the natives by the name of " Oigou." This yields an abundant supply of small seeds, which, when soaked in cold water, produce a firm, delicious, amber-coloured jelly.

The apartments in the rear, where the family dwell, are approached by means of a passage. This passage is protected from the heat of the sun by a walled screen of small bamboo. The entire structure, indeed, may be said to be built of the same material, for this plant nowhere grows in greater perfection than in the south of the island. A strong framework of bamboo supports the bamboo lath-work of the walls, the beams are of bamboo and so also are the rafters, while leaves of bamboo supply the thatch which covers the roof outside. The walls when completed are plastered over with mud, and sometimes also are lime-washed. The floor, as I have already explained, is formed out of hard-beaten clay. The furniture consists of a few bamboo articles of Chinese workmanship, supplemented with rough billets of wood for sitting on. One or two match-locks, some bows, arrows, spears and fishing-nets, garnish the rafters, and depending from these, as I have noticed elsewhere, are jagged hooks of bamboo used to protect provisions from the large species of rat that

Vol. II, Plate III

infests the Pepohoan dwellings. These rats are cleverly caught in a simple and ingenious bamboo-trap, which was to me the most attractive article the houses of this simple people had to show. It is, indeed, a most effective instrument, and as a plump rat is esteemed a choice delicacy, it must have been the reward promised by successful captures, that awoke a spark of genius in the mind of its inventor. Pity to think that he rested on his laurels ever after, a contented rat-catching, rat-eating Pepohoan! Many of the articles in use among the aborigines, such as matchlocks, spear-heads, gunpowder, and cloth, are of Chinese manufacture. The natives have no regular trades. To till the soil, and to prepare its produce for the Chinese market, are the only occupations which they know.

TYPES OF THE PEPOHOAN.

SMOKING is a favourite pastime among the Pepohoan of Formosa, men, women, and children all smoke alike. Their pipes they cut out of the nearest bamboo brake, carving and ornamenting them to suit their respective tastes. The pipe is their solace when labouring in the fields, and the companion which beguiles them when at rest. A pipe is among them as acceptable a love token as a jewelled ring would be with us. My readers therefore, looking at No. 9, will all allow that the pipe in the lady's mouth, which might, but for this explanation, appear a violation of good taste, is a characteristic as essential to her as a sunshade in summer to an English beauty. The two figures represent an old and a young woman of Baksa. The face of the younger is well formed and lit up with a mild and kindly expression, common to her race. Time deals hardly with the old women of Baksa; they soon become haggard with toil and exposure, and lose all trace of the comeliness which graces their early years; but there are many who, like the crone in the illustration, fight a stubborn battle against fate, dressing always with neatness and care, and gathering their jet black and glossy hair beneath their smooth blue turban folds. All honour to these matrons of Baksa. Theirs is a good honest struggle in the open field against the ravaging inroads of time. The most battered veteran of the tribe would scorn to shield her weakness and infirmities from the enemy behind the earthworks of paint and powder, false fronts, or dye. The bronzed and furrowed cheek, and the grey locks of old age meet everywhere with respect, and would even command a safe passport through the territory of a hostile tribe. The short blue or white jackets with their bright coloured borders are alike in both figures. The custom is to bring the flap of the jacket over the left breast and to fasten it. Whereas their Chinese neighbours bring the upper fold of the jacket over to the right and then button it. The lower robe or covering of the Pepohoan women resembles the Laos *longuti*, and the *sarong* of the Malays. The material is a dark blue cotton cloth. It struck me that in dress, in general appearance, and in many other points, the aborigines of Formosa bear a remarkable resemblance to the Laos tribes of Cambodia and Siam.

Unlike the Chinese, the marriage ceremony of the Pepohoan is a very simple rite, indeed, the woman seems most decidedly (in places where Dr. Maxwell's mission labours are unknown) to carry off the better half of the transaction. She it is who selects a husband to suit her own fancy. If provident she will choose a man noticed for his health and industry, as it will be his task to till the ground and to make himself generally useful in her father's household. Should he fail to come up to her expectations, she may divorce him at any moment and marry anew.

As to their religion, the fetish worship anciently practised is fast giving place before the zeal of one or two devoted Protestant missionaries, who have made many converts. According to their original faith the world has existed from eternity and will endure without end. They also believe in the immortality of the soul, and that the wicked will be punished, and the good rewarded, after death. Their chief idols are supposed to represent a male and a female spirit. The only example of their idols which I was allowed to view were in a house at Konganah, and were exposed to our vulgar gaze with the greatest possible reluctance. These images were standing against the wall of a dimly-lighted chamber, alive with spiders and festooned with cobwebs. The female idol looked like a stunted may-pole, with the skull of a deer fixed by the antlers to the top. The stem of the pole was wreathed with withered flowers. The male idol reminded me of a child's bamboo chair, it too supported a skull, as well as one or two wine-cups used in making offerings. The house in which I saw these idols was close to a Christian chapel which the natives were erecting for themselves. There are now over 1,000 native Protestants in the south of the island, and they build their own chapels, and make them as nearly as possible self-supporting.

These aborigines possess no musical instruments, but they sing simple and plaintive native airs full of minor passages. Such melodies indeed as one would expect to find among the captive or oppressed.

No. 10 shows the mode of carrying children, and the coiffure adopted by Pepohoan women of the more inland tribes, and among the purely savage mountaineers.

No. 11 is a full-length type of a Baksa girl, and No. 12 represents part of the village of Lalung, where we had hoped to fall in with a party of savages from the mountains. The son of our host, having lost his wife, had gone off to the neighbouring mountains to secure another bride. He was hourly expected to return escorted by a party of her savage kinsmen whom the lady would command as an escort. Here, as indeed at most of the places visited, we were hospitably entertained.

A COUNTRY ROAD NEAR TAIWANFU.

BEFORE I quit Formosa I must afford a glimpse of the sylvan groves round Taiwanfu, the capital, as shown in No. 13. In the old forts Zelandia and Provincia, and in the noble parks within the city walls, traces of the early Dutch settlers may still be discovered. A tragic history attaches to Taiwanfu. It witnessed that fierce struggle which closed with the final expulsion of the Dutch in the year 1661, and then on the 11th day of August, 1842, the parade ground beyond the northern gate was reddened with the blood of 197 of our countrymen who had been cast ashore upon the island; but before this massacre was over a fearful storm burst upon the scene, and raged without ceasing for more than three days, swelling the rivers and flooding the land, and destroying nearly 2,000 lives. An aged Chinaman remarked to my friend Dr. Maxwell, in allusion to the incident, "It was a black day for Formosa, that 11th of August." Many other events, no less calamitous, and of still more recent date, might be recorded of this city, which happened about the time of the storming of Anping, when our late and much-esteemed consul, Mr. Gibson, by his prompt and vigorous action, saved the lives and property of the foreign residents at the port. As we stroll through the parks or outer lanes of Taiwanfu, we shall discover nothing in their still and peaceful environs to remind us of the fierce conflicts that have raged within the city. The whole vicinage now wears an aspect of quiet repose, disturbed only by the drowsy hum of the produce-laden cart as it wends its way to market, or by the merry voices of children at play. The carts I have referred to are peculiar to the island, and I will therefore endeavour to describe one. The distant sound of a cart as it traverses the dry road on its drier axles, recalls, strange as it may appear, the full mellow tones of an organ. The whole contrivance is made of wood bound together with ratan. It is carried on two wheels, each a solid wooden disc of about four feet span. These vehicles are drawn by the huge Water buffalo, a brute alike remarkable for its sleepy aspect, its great working power, and for its docility among friends. But it is distrustful of strangers, and fierce, destructive and uncontrollable when its fury has been aroused. Then its giant horns become the most formidable and deadly weapons. Yet I have seen these unwieldy animals rolling in the shade with a group of children hanging about their horns, peering into their mouths and nostrils, or catching flies on their black, india-rubber-looking backs.

The lanes of Taiwanfu are commonly between two cactus hedges gay with the major convolvulus, the fuchsia and many other wild flowers. Their blossoms show out brilliantly against the background of green, while overhead the bamboo rears its stately plumes and branches to form a pointed arch of shade above the path. The slender stems nod to every passing breeze, and fitful gleams of sunshine light up the flowers and foliage beneath. A scene more bright and beautiful could rarely be found.

No. 14, the catamaran of Formosa, is an ingeniously constructed raft for landing in rough weather on the western coast. At Taiwanfu, there are several miles of shallow water to be encountered before we reach the shore, and the sea breaks with great violence there during, at least, four months of the year. The raft is made of bamboos which have been bent by heating them, so that they form a slightly hollow vessel. The poles are lashed together with ratan, and a space, or interval, is left between each for the free passage of the water. In the centre of the raft a block is fixed, and in this the mast is secured. Passengers are accommodated in a tub placed to the rear of the mast. This tub is merely laid on the raft, without any fastening whatever; it is therefore

not uncommon for the tub with its occupant to be carried off the raft and washed ashore. My own experience of the catamaran leads me to believe that it would be dangerous, and at times impossible, to land without it.

No. 15 was taken on the left bank of the Han river above Swatow. The banks of this, in common with the other streams of China, are high above the water during the dry season, and at those times chain pumps are employed for irrigation. A pump of this sort is simple and ingenious ; it consists of a long square wooden tube into which an endless chain is fitted, carrying a series of wooden diaphragms separated about six inches from each other. The diaphragms descend over guiding rods above the tube, and return again with a rapidity sufficient to raise the water in a continuous stream. At its upper end the chain traverses a wheel having a series of spokes, or treadles, outside, and it is by working these with the foot that the chain is made to revolve.

Bold rocks abound in and around the harbour of Amoy; inscriptions are to be seen on their most prominent surfaces. Plate No. 16 gives a specimen of these rock inscriptions, which usually relate to incidents of local history or tradition.

VOL. II, PLATE VI

SWATOW.

THE Chinese town which foreigners know as Swatow was first made an open port in the year 1858. It is built at the mouth of the Han river, on its eastern bank. The Han flows through a very populous and fertile section of the Kwangtung province, and affords at its entrance a spacious harbour where the largest vessels may anchor. Hence the great commercial importance of this place, which in 1842, for the first time, attracted the notice of foreign traders, and has, since that date, risen to be of considerable importance. But the progress of trade, as well as the development generally of this part of the province, has always been retarded by the lawlessness of the resident population. Of late years, as I have already noticed, the district has been reduced to comparative order by the vigorous administration of Juilin. The natives of Swatow speak a dialect which differs from that in use among the Cantonese, and, like the Hakkas, they appear to have sprung out of some stock originally distinct from the Puntis of Kwangtung, with whom they are continually at variance. Taken altogether, the people of this province, which is about as large as Great Britain, have probably been more difficult to govern than any other community throughout the vast empire of China. Moreover, this part of the country has ever been the favourite resort of robbers and rebel bands; constantly torn by internal strife and commotion, or overcome by foreign invaders. At one period a kind of republic was set up, at another it has constituted an independent kingdom, the nucleus of a southern empire which did not tender its full submission to the empire of the north till about the middle of the 10th century.[1]

It is to the Munchus, the present rulers of China, and to the close contact of Western civilization, that the province owes its greatest prosperity. Between the years 1842 and 1851 an unrecognized foreign community had established itself on Double Island, four miles, or thereabouts, below the present settlement of Swatow. The latter place was commenced in 1862 by the consent of the Chinese government, on a site opposite the native town and underneath the Kah-chio hills. No. 17 gives a view of the present state of the settlement just referred to, and was taken from the heights above the residence of Messrs. Richardson and Co. The hills of the locality are nothing more by nature than barren granite rocks. This granite is sometimes in a state of decomposition, but much of it also consists of solid boulders, bare and exposed, and resting like monuments on the tops and sides of the hills. In spite of these disadvantages, the rich soil of the plain has been imported, and round the foreign houses the sterile slopes and valleys have been transformed into flower gardens and close cropped lawns. As might have been anticipated, a thriving village has sprung up in the neighbourhood to supply the wants of the foreigners.

The European houses are chiefly built of a native concrete made of the felspar clay which abounds in that vicinity, mixed with shell lime. This concrete hardens in process of time into a stony substance. Within, these houses are adorned with a profusion of finely moulded cornices and panel-work in the ceilings. These are made by native modellers, who have carried their own branch of art to a high pitch of perfection, and have made it a speciality in Swatow. Birds and animals, flowers and fruit, are formed by these craftsmen with artistic skill, and in free and graceful designs. The artizans are paid but poorly for their labour,—so poorly that their condition is little above that of the ordinary coolie. I was much interested in watching these needy men at their work;

[1] Bowra, " History of the Kwangtung Province," " Fall of Canton Empire," p. 27.

they do everything by hand with the help of one or two small trowels, the thumb and fingers coming in for the most delicate touches of the design.

The fan-painters of Swatow enjoy a wide-spread reputation. There are, however, only two or three shops where the highest class of fan-painting is practised. The pictures on the fans of this sort are remarkable for the delicacy and beauty of their colouring, as well as for the variety of their designs, and for the grace and accuracy with which the drawings have been executed. I found the artists who engage in this work seated in small apartments, each one on his opium couch, and it is while under the exhilarating influence of the drug that the finest pictures are produced. The Swatow fans are not only greatly sought after by foreigners, but find a good and ready market in all parts of the empire.

The annual value of the trade of Swatow has been nearly tripled since 1860. In this part of the Kwangtung province sugar and rice are extensively grown. The cultivation of sugar-cane and the manufacture of sugar are industries modest in their aspect, and making but little outward show, as indeed is the case with most of those other pursuits which produce such great results in China. The total area of land under cane cultivation is great, but the farms are small. Each small owner tends his fields for himself, and has a small sugar-mill of his own in the midst of his farm. The crushing-stones of this mill are set in motion by buffaloes, and about one picul of raw sugar per day is the average yield of each mill. Thus, it requires many mills and many owners to furnish an annual supply of something like 800,000 piculs of sugar to the market.

Paper, china ware, pottery, grass-cloth and sugar, these form the chief articles of exportation from Swatow, while opium and piece goods are the principal merchandize imported. In 1870 the total value of the imports and exports at this town was about two and a-half millions sterling.

Every year sees an increase in the number of emigrants who leave this part of the province to work on the plantations of Cochin China, Siam, and the Straits of Malacca. More than 20,000 such persons are computed to have left the port in 1870, and we may be sure that the price of labour in China is at a very low ebb when we find that wages from two to three dollars a month are all the inducement held out to emigrants, and that such a sum as this is esteemed by the toiling poor sufficient to enable them to save money to invest in farming on their return to their own country. Chinese labour is much esteemed in the Straits, and I know from personal observation that coolies from China work much better on a plantation than do natives of India or Malays.

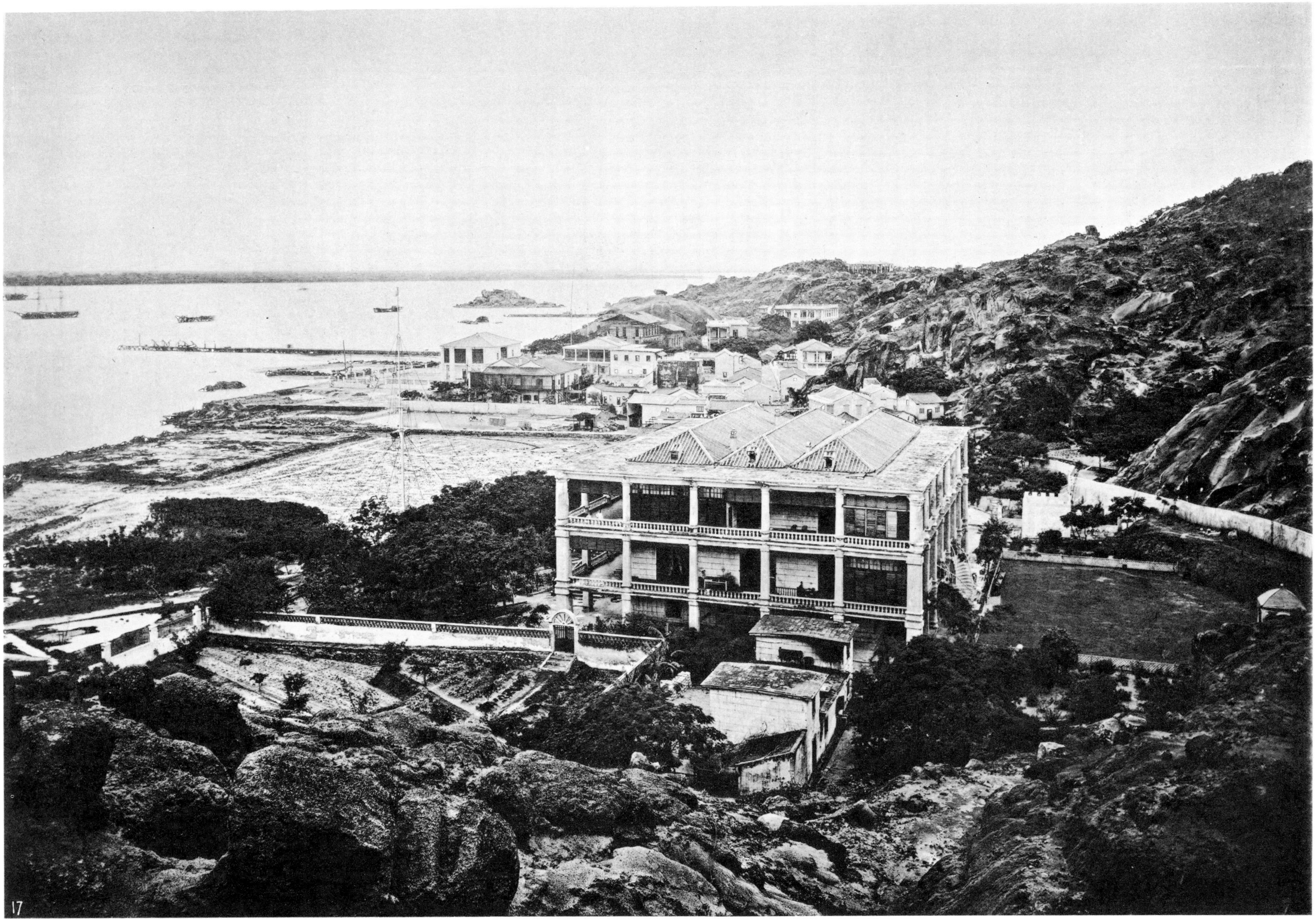

Vol. II, Plate VI

A PAGODA IN SOUTHERN CHINA.

THIS picture presents a type of the numberless pagodas which are scattered over the south of China. The one shown here stands on the right bank of the Han river, near Chao-chow-fu, and, like all the best examples of such edifices, the whole ground structure up to the first story is composed of stone. Within, a winding staircase gives access to the seven stories of which, as may be noticed, the tower is made up, and at each story there is an inner flooring or platform to correspond with the terraces outside. These terraces were originally surrounded by massive stone balustrading, resting on solid ornamental brackets of the same material. The balustrades have in many places been broken away, but what still remains is sufficient to show the beauty and skill with which the stone slabs are dove-tailed into the uprights of the balustrade. It may be computed from the figures shown in the upper terrace that the height of the structure is about 200 feet. This pagoda of course commands an extensive view of the river and the country around, suggesting the idea that such edifices were originally intended as watch-towers, whence the advance of an enemy could be readily discerned. This theory is corroborated by the circumstance that pagodas are much more numerous in those parts of Southern China which have been subject to invasion, and whose history, from the earliest times, is a record of warfare and strife. The positions in which these pagodas were built also seem to indicate that they were intended to serve as beacons and watch-towers, for they almost invariably are found to occupy some commanding height close to the banks of a stream. They are on all hands admitted to have been reared as monuments during the early history of Buddhism in China, and I contend that the promoters of the new faith must have profited by their hard experiences when driven out of India, and shown determination to guard their faith and the relics of Gotama from surprise in a new country. Pagodas appear to be confined solely to China. I have seen nothing like them in Cambodia, Siam, or in any other country where Buddhism prevails.

18

Vol. II, Plate VII

CHAO-CHOW-FU BRIDGE.

CHAO-CHOW-FU, the prefectural city to which Swatow forms the port, stands on the Han river, thirty-five miles above its mouth. The surrounding country is highly fertile and productive. When Swatow was thrown open to foreign trade, a British official was appointed to reside at Chao-chow-fu, as it is the seat of the local government. The attempt was made on several occasions to establish a consulate within the city walls, but the consul was repeatedly attacked by the turbulent mobs for which the place is notorious, and the project was ultimately given up. This tendency of the city roughs and villagers to attack foreigners met with a temporary check in January, 1869. A boat from H. M. S. "Cockchafer" had proceeded up the Han to Otingpoi for the purpose of exercising the crew. The villagers assembled, many of them "in puris naturalibus," and commenced chaffing and pelting the sailors. Efforts made to seize the ringleader were vigorously resisted, and as the villagers, armed with guns, spears, and other weapons, began to assemble in great force, our crew were at last obliged to take to the boat, where they were fired upon and eleven of their number wounded. In this disaster the Chinese mob had greatly the advantage of our men, as they could fire in security from the shelter of the high banks of the stream. This outrage was promptly redressed by our government, who dispatched a party of 500 men to storm the offending village. The result of this strong measure presents itself in the ruined houses and in the cringing civility of the natives about six miles round the spot. This part of the Kwangtung province has always given great trouble to its rulers; indeed, they have been obliged at times to leave their subjects to settle their own disputes by a system of clan and village warfare. As a rule the population in the rural districts are, when fairly treated, of a peaceful and inoffensive character. Under the strong hand of Juilin, governor-general of the two Kwang provinces, disturbances and riot have been summarily suppressed. These clan fights have done not a little to promote the China coolie traffic in its most revolting type, in supplying emigrants.

Chao-chow-fu is a walled city of considerable size and great commercial importance, as one may gather from its extensive warehouses, the busy traffic of its streets, the number of native craft that throng the river on which it stands. The bridge over the river is, perhaps, one of the most remarkable in China. Like old London Bridge, with its shops and places of business, the bridge at Chao-chow-fu affords space for one of the city markets. It will be seen from No. XIX. that the houses on it are built of light material, in a very primitive style, and are supported in such a way as to allow a maximum of market space on the causeway; while from a purely sanitary point of view, the house projecting as it does over the water, offers many advantages. The mode of supporting these structures displays considerable ingenuity. The only brickwork employed rests upon the bridge, and by its weight gives stability to the double brackets that project to support the lighter portion of the houses. I shall have an opportunity in another part of the work, of showing examples of the ingenious and beautiful modes, by which the Chinese support the roofs of their temples and palaces. Although these bridge-dwellings possess few attractions apart from their breakneck style of architecture, it is pleasing to notice some evidence of refinement in the flowers that adorn the verandahs, and that are to be found, indeed, in the humblest dwellings in China. If unexplained, it would be puzzling to find out the use of the two wooden frames which hang suspended from the bridge. They form a kind of moral or mythological drawbridge, which, when let down, is supposed to prevent the passage of boats and evil spirits beneath the bridge till darkness gives place to sunrise.

During my visit, the only foreigner in the city was the British vice-consul. When taking the illustration, I endeavoured to avoid the crowd by starting to work at daylight, but the people were astir, and seeing my strange instrument pointed cannonwise towards their shaky dwellings, they at once decided that I was practising some outlandish witchcraft against the old bridge and its inhabitants. The market stalls were abandoned, and for aught I know the shops were shut, that the barbarian who had come to brew mischief for them all might be properly pelted. The roughs and market people came heart and soul to the task, armed with mud and missiles, which were soon flying in a shower about my head. I made a plunge for the boat, which was fortunately close at hand, and, once on board, it told to my advantage when I charged a ruffian with the pointed tripod as he attempted to stop my progress. My camera lost its cap, and received a black eye of mud in exchange. For myself I sustained but little damage, while it may be fairly said that the bridge was taken at the point of the tripod.

MALE HEADS, CHINESE AND MONGOLIAN.

THE subjects of this plate are types of the male heads of China and Mongolia, No. 20 being that of a boy of the upper or most highly educated class, the son of a distinguished civil officer of Canton. He is a fine, attractive-looking little fellow, his full hazel eyes beaming with kindliness and intelligence. The almond form and oblique setting of the eye, so peculiar to the natives of the south, is well brought out in this picture. The face is altogether a pleasing one, but, as is common among children in China, it will gradually lose its attractions as it grows to maturity. The softness of the eye is then frequently replaced by a cold, calculating expression, the result of their peculiar training, and the countenance assumes an air of apathetic indifference which is so necessary to veil the inner feelings of a polished Chinese gentleman. No. 21 will convey an idea of what this bright little fellow may in time become. It shows the head of a full-grown Chinaman, though of a somewhat lower grade in the social scale — a man whose natural shrewdness and capacity for business have helped him on to a successful mercantile career. The cap he wears is that common in the south during the summer months. Nos. 22 and 25 give the profile and full face of a Mongol. This type belongs to the north of the empire, and the features here are heavier than those of the pure Chinese; indeed, the face, taken as a whole, approaches more closely to that of the European cast. The Mongols wear the head wholly shaven, and in this practice they differ from the Chinese, who invariably carry a plaited queue. No. 24 presents the head of an ordinary Chinese coolie, a fine specimen of the lower orders in China. A man of this sort has enjoyed no opportunities of taking on the polish which is acquired by study and by the high experiences of official life. He is, as a rule, a kindly-disposed person, quite alive to his own interests, and endowed by nature with a profound contempt and compassion for all barbarians who dwell without the pale of Chinese civilization. This will account for the expression he is casting upon me as I am about to hand him down to posterity to be a type of his class. He is thoroughly honest and sincere in his views, wishing in his heart, when kindly treated by a foreigner, that his benefactor had enjoyed the exalted privilege of being born a Chinaman, and that he may yet, in after periods of transmigration, luckily attain to that dignity of birth in some future state. No. 23 is a very old man, with the number of his years, one might almost fancy, registered in the furrows of his brow. He is a labourer, and, although over eighty, still earns a living as a porter; his white hairs and woefully curtailed queue gain him much respect and consideration among his neighbours.

CHINESE FEMALE COIFFURE.

THE hair of the Chinese is uniformly black, or very dark brown, which colour is clearly seen when a single hair is viewed beneath the microscope by strong transmitted light. Their hair, too, is uniformly straight, and the men all wear the queue, while the women dress their tresses into a diversity of artistic forms to suit the prevailing fashion of the locality in which they reside. Thus No. 26 shows a young Cantonese girl of the middle class wearing a head-dress which consists of an embroidered belt of satin, ornamented with artificial flowers, and kingfishers' feathers, and fringed with fine black silk depending from it in front to match the hair, which is cut straight across the forehead. It is a comely face, but before many years are over the natural peach bloom of her young cheeks will be replaced by the fashionable patches of vermilion which conceal the careworn features of married serfdom in China.

No. 27 shows the covering worn by the women of Southern China during the winter months. It consists of a square embroidered handkerchief of cotton or silk, folded diagonally and tied by two of the ends beneath the chin. No. 28, a young Swatow girl, exhibits one style of coiffure adopted in that part of the province; while No. 29 is another fashion belonging to the women of the same place, but of a different clan. The facial type presented in this picture is one peculiar to certain of the natives of Swatow. The nose is prominent, well-formed, and straight, the upper lip short, the teeth white and regular, and the chin well cut. As will be observed, the chignons are each of them different, and all alike deserve careful study by the ladies of Western lands. The dressing of the hair into fantastic forms is naturally a difficult task, and one which, most probably, would shut out spurious imitators in our own country, for few could throw their whole mind and energy into the work. In China, with these women, the hair is only done once or twice a week, necessity requiring the wearer to economize time. With a view to avoid injuring the elaborate coiffure during sleep, the lady supports the nape of her neck upon a pillar of earthenware or wood, high enough to protect the design from being damaged. In our land this device would imply a sacrifice of comfort, and here and there a case of strangulation would ensue; but no very grave objections could be raised to the novel chignon and its midnight scaffolding, when the interests of fashion are at stake. No. 30 is the chignon *par excellence*. The lady who wears it is of Ningpo extraction, and by profession a barber, who also makes wigs and chignons for sale. No. 31 gives the quaint mode of dressing the hair in vogue among the women of Shanghai; these conceal their raven tresses beneath a black velvet snood edged with white or pale blue, and remarkable for its quiet simplicity.

CHINESE ACTORS.

THE theatre and dramatic performances are highly esteemed in China as a means of entertainment during festive seasons.

The attraction of a play will draw business men away from their occupations for days together—a circumstance which proves that the well-regulated Chinaman, however actively he may be engaged, whether in the affairs of the State, or as a hewer of wood and drawer of water, has, after all, leisure at his command for enjoyment which, nowadays, in countries of Europe more enlightened than his, is unknown to more than a few. It has been incorrectly stated that there are no buildings expressly constructed for theatrical performances to be found in China. There are, indeed, none in the majority of Chinese towns; but in Peking, and in some other cities which I visited, edifices designed and solely used for dramatic performances do exist. Hongkong, for example, contains two large and imposing theatres, built by Chinamen and devoted exclusively to the representation of Chinese plays.

In style these two playhouses present a compromise between the plan of a European theatre and that of a native one. There is the pillared portico outside; the business-like check-taker planted behind a small window within; and there are one or two officers to keep order. The interior contains rows of private boxes, curtained and elegantly fitted, where gentlemen can enjoy privacy with their wives and families, and where tables, bedecked with fresh flowers in pots, are used for tea-drinking purposes. The arena is filled with benches; and, besides this, there are upper and side galleries, where cheap accommodation may be secured, and where vendors of cake, fruit, and tea, drive a flourishing business when the house is full. The stage, as in Europe, is illuminated by footlights; but no scenery of any kind is employed,—indeed, scene-painting and scene-shifting are arts unknown to the Chinese. The musicians sit upon the stage behind the actors; and the latter enter or make their exit by two curtained doorways through an ornamental partition which divides the stage from the green-room behind.

There are numerous bands of strolling players, and they may be hired to perform in private dwellings, in temples, or even in sheds erected in the public streets on the occasion of entertainments given by the wealthy to the poor of their neighbourhood. The duty of providing dramatic performances is also at times imposed by way of a fine upon some member of a guild for a violation of its laws. I remember witnessing the close of an open-air performance which had been given by a merchant on the river-bank at Hankow.

An audience of the unwashed and unperfumed had gathered in thousands on the bank of the stream, and were so closely packed together that the bare shaven heads reeking beneath the hot sun looked like a pile of wet turnips, each dotted with its point of bright sunlight. It was near nightfall, and the crowd had been collected there throughout the day. When it dispersed, old men were to be seen limping to their long-neglected duties. Women were bawling for their lost children, dogs that had been shut up in the throng, howled in the joy of freedom. Lewd fellows mocked the obscene gestures of the comedian, and of this motley crowd nothing in a few seconds remained. The scaffolding of the temporary stage was left to await a continuation of the play on the succeeding day.

Chinese actors, if popular, are well paid, They must, however, be men of considerable ability, and gifted with retentive memories, for when they are called on to perform at a feast, it is usual for some favoured guest to select one out of a score or two of plays to be then and there enacted; and many of these actors may have to sustain half a dozen different parts. Although well paid they enjoy few privileges, and are not even allowed to compete at the literary examinations.

The female characters are, as a rule, played by young men or boys, although on one or two occasions I have seen them enacted by women. The dresses usually worn are costumes belonging to the ancient Chinese dynasties, and the garb of the conquering mandarin is studiously avoided.

Nos. 32 and 33 represent actors attired, one as bride and the other as bridegroom, in the costume attributed to the period of the Mings.

Plates 34 and 35 exhibit dresses of the same epoch.

The dramatic parts assigned to females are sung in a shrill piping voice, while the tone of the male is pitched to suit the character represented. This peculiarity has obtained for Chinese theatricals the pigeon English name of " sing-song."

To the uncultivated foreign ear the effect of the band is extremely discordant, as each performer appears to confine himself to his own ideas of tune and time, irrespective of the efforts of his neighbours, some of whom appear to be making frantic efforts to blow their brains out through the brazen instruments. There are, however, occasional solo parts not devoid of a certain quaint charm to the European ear.

The Chinese drama more nearly resembles the romantic plays of modern times than any of the classical models of Europe. It has no heed for the niceties and refinements so prized by Athenian ears ; and its works are of a mixed character, in which tragedy and comedy alternate or combine. As was the case with Greece, some of their dramas are founded on mythology—the " Khan-tsieu-now," for example, where " la première scène du premier acte se passe dans le ciel, et la seconde sur la terre." [1]

---

[1] " Chine Moderne," par M. Bazin ; p. 395.

Vol. II, Plate XI

KULANGSU.

THE island of Kulangsu, in the Fukien province, forms part of the western boundary of Amoy Harbour, and presents a picturesque appearance when viewed from the granite heights of Amoy Island opposite. It was from these heights that the two photographs No. 36 were taken, but they lack the warm colouring and the green slopes which intersperse them. We miss, too, the bright patches of cultivated garden ground, and the belt of yellow sand which runs like a golden setting round this island gem. The girdle of the deep blue sea lends additional beauty to this charming spot, which owes so much to the effect of colour. Scattered over this small island is a native population of more than 3000 souls. Many of these are fishermen, and as Kulangsu is the place where the bulk of the Amoy foreigners reside, a considerable proportion of the local inhabitants are engaged in supplying the wants of the Europeans. Before the capture of Amoy by our forces on August 27th, 1841, this island, along with the others which surround the harbour, were strongly fortified with batteries, so as entirely to command the mouth of the harbour. Many of these defences had been thrown up only a fortnight previous to the time when they opened fire on our ships. The forts themselves could not be silenced until our men had disembarked and driven out their gallant defenders. The latter fought bravely enough, and it is recorded by Dr. Williams, that their heroic leader, Kiang-kiyun deliberately drowned himself in the harbour to escape the disgrace of surviving his defeat.

Vol. II, Plate XII

AMOY HARBOUR.

AMOY was one of the earliest ports to which foreigners resorted. About thirty-six miles north of this place is Chin-chew, known to Marco Polo by the name of Taitun, and, about the beginning of the ninth century, the centre of the local export trade. Amoy harbour is one of the finest on the Chinese coast, and at the points from which plate No. 37 was taken, is more than 800 yards across, thus it offers abundance of anchorage-ground for vessels even of the largest size. There is a maximum difference between high and low water mark here of about eighteen feet. The action of the tide has corroded the basis of many of the bold rocks inside the harbour basin, and a notable instance of this is to be seen in the upright mass of granite which stands in the foreground of this picture, and which is known by Europeans as "Six-mile Rock," and by the Chinese as the "Sail Windlass Rock."

To this pinnacle of stone, popular superstition is attached, for the natives look upon it as a kind of guardian genius who has control over the fates of Amoy. When this rock falls (say the credulous) Amoy will fall too. So year by year additional props are planted beneath its gradually diminishing base. In 1544 the Portuguese attempted to establish a settlement on this part of the coast, but the authorities there, more fortunate than they have been since in Macao, made the place too hot to hold the intruders. In 1624 a second attempt to tap the commercial resources of the district was commenced by the Dutch, who endeavoured to establish themselves on Fisher's Island. This position they afterwards exchanged for Formosa, and from the latter they were finally driven in Koksinga's time. Amoy was thrown open to foreign trade by the treaty of Nanking. The chief exports from this part of Fukien are sugar and tea, a great part of the latter article being grown in the north of Formosa. The import trade is now very much in the hands of the Chinese merchants, who avail themselves of the coast steamers to run to Hongkong to buy their wares, and who, if persons of respectability and standing, find every facility afforded to them by the banks in carrying on their commercial undertakings, however small their own capital may be. The irregular, illegal system of inland transit dues is very damaging to foreign trade, and effectually excludes European wares from many of the marts of the interior. Goods on being transported inland, although they have paid the legitimate port dues, are subject to a system of irregular taxation or squeezing, the amounts which are levied fluctuating with the need of the local officials at different points along the route.

During the war, a tax called le-kin was also imposed to meet the military expenditure. This tax is still levied on foreign merchandize at Amoy, while Swatow and the other ports on the coast, except Formosa, are none of them similarly burdened. Part of the carrying trade from this port to Formosa, Singapore and Batavia is still done in junks, for these, as I believe, are less heavily taxed than square-rigged ships.

The photograph shows that part of the native town of Amoy where the offices of foreign merchants have been built, the town itself stands on the west of the island from which it takes its name.

Vol. II, Plate XIII

VOL. II, PLATE XIV

AMOY WOMEN.

MANY are the old women whom I have seen, and many are the nationalities to which they have belonged; but, in justice to them all, I feel bound to admit that I have not found one who does not possess the little "tache" of nature which makes them akin — a predilection, that is, for sitting and talking about their neighbours' affairs, and for gossiping over the tittle-tattle of the place where they reside. The two old women of my illustration proved no exception to the rule. I fell in with them as they stood in confabulation, and suggested that they would find it easier if they were to sit down to their work. At the time I arrived the elder of the two—she with the black patch on her temple—was recounting the hours of suffering caused her by an acute headache, and how the physician had effected a cure by applying a small round piece of black plaister. This, when removed, she would stick dutifully upon the doctor's door, as a proof of its efficacy in alleviating pain. Her companion is employed by foreigners to nurse their children; she is a woman of a kindly nature, who does her own duty well, but carefully abstains from putting her hand to extraneous work, or drudgery of any kind. To her mistress she is cheerful, civil, and obedient; but her vocabulary to the children under her charge is not always the most select; indeed, she has a ready knack of showing her displeasure, by a free use of vile epithets which their fond mother is fortunately unable to understand. The pay of a good nurse in China is about £24 a-year, out of which sum she has to find herself in food. See No. 38.

SMALL FEET OF CHINESE LADIES.

THIS picture, No. 39, shows us the compressed foot of a Chinese lady, and I regard it as one of the most interesting in my collection. Who the lady is, or where she came from, I cannot say. I had been assured by Chinamen that it would be impossible for me, by the offer of any sum of money, to get a Chinese woman to unbandage her foot, and yet gold and silver are arguments in favour of concessions which operate in the Celestial Empire with more than usual force. Accordingly, all my efforts failed until I reached Amoy, and there, with the aid of a liberal-minded Chinaman, I at last got this lady privately conveyed to me, in order that her foot might be photographed. She came escorted by an old woman, whom also I had to bribe handsomely before she would agree to countenance an act of such gross indecency as the unbandaging the foot of her charge. And yet, had I been able, I would rather have avoided the spectacle, for the compressed foot, which is figuratively supposed to represent a lily, has a very different appearance and odour from that most beautiful and sacred of flowers. Nothing would persuade the lady to raise her dress just high enough to show her ankles. The process of compressing the foot begins in early childhood; the bones of the instep being gradually bent down by continual bandages till they meet the heel in such a manner that the smaller toes almost disappear and become entirely useless. The cripple is thus reduced to supporting herself on the great toe and the ball of the heel. Dr. Dudgeon says, " The os calcis from being horizontal becomes vertical, and its posterior surface is brought to the ground. The bones of the instep are pushed out of their place and made to bulge, thus giving a great prominence, and an arched crescentic form, resembling the new moon, to that part." The points, then, upon which the foot rests, are the heel in its new position, the ball of the great toe, and the fourth and fifth toes, whose upper surfaces have now become parts of the sole. Grave doubts exist about the origin of this artistic deformity of "golden lily feet;" some say it was a jealous husband, who, as already noticed, crippled his wife, that she might thus be more inclined to cultivate the pleasures of home. It is however related that his intentions were disappointed, for that the lady limped about upon her "golden lilies" and flirted abroad as before. The baneful practice is supposed to have come into fashion about the tenth century of our era. It is argued that it cannot have been of great antiquity, because Confucius and the early writers are silent on the subject. Tradition affirms that in 1122 B.C. an imperial lady had club feet, and that, in order to conceal her own defects from her lord, and keep him a stranger to the fair proportions of the feet of her maids, she ordered them to be bandaged. But, be the origin of the custom what it may, there can be no doubt, that it has been in vogue as a distinctive and peculiar institution among the Chinese for centuries past, and it is as much a mark of high breeding with their ladies, as vulture-claw nails are with their gentlemen. We despise so ridiculous a usage as this, but the following extract out of a native work will serve to show that the Chinese return us the compliment, and criticize us for deformities to which the inexorable requirements of fashion have given rise :[1] " The Yin-keih-le, or English females before marriage, bind their waist, being desirous to look slender."

The costume and general appearance of the men and women of Amoy are shown in Plates 40 and 41. The turbanned figure is an ordinary coolie, the type of the industrious labourer whose services are so highly rated in America and the other countries to which he emigrates. His habits of perseverance and economy gradually secure for him the reward of a modest competency, and if he resists the temptations of the opium pipe, and keeps aloof from the gaming tables, he will in a few years have amassed two or three hundred dollars, and with this he will embark as a farmer or a fisherman in his native land. Owing to the poverty of the people, in this part of Fukien, infanticide is still a common practice there, and it is of course the female children whom it is usual to sacrifice thus. In Amoy some of the wealthy Chinese do what they can to mitigate the evil by supporting a Foundling Hospital, where parents are paid a few cash, for bringing their children to be reared.

---

[1] " History of the Pirates," by F. Neumann ; p. 29.

Vol. II, Plate XIV

FOOCHOW ARSENAL.

HE site upon which Foochow Arsenal stands was formerly a piece of marshy ground. This spot, in 1867, when it was finally decided that an arsenal should be built, was raised a number of feet, so as to secure a solid and dry foundation. The work throughout was superintended by M. Giquel, a French gentleman who has shown his fitness for the duties committed to his charge in the undoubted success of the establishment which has been the result of his labours. This Chinese arsenal, or naval training school, as I might more correctly describe it, is to me a very great proof of modern progress in the empire, and marks the dawn of a new era in Chinese civilization. It is, indeed, a practical sign that some great change is at hand. Are we to suppose that the policy of exclusiveness remains unaltered, and that the arsenals at Foochow, Shanghai, Nanking, and Tien-tsin, are meant one day to provide for a great effort which shall drive the hated foreigners for ever from the Chinese shores? or are they designed simply to furnish materials for the maintenance of order within the vast territories of China? Whatever the conclusion to which we come, the active work that is daily going on in such establishments clearly indicates that the Chinese have become aware that to study their ancient classical literature, or to con the maxims of their sages, is not the kind of education which will fit them to cope with their near neighbours, who are adopting the customs, arts, and sciences of the West. These arsenals are not the only signs that light is breaking in upon the long night in which the Chinese race seems to have been sleeping in the bony embrace of her dead philosophers, for this exclusive but sagacious people are not only educating their students in the foreign arts and sciences, but are sending them abroad to foreign universities, in the hope that they may bring back with them the secrets of Western power. The Foochow Arsenal is, as I have said, a school where students are taught theoretical and practical science, and where, under able European supervision, transports and gunboats are designed, built, and fitted with engines manufactured upon the premises. Here, also, students are taught to navigate these ships according to the rules of modern science, as well as to drill and discipline their officers and crews, just as is the practice in our navy.

I visited the arsenal in 1870, and was shown over the different departments. In front of the engineering shops there was a tramway and trucks to facilitate the transit of materials and work from one shop to another. These workshops were fitted with every modern appliance : great steam-hammers, planing and drilling machines, and lathes of every variety. I felt most interested in the optical department, where the men were engaged in constructing portions of chronometers, ships' compasses, and telescopes. Some were busy at brass work, and others at grinding and polishing lenses. They had not, however, got to the length of making the achromatic object-glasses used for telescopes ; but, nevertheless, they were doing work which took me quite by surprise.

In front of the arsenal there was a patent slip for raising vessels broadside on to be repaired. This slip is capable of lifting ships of 3,000 tons.

The monthly expenditure at this arsenal is reported to be about £17,000.

This establishment does great credit to the Viceroy Tso, under whose rule it was built, as well as to M. Giquel, who has shown its uses by having already turned out several war steamers from the building yards.

42

FOOCHOW FOREIGN SETTLEMENT.

FOOCHOW, the capital of the province of Fukien, is situate about half-way between Hong Kong and Shanghai, thirty-four miles inland on the river Min. The foreign settlement is built on the south bank of the stream, about sixteen miles above the outer anchorage. The residences of the foreigners are picturesquely situated on eminences which command extensive views of the country around. The site of the settlement was formerly an old Chinese burial-ground, and abundant disputes arose in consequence, when steps were taken to purchase it for building purposes, the natives being loth to see the dwellings of living "foreign devils" erected over the resting-places of their dead. So whenever it became necessary to disturb a grave, these objections had to be overcome by liberal payments to the proprietors. These homes of the dead are built of granite and native concrete, and are of the omega shape. One of the foreign merchants showed me a fine example of their tombs, which, much to the disgust of his servants, he had transformed into a highly ornamental and cool piggery.

The settlement boasts an excellent club, library, and racket court, while the climate for six or eight months of the year is favourable to outdoor amusements. Many varieties of European flowers and vegetables are grown here to great perfection by the Chinese gardeners. It is altogether a sort of place where foreigners may well be content to reside. Here, as also in Amoy, there are a number of Protestant and Roman Catholic missions in active operation. There is also a prettily built English church, opposite which the Chinese have erected a small shrine, where incense is burnt by devout Buddhists to counteract the influences of the Christian place of worship. Close to the church there is an English mortuary chapel and cemetery shaded with a group of tall, dark pines.

It is only since the year 1853 that Foochow has risen to importance. The chief business carried on there at present is the collection and exportation of the produce of the Bohea tea-fields and of other districts. In 1863 over fifty million pounds of tea were exported from Foochow.

In the foreground of the illustration No. 43, the roofs of a number of Chinese houses are shown surmounted by platforms of wood, on which the families enjoy the cool breezes of summer. There are also rows of water jars filled ready for use in case of fire. This is common in Canton and in many other Chinese cities, but it affords very little protection against conflagration. It will further be observed that the blocks of native houses are divided by substantially built brick walls, which are raised with the object of confining a fire within the limits of a single section of the town. During my visit to Foochow this portion of the native suburb was burned down, but the fire-wall saved the extensive premises of Messrs. Olyphant and Co.

The highest point shown in the hills of the background is "Kushan," or "Drum Mountain," beneath which, in a finely wooded vale, there is one of the most celebrated Buddhist monasteries in China.

43

YUENFU MONASTERY.

THIS Buddhist monastery is remarkable rather for its romantic situation than for any historical associations. To reach it we must ascend that branch of the Min which falls into the main stream, on the south, nearly opposite the centre of the long island formed by the river dividing into two streams seven miles above Foochow, and re-uniting at Pagoda Anchorage.

The monastery is about thirty miles distant from Foochow in a very mountainous and richly-wooded country, which reminded me of the scenery of the Trosachs, the bold rocky outlines of the hills and glens on both sides of the river being here toned down by a profusion of foliage. The sacred edifice rests in a cavern on the summit of a mountain, and is only reached after a tedious and precipitous ascent. To this place many pilgrims resort, and I can well fancy the weary devotee pausing as he climbs to rest beneath the shade, and to admire the sublimity of the scenery around. Sacred texts from the classics are everywhere sculptured on the rocks, and it is in a dark recess, resting on a ledge of solid stone, with a frowning precipice of great depth in front, that this remarkable shrine has been constructed. The cave has been formed by the fall of a great mass of rock into the ravine beneath, where it has been overgrown with trees probably centuries old. A natural tunnel under this rock affords a covered way to the monastery, and above it the path leads us through a rocky chasm, roofed over with gigantic ferns. The quaint establishment, propped upon the stony projection, presents a very temporary and insecure appearance; this only applies, however, to the front of the monastery, as all the inner buildings are supported on a solid rock basis. There are three monks permanently attached to the building; one of them was a mere boy and full of vivacity, the second was an able-bodied, good-natured youth, and the third was very old, infirm, and blind. These recluses appeared to be extremely strict in their ritualistic observances; waking me every morning at sunrise by the wailing of their chants, by ringing their bells, and beating their gongs. Their meals, according to the practice of their order, consisted wholly of vegetable food, and tobacco was a luxury in which they freely indulged. Nevertheless I strongly suspect the old man to have been an opium smoker.

The water supply was obtained by a hollow bamboo rope, which had one end inserted in a spring above the projecting cliff, over which this bamboo duct was suspended, as shown on the left of the photograph No. 44, while the lower end communicated with a stone tank into which the water was allowed to flow.

44

Vol. II, Plate XVII

THE ABBOT AND MONKS OF KUSHAN MONASTERY.

IT is interesting to note how closely the dress of the Buddhist monk resembles the monastic garb of ancient Europe. In both we see a robe long, simple, and ample, falling loosely to the feet; and both carry a cowl for the protection of the head in cold weather, as well as a rosary to aid the wearer in keeping his debtor and creditor account of good and bad thoughts, words, and works.

This account the Buddhist devotee must privately balance during his hours of meditation, and at the close of every day, until he has reached that supreme degree of sanctity when the principles of good and evil will have ceased to combat in his heart, when the lusts of the flesh will no longer have power to torment, and all the weaknesses of his mortal body are absorbed in that perfect state of comatose ecstasy which is termed in their scriptures " Nirvana." The similarity between the Buddhist faith and the Roman Catholic churches may be traced even more minutely than this. " Buddhists everywhere have their monasteries and nunneries, their baptism, celibacy and tonsure, their rosaries, chaplets, relics, and charms, their fast-days and processions, their confessions, mass, requiems, and litanies, and, especially in Thibet, even their cardinals, and their pope."

These resemblances are probably accidental, as this vital distinction still separates the two phases of faith, that Buddhism in its original purity is a practical atheism, to which the Christian doctrine of atonement is absolutely unknown. The Buddhists have ten chief commandments which their great teacher left behind for their guidance. One or two of these I have subjoined :—

Thou shalt not kill any living creature.
Thou shalt not steal.
Thou shalt not drink strong liquors.
Thou shalt not eat after the appointed hours.
Thou shalt not have in thy private possession either a metal figure (an idol), or gold, or silver, or any valuable thing.

There are also a multitude of minor laws which have an important place in the regulations of the Buddhist priesthood. Thus at meal times :—

Every priest before he eats shall repeat five prayers for all the good things which have happened to him up to that day.
His heart is to be far from all cupidity and lust.
He shall not speak about his dinner, be it good or bad.
He shall not smack in eating.
When cleansing his teeth he shall hold something before his mouth.

In section eleven it is commanded you shall not take any meat with dirty nails. These, and many more such as these, make up the maxims of Buddha, and except he strictly observes them all no mortal can attain to the bliss of final absorption into Nirvana. If this be indeed true, then the disciples of Sakyamuni in China at the present day have, I fear, but slender prospects of happiness in a future state. See No. 45.

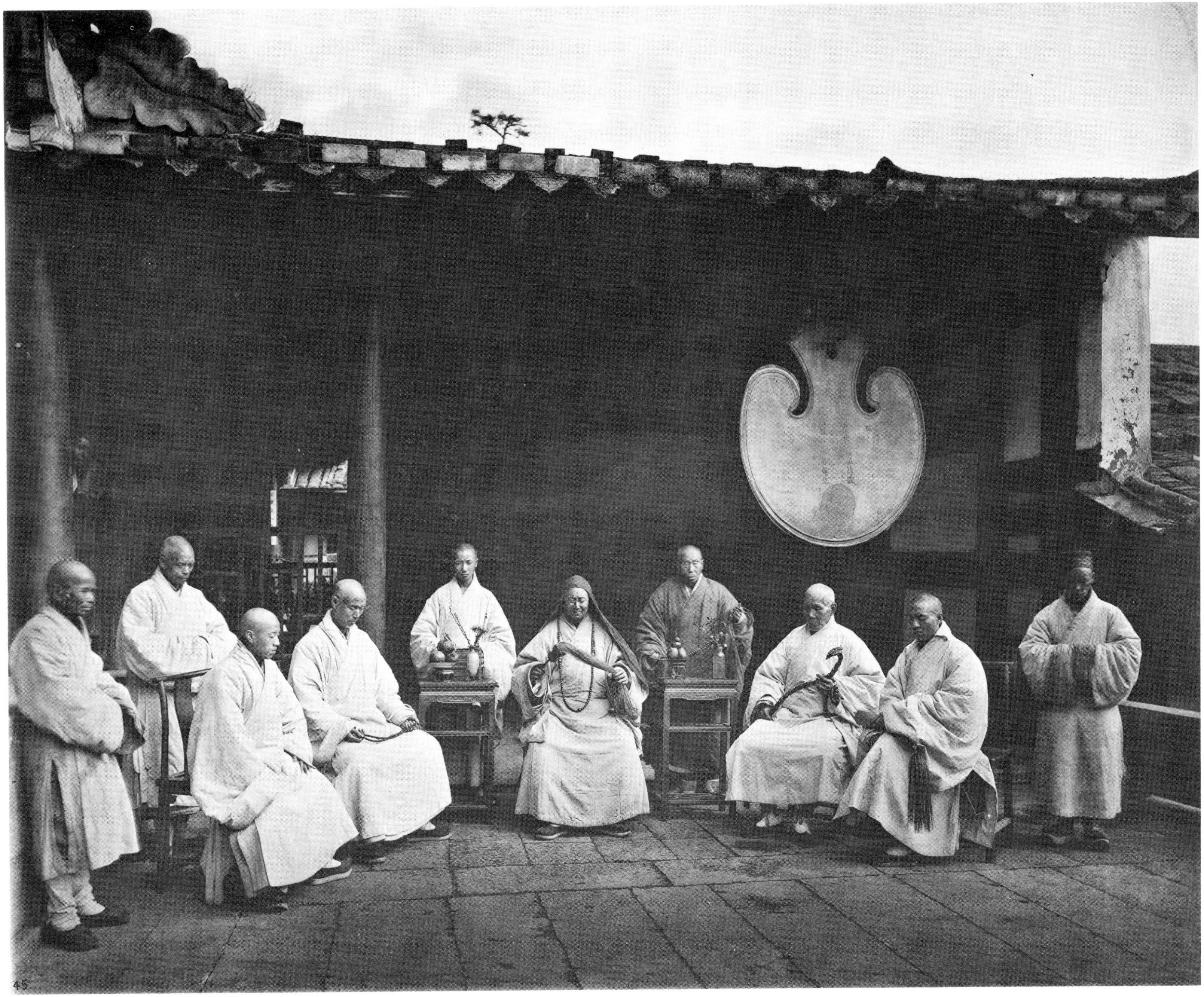

Vol. II, Plate XVIII

OLD JUNKS.

NTERESTING craft are the old weather-beaten junks which lie at anchor in the Canton river, waiting till the monsoon is favourable, to proceed upon their voyages. The usual destination of such junks is one of the ports on the China coast, or at furthest, Siam, Java, Borneo, or the Straits of Malacca. At their moorings, as represented in No. 46, these huge, clumsy vessels seem like mid-stream dwelling-places, fastened down by solid foundations to the river's bed, but when full rigged for sea, they look well, and even at times make good sailing before the wind; indeed, in every way they are more manageable than appearances would betoken. Yet the least favoured of our square-rigged ships will easily outsail the fastest of them. This is a fact which is making its way into the Chinese mind, but the process is slow and gentle, like that by which I have seen a pebble that had been caught in the hollow of a rock in the Upper Yangtsze, and that, with the action of the water and a few particles of sand, had drilled its way deep into the hard stone. Native builders have made a compromise between their old junks, and the foreign ship, and the new model, thus adopted, has been presented to the reader in Vol. I. Junks and junk-rigged craft are not uncommonly charged with lighter dues at their ports of destination. This spurious advantage is, however, ignored by the higher class of native merchants who trade at the open ports, and who readily avail themselves of the speed and security afforded for the transportation of merchandise by steamers and high-class sailing ships, many of which are jointly owned by foreigners and Chinese, and by companies in which Chinamen have subscribed for shares. The foregoing considerations will make it plain that the complete abolition of the ancient junk is nothing more than a question of time.

There are many evils in China which the governing class alone have power to redress, and which they will rapidly sweep away when it is their direct individual and collective interest to do so. One of these is the old tax, still levied in some quarters, on ships when they enter a harbour. This is a violation of treaty which is supposed to abolish all local dues on ships, yet at Takow and Taiwemfu, the district authorities collect one hundred and sixty-eight dollars on a ship, and one hundred and forty dollars on a barque, when arriving at port, taxing other vessels also according to a fixed scale.

The eyes of a junk, as has already been explained, are introduced to scare away deep-sea demons, and have nothing to do with the popular fiction, "No can see, no can walkee." The ports painted on her sides are blind, but there are a number of guns mounted on her deck, and these are kept in good fighting trim. Armaments of this sort are still necessary in the China seas, although acts of piracy there are not so common as of old. The hold is divided into water-tight compartments, and almost her entire capacity is used for stowage of cargo, even her deck being piled with bales and cases. Part of the crew are accommodated in berths, and the remainder are packed away among the merchandise. Her sails are of matting strengthened by and stretched on transverse ribs of bamboo. The anchor is of a wood that sinks readily in water, while the huge unwieldy-looking rudder is worked by a system of blocks and ropes which, at times, require the efforts of the entire crew of the junk.

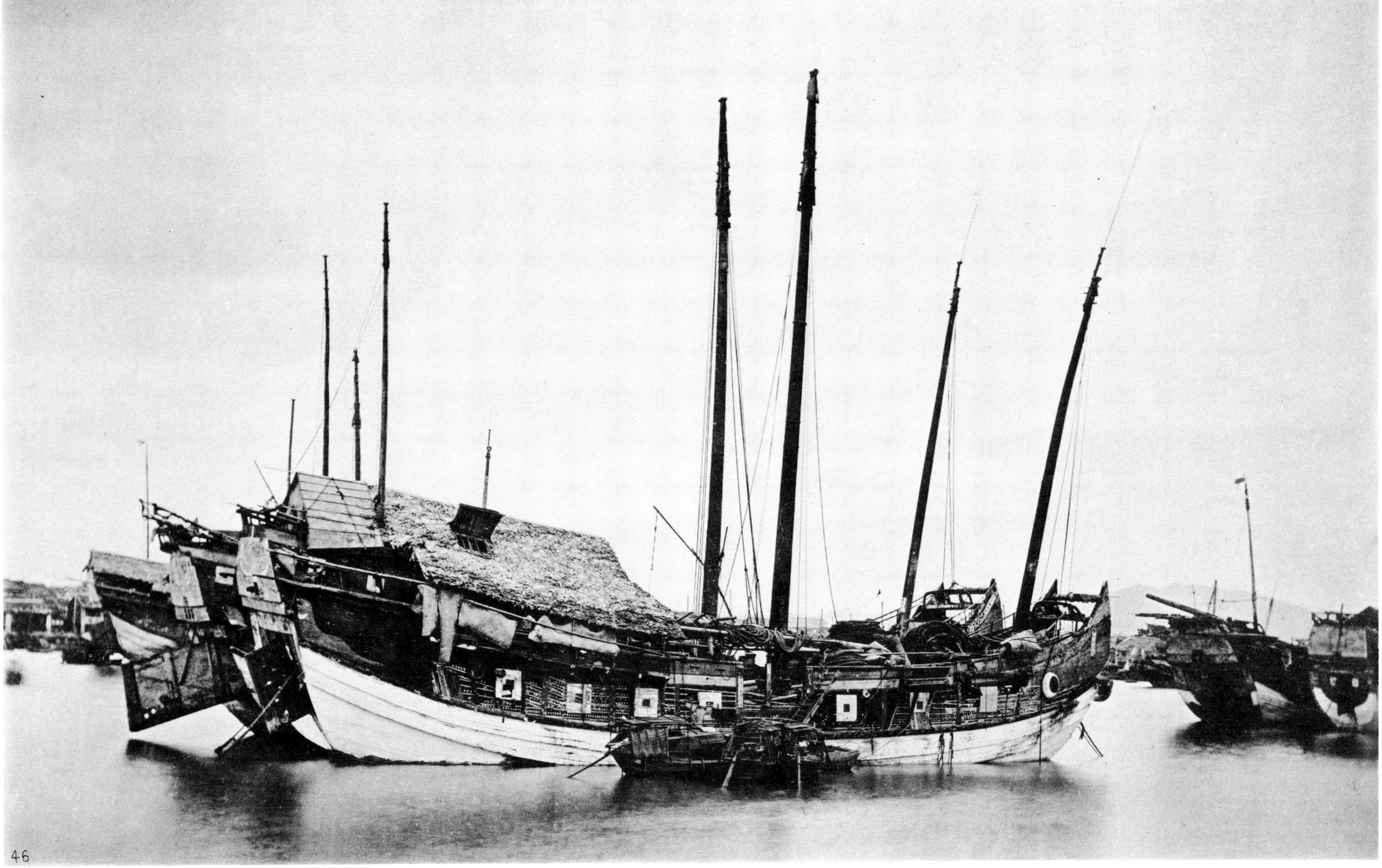

46

Vol. II, Plate XIX

PART OF THE FOREIGN SETTLEMENT, FOOCHOW.

THIS view, No. 47, is taken from the upper end of the foreign settlement, looking across the broad surface of the Min.

The picture is valuable, as it shows the plan of a Chinese house, general among the lower middle classes. The street entrance is unfortunately concealed by a wall cutting off the left corner of the foreground of the picture. The outer brick wall of the dwelling is raised to the height of the roof, and encloses a nearly quadrangular space, the front half of this being an open court, with apartments to the right and left, while to the rear, within the wall, is the dwelling where the members of the family reside. The outer doorway is the only opening by which access to this walled enclosure can be obtained. Light and air are admitted by the doors and windows that open into the court inside. Thus, when the outer entrance has been barred for the night, the family is completely secluded from the gaze of the world outside. Indeed, it is impossible at any time to see from the street what is going on within the court, even when the door is left open, for at three or four feet distance from the entrance a wooden screen intervenes. This screen is devised to guard against the importunity and annoyance of the spirits of the dead, which are supposed only to be capable of travelling in straight lines. To obtain the most perfect degree of privacy and seclusion is the primary object in the construction of all Chinese houses of any pretensions.

In many of the abodes of the poor this object is, from necessity, lost sight of, although, when it is attainable, they environ their humble dwellings with high fences of prickly bamboo or cactus. The best class of Chinese houses have a stone foundation and walls of brick, and the roofs are supported by crossbeams, which rest either on the walls themselves, or on wooden pillars whose tops are concealed beneath the broad eaves, and for this reason, as we may suppose, are devoid of capitals. The rafters consist of slender strips of wood, strong enough to sustain the weight of the red earthenware tiles above them. In some instances these rafters are hidden by a ceiling of coarse cloth stretched on frames and whitewashed. The interiors of the houses are highly ornamented with elaborately carved wooden partitions, and the walls are adorned with cleverly painted landscapes, groups of flowers, or fruit. Coloured tiles stamped with ornamental patterns run along the ridge of the roof; carved brackets support the eaves, while the water-pipes are of glazed earthenware, frequently so fashioned as to imitate the stems of the bamboo. In the centre of the court a deep-sunk well is usually to be found, and this is crowned with a single block of stone, pierced to admit a bucket. This stone is kept carefully covered; the door-posts and lintel of the outer entrance are also of stone, and a space on the wall above the doorway has some mythological design modelled in relief, and skilfully painted.

I shall endeavour to show, in a subsequent part of the work, the important position which the geomancer occupies in China—how his functions are called into request, alike in the cutting of roads, the building of houses for the living, and digging graves for the dead.

TERRACING HILLS.

TERRACING is greatly resorted to in China for the irrigation and cultivation of what would be otherwise waste land. No. 48 represents such a terraced hill taken on the roadside in the neighbourhood of Foochow, near a place called "The Plantation," which all foreign residents know well. Many of the hills are by this means, and by the skill and industry of the small farmers, made to yield three crops a year, and the land thus taxed is never allowed to lie fallow. The sewage of the city of Foochow is carried out by labouring women to fertilize the country. The women employed in this and other field work are represented in No. 49. They are strong, healthy, and many of them attractive-looking. Their olive cheeks are warmed with a glow of colour, and their glossy black hair is decked with silver ornaments and fresh flowers. Their dress is simple, and remarkable for its bright cleanliness. They never compress their feet, but rather draw the eye to their natural smallness by wearing prettily embroidered shoes.

THE PAILAU.

THIS is the nearest approach made in China to the triumphal arch of Europe. The Pailau or memorial arch is always erected by special permission of the emperor, and not always as with us, in memory of the noble deeds and virtues of the dead. A man, if he has done anything remarkable, and has funds at his command, may during his lifetime erect a Pailau for himself. A widow who has led an exemplary life to the age, say, of fifty, and abstained from marrying a second husband, may erect an arch to commemorate her virtues, and in this she will be aided by a small grant from the imperial treasury. In general design these monuments are similar to the triple gateways in temples and in the mansions of the great. The words "Shing-chi," signifying "erected by imperial favour," are inscribed over the central archway. The Pailau shown in No. 50 was erected to the memory of a virtuous widow.

FOOCHOW COOLIES.

PLATE 51 shows us that the Chinese coolies carry their burdens suspended from the two ends of a bamboo pole supported by the shoulders of the bearer. Socially the coolie is a very humble character. Poor as he is, nevertheless he is cheerful and contented, industrious and easily managed; he has a smattering of education, too; although he has not dipped into the classical lore of his country, he has a knowledge of the elementary characters of the language, which enables him to feast his mind on street literature, and revel in the simple books of folklore that are to be found in Chinese cities. His dress consists of a jacket and trousers of coarse cotton cloth, but if in prosperous circumstances he has one suit for summer, and a second for winter wear; the latter is the costume which is represented here. It is padded with layers of cotton, and has usually an eventful history attached to it, as the necessities of the poor wearer compel him often to place it in pawn during the summer, in order to release his lighter suit, but it frequently happens when money is scarce that he finds himself unable to redeem his clothes, and then they pass into other hands.

THE MA-QUI.

THE gentleman represented in No. 52 is known in the city of Foochow as a " Ma-qui "—" swift as a horse," and holds the subordinate position of detective officer attached to the magisterial establishment. I paid him a visit at his residence, and took his portrait in the central court. This man is reported to know the haunts of all the thieves in his district. He has been called " the king of the thieves," and he exercises an undoubted sway over the gangs that infest the city.

The liberal views regarding the ownership of property held by these unruly subjects of the Ma-qui meet with a degree of sympathy and consideration from detectives, which is at times apt to thwart the ends of justice.

Thus I myself once applied to one of these native detectives to aid me in tracing some property which had been lost; he coolly informed me that he thought he knew the thief, and that if I really wanted the goods, he was quite confident he could recover them on my paying about three-fourths of their value.

There are many expert professional thieves in China, men who would be profitable hands to any chief who would wink at their peculiarities and take them into his protection.

Housebreaking is practised with great address, particularly in foreign settlements. A gentleman with whom I was acquainted had the following experience with a Chinese burglar:—About midnight, as he lay awake in his bed, the lamp having gone out and the windows being open on account of the heat, he noticed a dark figure climbing up over one of the windows into the room where he lay. My friend remained quite still, and when the thief, believing all to be safe, had stolen into the centre of the apartment, he sprang out of his bed and seized the intruder. Both were powerful men, and a fierce struggle ensued; but the robber had the advantage, as his only covering was a thick coat of oil, so that slipping like an eel from the grasp of his antagonist, he made a plunge at the window, and was about to drop into the garden, when his pursuer made a final effort to catch him by the tail. This tail was coiled up round his head and stuck full of needles, but the thief got away after all, for even the queue was a false one, and as he dropped into the garden it came away by the weight of the fall, and was left an unprofitable trophy in the hands of the European whom he had vainly tried to rob.

BEGGARS.

PROFESSIONAL beggars are numerous in all parts of China, but it is in the larger cities that they more particularly abound, and their skill in dodges and deception would have furnished advantageous hints to the mendicants who used to infest our English thoroughfares. In China the beggar pursues his calling unmolested, and even has received for himself a recognition and quasi-protection at the hands of the civic authorities. The fact is, that the charitable institutions—of which there are many all over the country, and which are conducted in some cases with a fair degree of honesty—are yet totally unable to cope with the misery and destitution that prevails in populous localities. No poor-law system is known, and the only plan adopted to palliate the evil is to tolerate begging in public, and to place the lazzaroni under the local jurisdiction of a responsible chief. In Foochow the city is divided into wards, and within the limits of each ward a head man is appointed, who can count his descent from a line of illustrious beggars, and in him rests the right, which would seem to be, to keep the members of his order under his own management and control. During my visit to Foochow I was introduced to one of these beggar kings, and he it is, with three of his subjects, who are presented to the reader in No. 53. I found this man to be an inveterate opium smoker, and consequently in bad circumstances, in spite of the handsome revenue which he was known to receive.

I afterwards visited the house of another head man, and there I was much struck with many evidences of comfort, and even luxury, with which he was surrounded. The eldest son of the chief received me at the entrance, and conducted me into a guests' chamber; and while I was sitting there, two ladies dressed in silks, and with a certain degree of refinement in their air, passed the door of the apartment in order to get a glimpse of its inmate. My host informed me that these ladies were his mother, and his father's second wife or concubine; but the chief himself was unfortunately not at home. This king of beggars has it in his power to make an agreement with the shopkeepers of any street which runs through his district; and when a compact of this kind has been concluded, he will protect them from the pestering visits of his gang of beggars. Any shopkeeper who fails to come to terms is liable to have his establishment haunted by the most offensive class of mendicants. It was related to me that a silkmercer had failed to contribute his beggars' rate. One of the fraternity accordingly paid a visit to his shop, having his body smeared over with mud, and bearing in his hand a bowl slung with cords, and filled to the brim with foul water. Thus armed, he commenced to swing the bowl round his head without spilling a drop of its contents, but had anyone attempted to arrest his hand, the water would have been distributed in a filthy shower over the silks piled upon the counter and shelves. The shopkeeper paid his rate.

The worst class of beggars are the outlaws, who recognize no chief, and who live in holes and hovels about the burial grounds. I made the acquaintance of some of this class, and I have given a picture of them in No. 54. I found them dwelling, with many others, in a Chinese city of the dead, where the coffins containing bodies are deposited temporarily in mortuary houses or tombs till the geomanas has been paid to find a suitable place of interment. Many of these coffins are, however, never moved again, and then they rot in their places where they were stowed. In the first of these charnel-houses which I came to, I fell in with a living tenant, an old man so worn and ghastly that I fancied he had forced himself free from the mouldy, dank coffin that lay in the darkest corner of the sepulchre. He was seated at the doorway moaning, and striving to fan into flame some withered branches which he had gathered to make a fire. Further on I found the subjects presented in my photograph. These occupied another tomb, and had established a begging firm under the control of a lusty chief, who had just concluded a hearty meal, and who is seen standing in front of the entrance enjoying a pipe. His ragged partners were each discussing a reeking mixture of broken scraps which they had collected during the day. They had now laid aside their daily counterfeits of disease and deformity, and were laughing merrily, forgetful of the cares and coffins that surrounded them. The jester of the party was a man who made a good thing of it by acting the religious devotee, performing penance by driving an axe into his head; when I saw this impostor he was seated astride the highest coffin, cracking his jokes over the skull of its occupant.

Another of the party drove a flourishing trade with a loathsome skin disease. All of them, in truth, were dead to such of the finer feelings as usually have their home in a Chinaman's heart.

Vol. II, Plate XXI

THE SEDAN.

THE sedan-chair is one of the most useful institutions in China, and has been employed there from a very ancient date. Private sedans are kept by the civil mandarins, and by people of wealth and rank. In former days strict rules existed, which forbade certain of the lower orders, and even foreigners, from using sedans.

These rules are still in force among the Chinese, and with the civil mandarins the sedan is the official means of conveyance, their rank being denoted by the covering and furniture of their chairs, as well as by the number of bearers, and of the footmen in attendance. Military mandarins, on the other hand, travel, or pay their official visits, on horseback, as is shown in No. 56. Public chairs are now in use in different parts of the empire, and these I have already described in Volume I.

THE PLOUGH.

THE Chinese plough, like that in use with us, is furnished with a share and mould-boards of iron. The one shown in No. 57 has, however, only a single lever fastened to the beam in place of the two which are employed to guide our ploughs. It will be seen that the ploughman is enabled by this means to direct his implement with one hand, while the other is left disengaged for managing the ox, which is yoked to the plough. This ox, in the Fukien province, is of a very small breed, and is employed for light work, such as the ploughing of orchards and gardens.

NORTH CHINA PONY.

NORTH China pony, one that was trained successfully as a racer, is shown in No. 58. Most of these ponies are bred on the Mongolian plain, and are brought down during the winter months to Peking for sale. There they fetch from £5 to £50 apiece, and are then commonly transported by their purchasers to the ports on the coast, and re-sold at much higher prices. They are hardy and strong-limbed animals, and the example in the photograph affords a handsome type of its class; although, in common with all the ponies of Mongolia and China, it has the head large, and a frame which inclines to be heavy. No horses are either bred or made use of in China; even the cavalry there are mounted on ponies such as this one, and mules are held in greater esteem than horses among the Chinese. It seems strange that they should not have endeavoured to improve their own stock by making use of some of those high-bred horses which were left by our troops in the country at the close of the last war; but it is clear they have not done so, as they have still nothing better than their own heavy-limbed ponies to show.

Vol. II, Plate XXII

THE FRUITS OF CHINA.

THE majority of the fruits grown in China are indigenous to the country, and there are many which have not yet been introduced into the orchards of Europe. A proportion, however, of the Chinese fruits are common also to the more temperate climates of the west. although, with one or two exceptions, these varieties are not reared to a perfection in China, equal to that obtained in other countries, where the same fruit is to be found. This remark applies especially to the apples, pears, peaches, plums, and grapes in the southern provinces, where the gardeners show a strange tendency to gather and dispose of their fruit before it has fully ripened. It is less true of the northern provinces, where these fruits are nearly equal in quality and flavour to the produce of our English gardens. The principal fruits of China, as given by Dr. Williams, are comprised in the following list :—The pomegranate, carambola or tree gooseberry, mango, custard apple, pine apple, rose apple, bread-fruit, fig, guava, and olive. The whampe, lichee, langan, and loquat are the native names of four fruits, the second of which is said to have been introduced, while the others are indigenous. The lichee, probably the finest of these, has a rough and granulated skin of a bright red colour. The pulp is whitish, opalescent, and juicy, and covers a hard seed, which, in fruit of inferior quality, is often of considerable size. A lichee may be seen in the right-hand corner of No. 59, with its skin broken and hanging away. The Averrhoa carambola, known to foreigners as the Chinese gooseberry, is shown in the same picture to the extreme left. This fruit grows in great abundance in Malayan India. To these we may add the plantain (*Musa paradisea*), of which there are many varieties in Southern China and Formosa ; the papaya (*Carica papaya*), the seeds of which are used as anthelmintics ; oranges and limes of numerous kinds ; and the persimmon, which looks like a huge tomato, and has its polished skin filled with a sweet succulent pulp of a pinkish colour. Wild raspberries grow in abundance in Formosa, and have a flavour equal to those of our home gardens.

Vol. II, Plate XXIII

THE TEA PLANT.

THE geographical limits within which the cultivation of the tea plant has in modern times been carried probably lie between the 25th and 37th parallels of north latitude, Japan being the northernmost country in which the shrub is grown, and Assam the furthest point south to which its culture has been at all successfully extended. Fortune considered that the districts in which tea can be grown to greatest perfection are those between 27° and 31° north; and it seems probable that the finest qualities of tea are still to be found on the slopes, terraces, and steppes of the Bohea range of mountains. The two varieties of this plant which are best known in China are *Thea Bohea* and *Thea viridis*. From the former black teas are manufactured, while *Thea viridis* supplies the best descriptions of green. The tea plantations, with few exceptions, are small in size, as is the case also with the plantations of mulberry in the districts where silkworms are reared. The fact is that the growers are most of them small farmers, men who possess little or no capital of their own, but obtain advances on their crops through the landowners, or the agents of the native tea merchants, to whom they dispose of their tea. Most of the capitalists engaged in the tea traffic are sharp-witted, far-seeing traders, belonging to Canton.

The tea plants are reared from seed sown in a nursery, and when they are sufficiently matured, the finest of them are selected, and planted out in rows about four feet apart, a like interval being left between each of the plants, so that every clump enjoys an equal share of soil and sunshine. See Nos. 60 and 61. Manuring is rarely resorted to, as the plant is a hardy one, which, if kept free from weeds, will mature in about three years' time. It is then ready for picking, and is never allowed to flower. The first crop of the early leaves is gathered in the month of April, the young leaves then yielding the finest teas, while the older leaves are collected in May and during the early part of June. The leaves thus gathered are sold to the tea agents, who, when they have obtained a sufficient quantity to make up a parcel of say 600 chests, so mix the leaves together as to secure that degree of uniformity in the manufactured tea which will admit of its being brought to market under a specific name. In the production of a good sound tea a great deal undoubtedly depends upon the quality of the leaves, but the marketable character of the article owes quite as much to its subsequent manipulation in the firing and sifting rooms. Black teas are produced by first allowing the fresh leaves to ferment and blacken by the oxidation which follows their exposure in the open air and light, while green tea is obtained from the same plant by arresting the exposure of the leaves while they are still green, and before the process of fermentation has set in.

It has been reported by Mr. Fortune that certain green teas owe their hues to an admixture of deleterious colouring matter; I have, however, never seen this process of tea-dying in operation.

There are spurious teas exported—those made up of tea-leaves that have been already in use. It is impossible to say what foreign matter, either designedly or by accident, may have been introduced into such as this, but the teas that are bought and sold at fair prices are remarkable for their purity.

THE YENPING RAPID.

THE Min is the great artery down which the produce of the central tea districts of China is conveyed to the Foochow market for exportation. Several rapids are to be found on this river, and of these the one represented in No. 62 is by far the most dangerous, for the channel at this point is interspersed with huge masses of rock, on which many a cargo-boat is wrecked during the year. At all seasons the greatest pluck and dexterity are needed in the steersman to bring his boat in safety down this rapid. When I descended it in December, 1871, there were evidences of recent wrecks strewn over the rocks, and in portions of the cargo that had been saved and piled up along the banks. At one time I thought that our boat would have been dashed to pieces, for it seemed to be flying down the rapid and on to a jagged rock, and the helmsman appeared incapable of bringing her round in time to clear the danger. His appearance, however, was reassuring; calmly and impassively he stood at the helm, and just as I was prepared to make a spring for the rock, he cast his whole weight on to the rudder, and brought the boat round with a swoop within a hair's breadth of the rock, and we escaped with the side of the boat slightly grazed.

SMALL RAPID BOAT.

THE scene represented in No. 63 was taken about 100 miles above Foochow, and shows the boat in which I ascended the river Min for a distance of about 260 miles from its mouth, as far as the city of Yenping. The boat is strongly built, and is as nearly as possible flat-bottomed. Its frame is of hard wood, planked with pine, a tree which grows in abundance on the hills of this portion of Fukien.

VOLUME III

VOL. III

LIST OF ILLUSTRATIONS.

LIST OF ILLUSTRATIONS.

NOTE.—*The numbers corresponding with the above list will be found marked in the lower left corner of each subject.*

The Photographs are printed in Permanent Pigment by the Autotype Mechanical Printing Process, by MESSRS. SPENCER, SAWYER, BIRD, AND CO., *London.*

VOL. III, PLATE I

NINGPO, PROVINCE OF CHEH-KIANG.

CHEH-KIANG is the smallest among the eighteen provinces of China, but for all that it has a history of considerable importance, its products are numerous and valuable, and its commerce great. Hang-chow-fu, the capital, has long been renowned for its magnificence. The great Venetian traveller pronounced it an Eastern paradise; but, in common with most places of note in China, it has experienced many vicissitudes of fortune, there have been seasons of trial and suffering when its ancient glory was like to depart from the city, and the culminating catastrophe overtook the place in 1861, when the Taiping rebels overthrew it. On that occasion the leader of the "great peace" sent his army to besiege the city and to lay it waste, a task which was most effectually carried out by the motley followers of the "Tien Wang," or "Heavenly King," as he styled himself. Famine, with a train of horrors such as recall the history of the siege of Jerusalem, was followed by the fall of the town, and then the populace were unsparingly slaughtered, and the palaces were destroyed. But there is something to be told of Cheh-kiang of deeper interest even than this, for in that province, at a spot called Huang-ke, Yu,[1] the famous founder of the first dynasty of China,[2] is reported to have met his end. If the records of the "Shoo King" are to be credited, Yu was one of the greatest men that ever lived. When he entered upon his labours the Empire had been desolated by a great flood, and he is said to have shown an engineering capacity almost superhuman by deepening the rivers, draining the land, and conducting the streams into their original channels. Yu flourished perhaps something more than a century subsequent to the period of the Noachian deluge; the flood which Yu successfully dealt with may probably have been caused by a change in the course of the Great Yellow River similar to what occurred for the ninth time (according to Chinese accounts) between the years 1851 and 1853. At any rate, the overflow of the river during Yu's time is referred to in the "Shoo King."

The province of Cheh-kiang is rich and productive, and in its mountain regions presents some of the most charming scenery which China has anywhere to show.

Ningpo, the port now thrown open to foreign trade, was one of the first places to which the Portuguese resorted after their expulsion from the south. At that spot they established themselves on the river Yang in 1522, and there, according to Chinese records, owing to their barbarous conduct, some twenty years later met with a fearful retribution at the hands of the Chinese. Their settlement was then destroyed, their ships were burned, and 800 of their detested race were slain.

Ningpo stands on the left bank of the Yang, about twelve miles inland. On the 3rd April, 1872, I crossed over to the place from Shanghai in the steamer "Chusan." It was daybreak when I entered the river, and the somewhat harsh outlines of the islands and the Chinhai promontory were mellowed in the morning light, while a multitude of fishing boats with their sails spread to catch the gentle breeze contributed to enliven the scene. Fukien timber junks, laden till they looked like floating wood yards, were labouring on their voyage up the stream. One feature full of novelty to the foreign visitor is the endless succession of ice houses lining the bank at short intervals, and stored with ice for use in the exportation of fresh fish during summer.

FUKIEN TEMPLE.

AMONG the chief attractions of the town of Ningpo, is the Tien-how-kung, or "Queen of Heaven" Temple, the meeting house of the Fukien Guild. I have chosen this edifice as the frontispiece of this volume partly because it affords one of the finest examples of temple architecture in the Empire, and partly because the subject of Chinese guilds and trades unions is exceedingly important in connection with the social economy of the people.

The student of architecture will find the picture worthy of the closest scrutiny, for even the minutest details among the ornaments of the building are full of deep significance in reference to native art and the Buddhist or Hindoo mythology.

[1] "Chinese Classics," by J. Legge, D.D., vol. iii. p. 61.　　　[2] "China," par M. Panthier, p. 466.

It will be noticed that the stone pillars of the central edifice are remarkable for grotesque yet beautiful designs, where the dragon, the national emblem of China, is seen to be the leading figure. This dragon has been cut in high relief round each pillar, and made by this means to appear as if sustaining the temple; the same reptile may be discovered carved in low relief on the blocks of stone between the steps, and supporting also the ornament which forms the apex of the roof above. The dragon wields a potent influence over the people of the Empire; it forms one of the fundamental principles of their system of geomancy, and is supposed to exist in every mountain and stream throughout the land: its control is as firmly believed in by the Chinese masses as are the benign effects of the sunshine upon the earth. The dread of disturbing the repose of the dragon spirit as he broods over the soil of China, forms one of the chief obstacles to the advance of Western science, to the opening of mines, and to the construction of railroads and telegraphs across the interior of the country. It will be seen that the pillars of the temple here shown have no capitals, and that they are furnished by way of substitute with ornamental brackets made so as to throw the weight of the massive roofs down the centre of the shafts. Brackets such as these are in common use, and are applied to a variety of purposes. The central roof, for example, is supported by a system of ornamental triple brackets, which combine great strength with lightness and elegance of design. They are strong enough to prop up the heavy superstructure, by which a cool shade is obtained, and, at the same time, sufficiently open to admit light and air into the inner hall. It is impossible to describe in detail the fitness and charm of such a building as this. I must rather allow the picture to speak for itself, and conclude with a few remarks on guilds.

There is no country in which the benefits of union and combination are better understood than in China. Here, first of all, we find the principle of unity in the government of the land, the officers being chosen from the people, and owing their positions solely to their knowledge and high attainments. In the same way every profession or trade has its guild or union, governed by men distinguished for their wisdom and high standing in their several crafts; and every individual member of each trade, if he desires peace and prosperity, must subscribe to the rules laid down for the common interest of the whole. These unions have each their temple or guild hall in every city or village, and are under the protection of some local god. In these temples they hold their gatherings, frame their rules, and enjoy their feasts.

There are masters' guilds, where, at stated times, the current prices of products and manufactures are fixed, and there are servants' guilds, where, in like manner, the wages of labour are regulated. Judging from the great antiquity of some of these guild houses, trades unions and combinations, which are of recent development in our own land, have been in operation in China for many centuries.

The Fukien Temple was originally founded during the twelfth century. It was at different times destroyed and rebuilt, and was finally raised to its present magnificent proportions about the beginning of the eighteenth century.

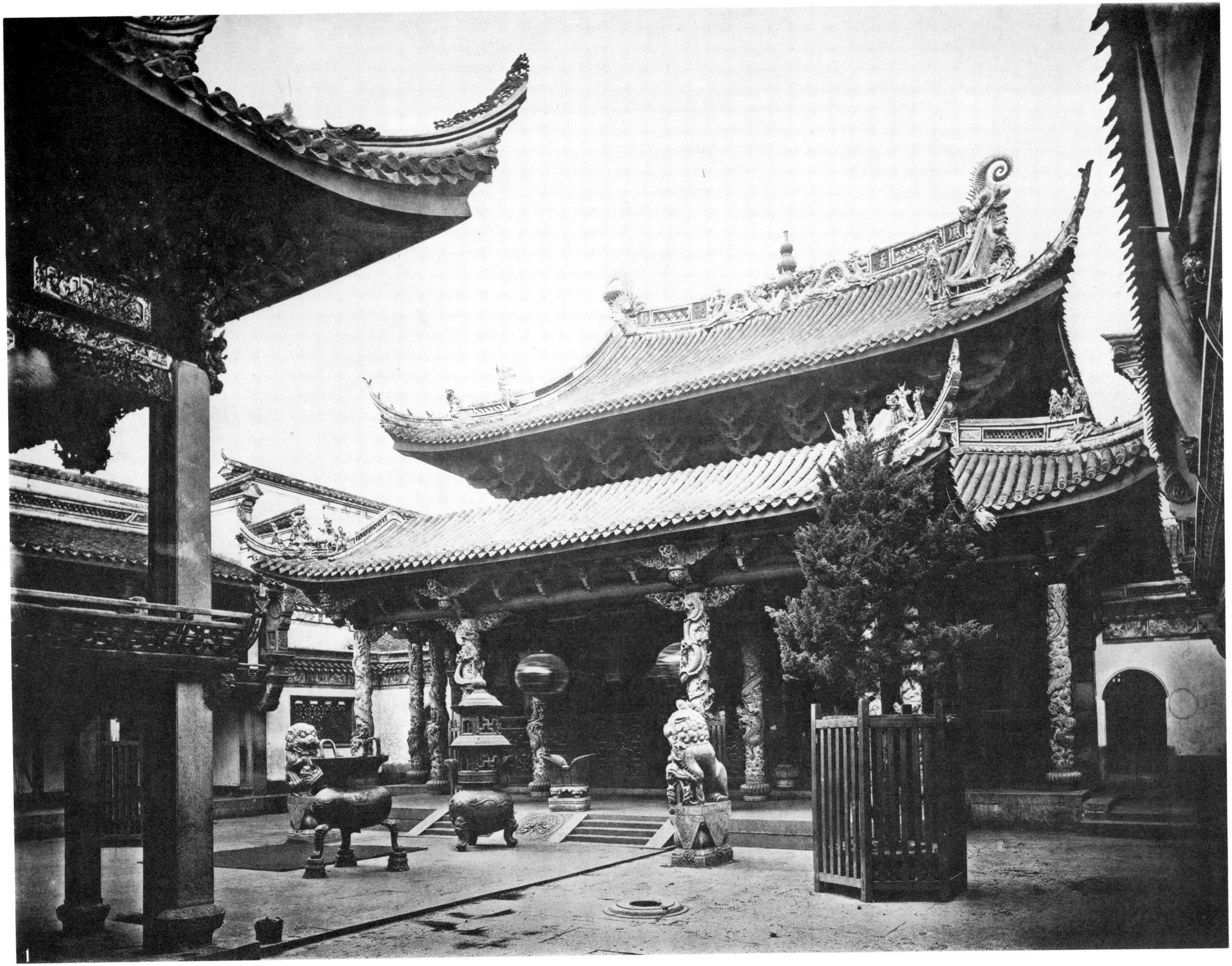

Vol. III, Plate I

SNOWY VALLEY.

LEFT Ningpo for Snowy Valley on the 4th of April. My conveyance was a native house-boat hired to take me some eighteen miles up stream to Kong-Kai. It was nearly midnight when I started from the Ningpo wharf, and we hoped to reach Kong-Kai village about 9 o'clock next morning. But, as usual, the boatmen no sooner got clear of the floating bridge and city than they dropped anchor to wait, as they pretended, for the tide, but in reality to gain time and money. Induced, after much delay, to stick to their bargain and proceed, they landed me at the allotted time at Kong-Kai. My party was made up of four coolies to transport my baggage, together with two Chinamen who had been in my service for some years, and who were the constant companions of my travels. We set out for the hills, enjoying as we advanced the sweet perfume of bean and of rape fields, which stretched in a golden meadow to the distant margin of the uplands in front. Everything shone with freshness and beauty in the morning light; the country around us seemed a perfect garden of cultivation. In the midst of a scene such as this it was painful to find, in the village of Kong-Kai, a festering sore on the face of the landscape, and to be forced to exchange the balmy breath of the fields for the foul air of mud-polluted alleys. As I stood at this hamlet on its old bridge, a striking contrast presented itself to my gaze. Looking towards the hills through the pale green foliage of an overhanging tree, you might discern the river flowing between its reedy banks and reflecting the feathery plumes of bamboo and the more distant objects of the landscape. There, too, gliding on his loaded raft down stream, was the owner of a cargo of earthenware, resting on his oar, basking in the sun, and smoking the pipe of leisure and contentment. To the left, towards Kong-Kai, a small temple reposed in the deep shade of an ancient tree, and there were squalid villagers trooping out from the mire of a lane that formed the leading thoroughfare. One group had scaled the treacherous height of a dung-heap which had sunk, faint with its own odours, against the gateway of the shrine. The temple, the lanes, the shops and houses of the village, wore an air of dreary decay and blight thoroughly in keeping with its opium-wasted inhabitants. Here we procured mountain-chairs for the eighteen-mile journey to Teen-tang Monastery. The chair-bearers looked worn and feeble, but as I walked a good deal they were not overtaxed.

It was a great relief to turn one's back upon the village and inhale the pure air of the plain. We passed several hamlets on the way, and in these the people seemed cleaner and in better condition. The women and children of this district adorn their raven tresses with the bright flowers of the azalea, a plant found in great profusion on the surrounding hills. The halting-places were little wayside temples. In one I met two old women, the priestesses of the shrine; they were most haggard, ill-favoured crones, and it was with grave forebodings that I allowed them to prepare my repast. As they leant over a fire of reeds in the dim light of an inner court, with hideous idols glaring around, I should not have been surprised had I seen them vanish in the smoke, and once I half suspected that I was being made the victim of some spell or incantation, for I observed one of these beldames stretch forth her withered hand to pluck a leaf from some strange plant which grew in a pot near the altar, and then she dropped the herb mysteriously into the cup of tea which she handed me. I sipped the decoction daintily, eyeing the old priestess the while, but nothing came of it. Probably she divined the drift of my thoughts, for her oaken face shrank up into a weird grin. The tea was good, but the cakes brought from behind a smiling goddess were as preternaturally tough.

The dilapidated outer porch of one of these wayside temples is represented in No. 5. Skilfully modelled images, the size of life, are here seen guarding the portals, and my lean chair-bearers are also pictured gambling with an itinerant fruit-seller.

Farms and clumps of fine old trees studded the well-tilled plain, and the haystacks piled up curiously round the trunks of trees added to the peculiarity of the scene.

The ascent of the mountains to the Monastery of the Snowy Crevice afforded a succession of the finest scenery to be met with in this part of China. The azaleas, for which the place is celebrated, were in full bloom, mantling the hills and valleys with rosy hues, and throwing out their blossoms in clusters of surpassing brilliancy against the deep green foliage which binds the edges of the path. The mountains in many places were thickly wooded,

Vol. III, Plate II

while jagged rocks from amid the folds of the foliage shot up their bold cliffs in striking contrast. But it was just before reaching the richly-tilled lands of the Monastery that we came across the finest scene. Here, as we looked back, from the altitude of about 1,500 feet, the eye wandered over an endless multitude of hills. A single cloud rested on a distant summit, as if to watch the windings of a stream which ran, wrapped in the glory of the evening sun, like a belt of bright gold dividing the valleys, and girdling the far-off mountain sides. As the sun declined, the hill-tops seemed to melt and merge into the fiery clouds, deep shadows shot across the path, swallowing up the woody chasms, and warning us that night was near at hand. Darkness had set in before we reached the Monastery. Here we met with a cordial welcome, a hooded bonze in holy stole leaving his evening reckoning on his amber rosary to light us to our quarters. From him I gathered the startling intelligence that foreign champagne was better than Samshu, and with a parting salutation he left us for the night.

The Monastery of the Snowy Crevice (see No. 3) rests in a fertile valley on the margin of a pure mountain stream, and is overshadowed by hills clad in pine forests and bamboo. The stately tree in front is supposed to have been planted by the pious founder of the shrine about the end of the ninth century. The building has been often renewed since then, and so, perhaps, has the tree.

Every monastery is popularly supposed to be ancient, and some, according to tradition, were never built at all, but created for the pious of pre-historic times. One of the stories connected with this place relates that in 1264 A.D. the Emperor Li-tsung dreamed a dream about the temple, and accordingly named it "The Famous Hall of Dreams." This formed one of the most important events in its history, for the dream was followed by substantial presents. There is also another legend which tells us of an anchorite, and of an emperor, who essayed in vain to slay the holy man, till at last he fell down and worshipped him because he had never come across anybody whom he could not slay before. This monarch had just put a million of the common sort of his subjects to death, and he was athirst at that time for some victim of rarer eminence and sanctity than any of the others whom he had brought to their end. He died a pious priest, and left some suitable presents behind him too. Something like this is not unknown even at the present time. There are monks, I am told, in those places, who have lived lives of crime, and who find it expedient to retire to these choice retreats to die pleasantly, chanting "Ometo Fuh." Such holy ones, rescued from the grasp of justice and the jaws of the pit, take good care to live as long as they can. Many of the priests of the Buddhist faith are doubtless, judged by its laws, good and true men, and the majority are hospitable, and civil to strangers. They seldom neglect, however, to let one know the value of the presents they have received from other foreigners who, on previous occasions, have visited their abodes.

At this place I was conducted by an aged monk to view the "Thousand Fathom Precipice." I had to cling to a tree and then look down into the abyss. In this position I was deafened by the roar of the Tseen-chang-yen Fall (see No. 2), but could discern nothing for a cloud of mist that floated beneath my feet. At last I was startled from my contemplation by a vulture that shot out from the face of the rock, and caught a tiny bird as it hovered above the cloud. I afterwards descended to the fall through a steep, shady path in the woods. The great height of the fall may be guessed by looking at the full-grown trees above. It exceeds 500 feet, and descends about as many more in cascades over the rocks before it reaches the valley. No picture can convey an idea of the romantic beauty of the place. The variously-coloured rocks were covered with ferns and flowering shrubs, and the water, broken over the mossy ledges, fell like the delicate folds of a bridal veil. Climbing over huge boulders and beneath bamboo clumps, I reached the stone basin below, where the spray was lit with a hundred rainbow hues, scattering a thousand gems on the ferns, which seemed to bend their leaves and catch the burden of the fall.

No. 4 presents another striking scene in Snowy Valley, the fall commonly known as "Sung-ing-day," and approached by a picturesque bridge of a single arch concealed beneath the creepers that overgrow it. The water here descends into a deep, narrow chasm, and groups of tall, dark pines look sombrely over the verge of this precipice into the dark abyss below, where the river seeks a new channel through a rough and broken bed. The peaceful cultivated hills above and the rugged foreground present a combination as rare as it is striking.

The costume of the women of Ningpo is represented in No. 6. Almost the only point in which this attire differs from that worn by the ladies further south is the fashion of dressing the hair.

Vol. III, Plate III

SHANGHAI.

HE treaty of Nanking was concluded in 1842; but even before that time Shanghai was a place of considerable trading importance. By the treaty referred to, the port was thrown open to foreign trade, and its advantageous position led to so rapid an increase of its commerce, that it soon became the chief emporium of China. Shanghai city stands on the east of the province of Kiangsu, and on the verge of a vast productive plain, which, prior to the accession of the Chow dynasty, formed part of the old province of Yang-Chow, itself one of the nine provinces under the administration of the famous Yu. During the time of Yu, however, this part of the province was probably under water; at any rate, it was not until the beginning of the eleventh century, when the Sung dynasty occupied the throne, that Shanghai became a trade resort. Previous to this date the port was at a place called Tsing-lang-chien, twenty-five miles inland, on the banks of the Woosung Kiang, at present known as the Soochow Creek, but in those days a considerable stream, and navigable for sea-going vessels. When the present Wong Poo was nothing more than a small canal, the latter gradually deepened, while the former got filled up, and this necessitated the opening of Shanghai as a trade mart. During the Mongol dynasty it was a place of great importance. Under the Ming, it had a troubled career, for its wealth drew down upon it periodical raids and invasions at the hands of the Japanese. For this reason it was converted into a walled city, at the request of the landed gentry, in 1544, and from that time it made gradual progress, and was raised in 1842 to the dignity of a treaty port, since which event it has enjoyed almost uninterrupted prosperity. The Chinese records of the successful raids of the Japanese are not without interest and significance. At that early time the Japanese successes over their Chinese foes, who always greatly outnumbered them, were due to their discipline, daring, and weapons. In connection with this subject let us glance at the relative positions and prospects of the countries. The geographical situation of Japan with respect to China bears a striking resemblance to that in which Great Britain stands to the Continent of Europe. In the one, progress is being fostered with a swift and nervous energy, with an impetus that may carry it too far, while the other remains almost *in statu quo*, or else adopts, with proud reluctance, those tardy measures of reform which have been pressed upon her by a closer intercourse with foreign nations, while, with rare exceptions, her rulers and people remain blindly wedded to their ancient petrified policy of exclusiveness, looking back for inspiration to the doctrines which their dead sages have handed down. But some of my readers will point to the arsenals and shipbuilding yards of Shanghai, Foochow, Nanking, and Tientsin; to the foreign college of Peking, and to the foreign customs administration. These they will count as signs of slow, determined progress. They may be so, and yet the arsenals and their products may, after all, be only intended to defend the ancient state of things. The foreign customs administration pays, whereas, if it were left in the hands of their own officials, there would be a lack of revenue. The Peking College has its native supporters in high places, but they have to fight against great odds for its maintenance. Adam Schaal and Ricci had greater and warmer supporters two centuries ago, and what came of it all? I found a coolie drying his jacket on one of their finest astronomical instruments, on the wall of Peking. China will sooner or later be forced to press forward in the march of civilization, as her Japanese neighbours are fast discovering the secrets of Western power. When that time arrives, the Chinese will find the elements of all they are in search of at the foreign settlements in Shanghai, where the schools, the splendid commerce, the merchant palaces, the fleets of steamers, the local foreign government, the opulence of the inhabitants, and the condition of the streets and dwellings, offer an instructive contrast to the condition of the Chinese walled city which lies to the south of the foreign settlements. The labour of centuries has brought this city to its present state, and the result is little to the credit of the authorities who rule there.

The site granted for the erection of the foreign settlements was partly a marshy waste in 1843; it was, however, eagerly accepted by Capt. Balfour, then consul for Britain, and the transformation wrought there within little more than twenty-five years is one of which the settlers have just reason to be proud. It was here, too, that the system of a foreign inspectorate of customs was inaugurated in 1854; and owing to the success of the innovation, it has since been extended to all the treaty ports.

The Taiping rebellion placed a temporary check upon the trade of Shanghai, although at the same time many and rapid fortunes were made in supplying house accommodation to the Chinese, who flocked thither for protection. The relief of Soochow, however, by the troops under Colonel Gordon, brought with it a time of reaction, as the new Chinese quarter was deserted by the refugees, and the houses left tenantless. The place, however, soon recovered itself, and has since continued to progress. The published trade statistics show that the commerce of Shanghai has been steadily on the increase. The nature of the trade has, however, changed, as a part of the foreign trade is passing into the hands of Chinese merchants, who have readily adopted the use of telegraphs and steamers in carrying on their business operations. No. 7 shows the condition of the Bund in front of the British concession in 1869. It has been much improved since that time by the erection of imposing buildings, and by the laying-out of a public garden on the waste land in the foreground. The foreign houses, when seen from the river, present a very striking appearance, partaking, as they do, of a variety of massive and graceful designs. The British concession occupies a space nearly square, facing the stream, and surrounded by creeks; the roads run almost parallel to the Bund, and have others which cross them at right angles, and thus the actual settlement is divided into all but rectangular blocks. The roads parallel with the Bund are now named after the provinces of the Empire, in proper order from east to west, while the cross streets are called after the chief cities, following in similar order from north to south. Thus we have the "Flowery Land" in miniature, with these important differences—good roads, properly paid officials, and a responsible and efficient local government. The American concession is contained in a strip of land on the north, to be approached by a bridge over the Soochow Creek; while the French are found on a plot to the south between the British concession and the native city. The settlement has now extensive suburbs dotted with picturesque villa residences standing in their own garden ground. It also boasts a splendid club, and other societies of various sorts for the promotion of art, science, literature, and good fellowship. During the proper season, shooting is a favourite pastime among the residents, as the surrounding country abounds in hares, pheasants, partridges, quails and snipe, while water fowl may be met in numbers on the creeks and inland lakes. During the winter months the climate is cold and bracing; in summer the temperature averages 90° Fahrenheit. Shanghai, notwithstanding the summer heat, is in all respects one of the most agreeable ports in China.

NOTE.—I am indebted to Mr. Smith, of the Shanghai American Mission, for a translation of facts connected with the early history of Shanghai, taken from the Chinese work, "The Mirror of History."

Vol. III, Plate IV

PART OF SHANGHAI BUND IN 1872.

SINCE 1869, the date at which the previous illustration was taken, the foreign settlement at Shanghai has been steadily improving. No. 8 is a photograph executed in 1872, and designed to give some notion of the improvements to which reference has been made. At least two new buildings have been erected within the past four years, one being the Oriental Bank, bisected by the flagstaff in the picture. The view was taken from behind the gate of the public gardens.

No. 9 shows the style of buildings at the southern extremity of the Bund, and the state of the ground fronting them in 1869.

Among the few objects of historical note to be found in the neighbourhood of Shanghai is the Lung-hwa-ta, or "Pagoda of the Dragon's Glory," to the east of the village of Shi-ka-wei, on the banks of the Hwang-pu. This pagoda is one of the most ancient structures in the province, and the temple to which it belongs is a favourite native resort during the Ching ming or spring festival, the time for offering sacrifices to the spirits of deceased ancestors. Tradition tells us that the pagoda was erected about A. D. 230, when the Han dynasty occupied the throne. But this statement is untrustworthy, and information much more reliable assigns the edifice to a considerably later date. A distinguished emperor of the Sung dynasty, about A. D. 800, conferred upon it the title Kung Siang, "total resignation." This practice is one of the remarkable features connected with those ancient shrines. Emperors have invariably given names to them, and these names form the starting-points of their history. In this instance the name has proved inapplicable, as the monument has been at various times battered, broken, and levelled to the ground by the ruthless Japanese, and has risen again on the old site to its old proportions. The great Yunglo rebuilt it once about the beginning of the 15th century, and at another time the temple enjoyed imperial favour at the hands of a Ming empress. On this last occasion the present was not an empty name, but gold and silver, as well as a god, for it seems that at that time the old gods of the temple had fallen out of repair. The pagoda shown in No. 10 is 120 feet high. It is ascended by a winding staircase, and from the summit a commanding view of the surrounding country can be obtained.

Vol. III, Plate V

THE SHANGHAI WHEEL-BARROW.

IT may seem incredible to some of my readers when I inform them that, in Shanghai, wheelbarrows are substituted for cabs! Such a conveyance is shown in No. 11, and, after all, is not unpleasant, when one has grown accustomed to its use. These wheelbarrows, if they have no other advantages to recommend them, are at any rate cheap, and comparatively safe. There is here no risk lest the steady-going coolie who propels the vehicle should shy at a sheet of paper, or lamp-post, or bolt with his burden. For all this, the wheelbarrow is not in much favour with the foreign residents, and at one time, indeed, was threatened with abolition, as the screeching of the wheels on the dry axles disturbed the even flow of business in the offices of the foreign residents. To ensure silence the constant use of oil was enforced, and thus the difficulty was got over. There are a number of wheelbarrow stands scattered over the settlements, for these conveyances are in constant demand among the natives, and present a striking feature on the Bund, when the hours of business are at an end. Then the Chinese merchants and their servants are wheeled along in their bright silks and satins to enjoy the cool breezes off the river, their faces aglow with good humour and enjoyment. I have frequently seen the filial feeling and economy of the race displayed in a fearfully overburdened wheelbarrow, laden with a whole family, who thus reaped the full benefit of a single hire. The unfortunate coolie, streaked with perspiration over his dusty face, was all the while straining every nerve with the effort to propel his patrons and doing his utmost to make the ride agreeable in order that he might secure a regular hire. The Chinese coolie is a willing and constant labourer in whatever sphere you find him at work. He has to fight a hard battle for existence, and he fights it manfully, conquers, and is, as a rule, contented, although he has nothing to show for it all, when the day is done, except the barest necessaries. Who, therefore, can wonder at him if he seeks a cheap elysium in the dreams of the opium pipe? Wheelbarrows are not only used for passengers, they are also extensively employed for the inland transport of goods; I have met with them in different provinces, travelling in trains, laden with native and foreign produce, armed each with a long matchlock, and, in some instances, partly propelled by a sail.

COTTON SPINNING MACHINE.

IN China some of the finest mechanical appliances are found in a rudimentary form, containing, so to speak, the germs of our own more complex machines. No. 12 presents to the reader a simple spinning machine driven by the foot. To me it was full of interest, as its work is very effectually performed. The left foot is placed upon the beam, which rests in a crescent-shaped axis of iron, so as to keep it in position, while the other extremity of the beam has a pivot which works in an aperture in the wheel. The right foot of the spinner imparts to this beam the eccentric motion which sets the wheel agoing, a belt on the wheel communicating the rotation to three upper spindles whose motion is as many times accelerated as the circumference of each spindle is contained in the circumference of the wheel. By this contrivance a great velocity is obtained The spindles not only spin the cotton, but they act as bobbins, and reel the thread as it is spun. Here we have the early dawn of that complex system of mechanism, which now feeds the looms of Bradford and Manchester. The picture has an additional attraction as showing the winter dress of a Shanghai mother and child of the labouring class.

In a great cotton-growing province like Kiangsu, cotton may be had cheaply in the cities, and it is therefore used freely to pad the winter costume of the poor; while in the country it is raised by the small farmers, and then dressed, spun, and woven by the women and children of their households into domestic fabrics. The band round the head is that commonly worn by the women of Shanghai, and the ample hood of brilliant coloured cloth is in use for children all over China.

CHINESE LAW COURTS AND PUNISHMENT.

THE administration of justice in Chinese courts of law is conducted on principles different from those which prevail among Western nations. There are no counsel for the prosecution, or to defend the accused. Instead of these, certain officers attached to the Yamuns of the Mandarins, and in the pay of the presiding judge, make law their special study, and are expected to guide him in all technical points. These men, however, are not recognized by their government. In addition to these functionaries there are clerks, or Shiye, who attend to the business of the courts, and draw up the depositions; but there are other persons to be courted by the parties in a suit, who arrange the gifts and bring the case before their superiors. In a Chinese court no oaths are administered to the witnesses, and the truth, or some convenient substitute for it, is only disclosed under the dread of punishment, or by actual torture. Should money flow freely from the friends of an offender, truth and justice, it is said, run a fearful risk of being shunted to the wall, and crime condoned. Poorer culprits, who have no rich allies to aid them, frequently come worst off. In dealing with these offenders, virtue, justice, and purity assert themselves in the righteous judge. Penniless pilferers are bambooed, caged, triced up by the thumbs, or suspended by cords, while lying lips are beaten to a pulp, as a suitable lesson to the deceitful and dishonest pauper. I have in my possession a photograph, which I took in Amoy, of a poor and therefore profitless thief, who was strung up by the thumbs until the flesh rotted from the bones. He had been a bungling robber, and, unfortunately for himself, had nothing in him of the daring burglar, who could share his rich booty with conniving detectives. It is an easy task to write about one's impressions of the imperfect administration of justice, gathered from one's own experience in the country and from books. I have no doubt however that any native official thoroughly acquainted with Chinese law and its administration could, with equal ease and honesty, point out many advantages which their system offers in dealing with the criminal class of their countrymen, and be able to prove that it is quite common to find judges, and magistrates, actuated in the discharge of their duties by a simple desire to do what is deemed right, according to the usage of their land. The people dread their courts of law, and call their prisons hell. The following is a description from a native source of the duties which a magistrate and his subordinates may be required to perform during a season of local tranquillity. The underlings of the Yamun, or magistrate's office, found it expedient to foster a dispute between two peaceably-disposed neighbours named Hang and Chang. The quarrel at length broke into open hostility, and Hang was advised by these underlings to prosecute Chang; Hang therefore paid them a small fee, and proceeded to the Yamun dressed in his best attire. Hang, having bribed the gatekeepers, was admitted to the presence of the magistrate, who received him with marked courtesy, and informed him that he had heard of his renown as a man esteemed among his neighbours for his lovingkindness and filial piety. Hereupon Hang craved pardon for the liberty he had taken in coming before a man of such transcendent virtue and wisdom, assuring him how the thought, that one of such rare qualities should be so poorly paid, had caused him weary days and sleepless nights. Hang further begged as an honest citizen to lay a gift at the great man's feet. This was too much for the magistrate, who replied with an air of scorn, "Never, Hang, never! My wants are few. Your kind intention is sufficient. But stay; should you wish to share your savings with the poor, leave the present, and I will divide it among my many charities. Is there anything I can do for you in return?" Hang then stated his case. "Ah!" said the irate judge, "Chang—you say Chang assaulted you? That arch-disturber of the peace shall be speedily brought to justice." Chang, who had been posted up in all that passed at the interview, proceeds to lay his complaint, and the fees and presents bestowed by him exceed those of Hang. Chang in his turn is received with marked respect, and informed that the official eye had long rested on and sought out the vile haunts of Hang, who was a dangerous and desperate ruffian. Chang's virtues were extolled, and his presents received in the same spirit of resignation. A day was appointed for the trial, Hang confidently expecting to find Chang a manacled prisoner, while Chang felt sure of gazing upon the fettered Hang. But the merciful judge informed them of the bitter regret it caused him to think of such a feud existing between two distinguished citizens, and advised them to save their good name, and settle the difference between themselves. The fees and presents were not returned, and, strange as it may seem, the needy poor remained as needy and as poor as ever.

THE CANGUE.

THE cangue, or collar of wood, is one of the lighter punishments of China, inflicted for minor offences, such as petty theft. The nature of the crime, as well as the name and residence of the delinquent, if he has any, are inscribed in prominent characters on cards, and fixed to the cangue. The wearer is usually located in front of the house or shop where the offence was committed, and is forced to depend for food on the charity of passers-by as the imposing dimensions of the wooden encumbrance prevent him feeding himself.

THE CAGE.

CRIMES of the worst order are sometimes punished by starvation in a cage (see No. 14) so constructed that the prisoner has the choice of either suspending himself by the neck to relieve his toes, which just touch the board, or of standing on his toes to relieve his neck. During my short visit to Foochow a murderer was executed by this process, his cage being exposed on the great stone bridge across the river Min. His crime was one of a most revolting and fiendish type. He had murdered a little girl, mutilating her to a fearful extent in order to secure the gold bracelets and bangles with which his victim had been adorned. The people were forbidden to minister to his wants with even a drop of cold water, so that he became maddened with agony, and strangled himself in his wild ravings at last.

Vol. III, Plate VI

VOL. III, PLATE VII

THE ISLAND OF PUTO.

PUTO is one among a group of more than one hundred islands which stud the Chusan Archipelago. With the single exception of Puto, all the rest of these isles are included in the jurisdiction of the district of Tinghai, in the Ningpo dependency. Puto is under the independent rule of the abbot of the great Buddhist monastery dedicated to the goddess Kwanyin, an important deity in the theogony of China, and whose name the monastery bears. This islet, which is not over four miles long, forms the chief Buddhist centre of the Empire, and is peopled solely with bonzes and nuns, the inmates of some sixty temples scattered among hills and dales there. This ecclesiastical population is said to number 2,000 souls, and its ranks are recruited from time to time by the purchase of young slaves, who are trained by the monks to devote their lives to the spirit-crushing service of the Buddhist faith, and finally are drafted, many of them, as mendicants to the mainland to seek support for the maintenance of the monasteries, and of the lusty, lazy monks, the pious paupers who spend their years in drowsily chanting to Buddha, and who, if dirt and sloth will foster the growth of piety, must indeed be accounted holy men. The lives of these Buddhist recluses are very low-pitched. They are not engaged, as a rule, in any active works of charity or benevolence, and the highest praise that can be accorded to them is, that they refrain from inflicting harm as well as from doing good. The greatest among them I ever saw was said to be a living Buddha; he was very dirty and very silent, looking more of a mummy than a man. A spider might have crawled down his capacious throat, or woven its silken curtain over his half-closed eyes, and yet not have disturbed his tranquillity, or roused his dormant faculties into action, so thoroughly, judging from the comatose signs of his Buddhahood, did he seem to have attained perfect repose. But I dare not be too severe, as I have met with hospitality at the hands of many of the less devout members of the creed. At the same time, I am bound to state with equal candour that the faithful mendicants, or Buddhist touters, never failed to seek a recompense.

The chief monastery of Puto is shown in No. 15. The group of sacred buildings, embowered in rich foliage, and backed by the granite-topped hill, the bright colours of the roofs and walls, the sacred lotus lake spanned by a bridge of marble, together make up a picture of rare, romantic beauty. But the monks of China have always surrounded their retreats with the elements of the beautiful in nature, and have exhausted the resources of native art and architecture to embellish their shrines. Puto, the sacred isle, with its picturesque rocks and ravines, its woods and its temples, forms no exception to the rule. As we cross the marble bridge, and enter the wide portal to explore the multitude of courts and dormitories, the romance of the scene vanishes in the thick vapours that float above the altars, and which veil the smiling or glaring gods or goddesses, emblems of the holy ones, or of the fierce guardians of the Buddhist faith.

Temples were for the first time erected on this island as early as 550 A.D. The revenues for the support of these various religious establishments are derived from three sources:—the rent of church lands, the contributions of pilgrims, and the labours of the mendicant priests. The buildings seem to be gradually falling into decay, but in this respect the temples of Puto by no means stand alone. It is only fair, however, to add, that among many earnest Buddhists it is deemed a more pious act to build a fresh edifice than to restore an old one; and as to the resident priests, even if they had the means and energy to repair the buildings of their temple, they yet regard any zeal on such matters as indicating too marked an anxiety about purely mundane affairs. This, however, applies more especially to Buddhism in the countries where it probably retains more of its original purity than in China.

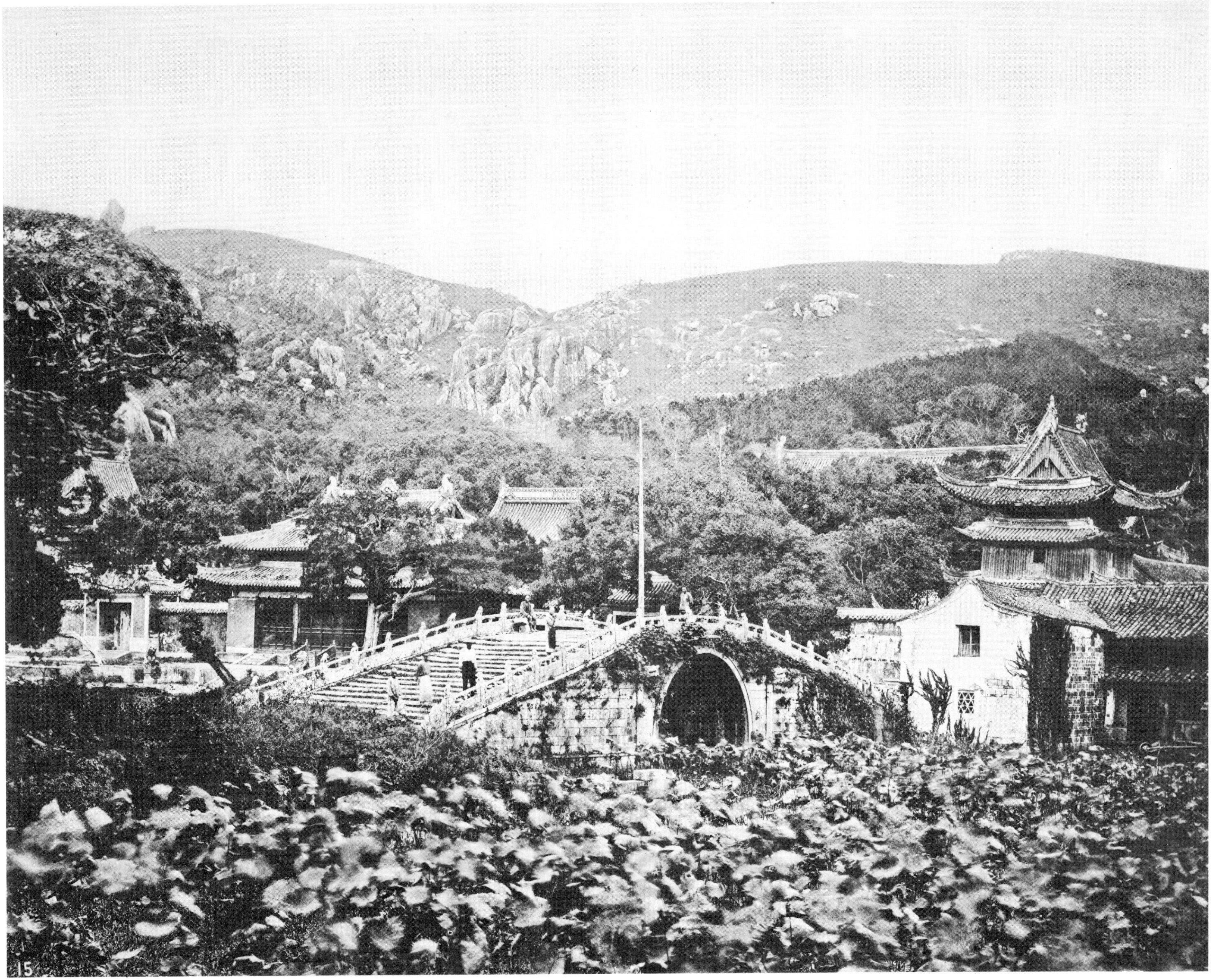

Vol. III, Plate VII

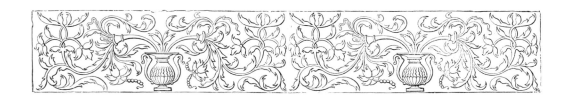

THE RIVER YANGTSZE.

 HE introduction of railways into China has found many earnest advocates, and no one can deny the advantages which may be expected from the accomplishment of such a project. But there are numerous obstacles to so sweeping a measure of reform, and one which the Chinese might urge, with some fairness, is that their rivers, creeks, and canals already supply them with a vast network of intercommunication, extending over the richest provinces of the Empire.

The Yangtsze is the greatest river in China, and the longest but two in the world. It flows from an unexplored source in the mountains of Thibet for about 3,000 miles, and discharges into the China Sea. At present it is known to be navigable for steamers to the I-chang Gorge, a distance of over 1,100 miles above Shanghai, but I have no doubt that ere long it will be found possible, with suitable vessels, to ascend the gorges and rapids, and extend the steam-traffic over two-thirds of the entire length of the stream.

From the earliest times the watercourses of China have occasioned trouble to the people, and perplexity to their rulers. Ever since the days of Yu, the first emperor of a known Chinese dynasty, the channels of the rivers have been subject to constant change. Summer after summer, when the mountain snows have melted in the north, the flooded streams have burst their banks, and carried death and destruction over the vast and fertile districts of the plains below ; indeed it appears to me that the prevention of disaster, and the security of the Empire in prosperity and peace, have always been directly dependent upon the exercise, by the government, of a vigilant and effective super-vision over the watercourses and embankments throughout the country. The shifting of the Yellow River in 1851-3, with the calamities necessarily consequent upon the deviation of that stream, might have been avoided had efficient measures been adopted during the dry season for strengthening the bank and deepening the original channel. Mr. N. Elias, who explored the breach, says : " The main pressure, during the flood season, had come to bear on the upper or weaker part of the embankments and, no measures having been taken to strengthen them, or deepen the channel, the great catastrophe happened which, with its consequences, had been predicted by the Abbé Huc some years before." In Pechihli, a year after the Tientsin massacre, an inundation arising from similar negligence laid waste part of that province, and the distress which that disaster inflicted upon the people, and which I witnessed on my way to Peking, produced an impression which will never be effaced from my memory. It seems to me, then, that before the introduction of railways can be urged with any degree of force, pressure ought to be put upon the authorities to induce them to throw open the interior to trade, and to grant foreign merchants, and their commodities, unrestricted use of the arteries of communication which already exist in the lakes, the rivers, and the canals. Such a step would pay the government, besides tending to secure the people against floods, and to prepare them, with the expansion of commerce, for the railroads and telegraphs that must follow in the end. The Chinese would not be slow to appreciate the substantial advantages of such a concession.

SILVER ISLAND.

 WILL now carry the reader with me on a journey to the gorges of the Upper Yangtsze, about 1,200 miles from Shanghai. In the spirit of a faithful cicerone, I will present to his notice the usual objects of interest, as well as a host of others, which, from their grandeur or novelty, will have superior claims upon his attention. Starting from Shanghai in one of the Shanghai Steam Navigation Company's commodious steamers, with a saloon which offers the ease and luxury of a drawing-room, and where the agonies of *mal de mer* are quite unknown, we proceed for about 140 miles up the river to Chinkiang. A few miles below that city we pass the mouth of the Grand Canal, perhaps the greatest of the public works in China ; at any rate, one which has proved infinitely more useful than the famous Chinese Wall. Here in mid-stream, just below the town, we come upon the rock known among foreigners as Silver Island (see No. 16). This is one of the most picturesque objects on the lower river, and, like Puto, is entirely occupied with Buddhist edifices, over which a chief priest or abbot exercises supreme control. The monastery there is an imposing pile of buildings above the broad granite steps of the landing, while other quaint temples and shrines are to be seen peeping out from among the woods which cover this sacred and beautiful retreat.

16

Vol. III, Plate VIII

GOLDEN ISLAND.

KIN-SHAN, or Golden Island, has attractions of its own no less remarkable than those of the sister islet below Chin-kiang. It is, however, an island no longer, for the alluvial deposits of the Yangtsze's floods have joined it so completely to the right bank of the river, that I had no difficulty in finding room on dry-land for taking the photograph here numbered 17. The pagoda-crowned rock presents the boldest and most striking object in the neighbourhood, and it is almost surplusage to say that it has on that account been appropriated as a suitable site for Buddhist buildings. During the rebel occupation, which extended from 1853 to 1857, these edifices were destroyed by the so-called Christian followers of the Tien-Wang, who left wreck and ruin behind them on every spot where they had carried on their operations. It is strange that they should have allowed this pagoda to remain upright, yet they did so, but not until they had stripped it of its costly ornaments, so as to leave it standing like a battered and broken obelisk, a monument which will testify to future generations that it is desolation and destruction, in vulgar parlance, which have been described as " heavenly progress" in the language of the Taipings. The temples are now in better repair than they have been for years.

Chin-kiang-fu stands at the junction of the grand canal with the Yangtsze, a site of great importance. For this reason the place was one of those most desperately defended during the hostilities of 1842, and its fall materially hastened the negotiations for peace which ended in the conclusion of the treaty of Nanking. But as to the three Treaty-ports on the Yangtsze, it was not until 1861 that they were formally opened to foreign trade, the delay arising from the disturbed condition of the country so long as the Taiping rebellion remained unsubdued. The foreign settlement stands on the bank of the river, close to the Grand Canal, while on the western extremity is the Yin-shan, the true Silver Hill, whose name is sometimes erroneously applied to the island in midstream. There is the usual Bund in front of the foreign houses, facing the river. Some idea of the position of the settlement in relation to Golden Island will be gathered from the distant view of part of the river in which the foreign houses are to be seen. The trade of this port suffered during the rebellion ; it speedily, however, recovered, and was greatly aided by a system of transit passes, which was introduced for the first time in 1864, and which has operated favourably in the development of foreign trade. The value of the trade of the port was £1,840,769 in 1868, and £3,212,769 in 1871. During the past year the trade again appears to have decreased, but this is a depression which has been felt, more or less, all over China.

Vol. III, Plate IX

NANKING ARSENAL.

ANKING is not open to foreign trade; if it were, the mode by which strangers disembark from the steamers would be different from what it is. Three officers of the Viceroy's household, with myself, my servants and baggage, had to scramble into a small boat after dark, and were landed at the dryest part of the bank, whence boatmen led the way up to a straw shed, erected for the accommodation of passengers who might be waiting for the departure of the steamers. A few dim lanterns flickered about the walls of this building, and lit up the faces of a crowd of Chinamen, who were squatting on the earthern floor, or reclining on wooden benches. In this place I was constrained to spend the night, in an atmosphere of garlic and tobacco smoke; and here, too, I learned, to my deep regret, of the death of Tseng-quo-fan. This great man, one of the foremost statesmen of his time, died on the 14th of March. Through the kindness of our Minister at Peking, I had obtained a letter of introduction to Tseng-quo-fan, from Li-hung-chang, a comrade who had fought with him during the Taiping campaign, and now the Viceroy of Pechihli, and it was most unfortunate that I had deferred my visit to Nanking until my return from the Upper Yangtsze. My letter was now forwarded to his son, who sent a courteous reply, expressing regret that I had not arrived in time to take his father's portrait. Tseng-quo-fan, a native of Siang-Hiang, in Honan, distinguished himself during early life at the literary examinations, and rose rapidly to the highest rank as Commander-in-Chief of the troops in the Yangtsze Valley and southern provinces. He aided Col. Gordon against the Taipings, and was instrumental in crushing the rebellion. He was a member of the Grand Secretariat, and after the fall of Nanking was created a noble of the second class. He was then at the zenith of his power, and it was even said that his wide-spread influence was dreaded at the Court of Peking. In 1868 he became Governor-General of Pechihli; but he was removed from that office immediately after the Tientsin massacre, and for the third time appointed Governor-General of the Liang Kiang.

The Arsenal was built under the auspices of Li-hung-chang. It was the first of its kind in China, and stands near the site of the great Porcelain Tower outside the south gate of the city. The "Monastery of Gratitude," as well as the tower, were destroyed by the rebels, and the present Arsenal is partly built out of the bricks which had been employed in these structures. The chants of bygone days that used to issue from the Buddhist courts, filling the air with their dreary monotones, are to-day replaced by less peaceful sounds—by the whirr of engines, the clang of steam-hammers, and the reports of guns or rifles, which are being tested for use. The Arsenal is conducted upon the most advanced scientific principles, and superintended by Dr. Macartney. It is a startling innovation on the old style of things in China. If the Chinese first taught us the use of guns (they are said to have employed them at the siege of Khai-fung-fu, in 1232), we are certainly repaying the obligation with interest by instructing them how our deadliest weapons are to be made. In this Arsenal many hundred tons of guns and ammunition are yearly manufactured, and I have no doubt its products have proved of great service in the prompt suppression of the Mahometan outbreak in the Provinces of Kangsu and Shensi. In No. 18 my readers will recognize a mitrailleuse; on the right of it a torpedo, and rocket tube, a pile of shells, a howitzer, a rocket-stand, and a field-gun carriage. The mitrailleuse had just been finished, and was fired in my presence. A native workman is engaged in describing the instrument to one of his officers. This picture shows that, however much the Chinese may have neglected to cultivate the Western sciences which pertain to peace, they have sought to make themselves masters of those which relate to war.

18

VOL. III, PLATE XI

NANKING.

ANKING became the imperial capital during the fourth century of our era. China was split up at that time into a Northern and a Southern Empire; but Yang-Kien, an emperor of the Soui dynasty, united the two divisions, and removed his court to Peking. Hung-Woo, the first of the Ming emperors, made Nanking again the imperial capital, and restored it to its former glory. This monarch was one of the most remarkable rulers which China has ever possessed. Before his advent, the empire groaned under the yoke of the successors of Kubli Khan, and longed to get itself free. Then Choo-Yuen-Chang, better known as Hung-Woo, arose, and was accepted as the deliverer of his country. His name is still much revered as a wise and just ruler, under whose sway the kingdom prospered. He had raised himself from the lowest ranks of the people, his father having been nothing more than a poor labourer. He was succeeded by his grandson, who, after a troubled reign of four years, was driven from the throne by Hung-Woo's son, Yung-lo, "the Successful," and the latter again removed the court to Peking. Since Yung-lo's time Nanking has had a troubled career. It once more enjoyed the honour, this time a questionable one, of being raised to a capital by the Tien-Wang, the Heavenly King, or, to call him by his most familiar title, the Taiping rebel chief. This event occurred in 1853. Probably the past twenty years have, on the whole, been the most notable in the history of the city, yet thirty years ago it was the scene of the signing of the treaty which secured the opening of a number of ports to foreign trade. The ground in front of No. 19 has been inch by inch contested between the imperial forces and the rebels, and it is strewn with the graves and bones of Taipings and Imperialists, mingled together in kindred dust. Here in 1864 the rebellion received the decisive blow, and the city, in the background of the picture, fell into the hands of the conquerors. When things were at the worst for the rebels, the Tien-Wang sat calmly within the city walls, confident in the Divine origin of his own mission, and assured that deliverance would, therefore, be sent from above. He believed in God, in Christ as a messenger from Heaven to mankind, and in himself as an instrument appointed by the Almighty to work out the redemption of China. He built himself a sumptuous palace in the imperial quarter of Nanking, and there he dwelt in sublime serenity, looking down upon his enemies with pity and disdain, as they mustered in the tombs of the great Ming rulers for the final attack upon his capital. When his soldiers were famishing around him, he still trusted in God; and when they asked for bread, he filled their mouths with a new doxology, enjoining them to sing it until heaven should send relief. One of the last commands of this prince of peace was, that in the wording of all documents his generals and others should use the terms, " Heavenly Father, Heavenly Brother, and Heavenly King."[1] This was his heavenly Trinity, and according to his own modest estimate he was himself the last person of the three. Whoever disobeyed this command was to be drawn asunder by horses—a truly mild and merciful way of disposing of unruly heavenly subjects. The state of the city became hourly more like hell than heaven, and at length, three days before its capture, the king is said to have perished by his own hand. The Imperialists laid the town waste, and devoted three days to the slaughter of the rebels. But many had already committed suicide before the Imperialist troops were in possession, and the bodies of numbers of the women of the Tien-Wang's household are said to have been found outside the palace gate. The son of the rebel emperor is supposed to have been cut to pieces in attempting to make his escape.

The photograph numbered 19 was taken from a hill outside the southern gate. The wall, it will be perceived, is of great height here, in some places seventy feet, and thirty feet at its base. Very prominent among the groups of buildings seen above the wall are those towering over the south gate, restored to their ancient splendour, while outside the ramparts an extensive suburb has sprung up around the Arsenal, on the site once occupied by the " Porcelain Tower." The most conspicuous object among those which still remain in connection with the " Monastery of Gratitude," is a huge white marble tablet on the back of a tortoise. This is seen in the picture just below the south gate, outside the wall, and about half an inch to the right of the gate. The wall has a circumference of about twenty-two miles, being nearly two miles greater than the circuit of the walls which enclose the Imperial and Chinese cities at Peking. But in Nanking a considerable part of the space within the wall is under cultivation. Much of the city has been restored, and its old trade was reviving during the time of my visit, but there was still a wilderness of ruin in the Tartar quarter nearest the Ming tombs, bearing a deplorable aspect of desolation. I saw a brace of pheasants rise from the ruins of an old homestead. The people were building new streets of the old material in the places furthest from the wall. Nanking is still celebrated for the rich quality of its silks and satins.

---

[1] " The Autobiography of the Chung-Wang," p. 64. Shanghai, 1865.

19

Vol. III, Plate XI

THE MING TOMBS, NANKING.

HE Ming Tombs at Nanking contain the remains of Hung-woo, the first emperor of the dynasty, as well as those of his grandson, who followed him on the throne. The tomb of Hung-woo, who died in 1398 after a reign of thirty-one years, stands on the western slope of the hills near the eastern wall of Nanking. A portion of this splendid mausoleum is shown in the distance on the right of No. 20, while the approach to the once imposing structure is guarded by stone statues of warriors in full panoply, and by a double row of colossal animals, also sculptured in stone. These ancient examples of Chinese sculpture will, however, bear no comparison with the productions of cotemporary European art, yet there is a native ideal in the whole which shows itself most conspicuously in the calm, majestic repose and benign expression of the warriors, who seem pleased with the task imposed of guarding the ashes of the dead. The statues probably represent the life-guards who in those days waited upon the emperors. Their weapons and armour look heavy and cumbrous, although in active war they might have proved as formidable as any in use at that period in Europe. A poor native assured me in confidence that giants, tall as these statues, existed in those days. Be that as it may, Hung-woo must have had brave and disciplined soldiers to aid him in fighting his way to the throne, though the arms of the mailed guards where he sleeps offer a strange contrast to the weapons now manufactured at Nanking Arsenal close by.

FOREIGN DRILLED TROOPS.

O. 21 shows a company of Chinese troops, a remnant of the "Ever-victorious" Anglo-Chinese force who have been trained to European discipline and drill. We miss the solid bearing and benign expression of the old stone warriors, but opium when the latter flourished was probably unknown. There are 150 of these foreign-drilled and foreign-equipped soldiers at Ningpo, under the command of two foreign officers, Colonel Cook and Major Watson. During the rebellion there was a regiment of them 1,000 strong, but now they are used as the Ningpo city guard. Of native officers there are to the Ningpo force a sergeant-major, two corporals, two lance-corporals, one artillery sergeant, one corporal, and a lieutenant of infantry.

The police of Nanking are also under four foreign inspectors.

Large bodies of foreign-drilled troops are stationed at Canton, Foochow, Shanghai, and other parts of the Empire, and these forces are supplied with modern rifles, guns, and ammunition. The pay of privates (and in Ningpo they are regularly paid), is, in the Ningpo force, six dollars a month, or about one shilling a day, including a summer and a winter suit of clothes. The summer suit is white with blue facings, and the winter dress dark blue with green facings, and a dark green turban.

One of the workshops in the Nanking Arsenal is shown in No. 22, where guns are turned, drilled, and rifled. A native workman may be seen at his post guiding a great foreign turning-lathe.

The departments most interesting to me were the one where rifle-caps were being punched and filled by machinery, and another where the guns were being cast with such solidity and perfection as to rival the finest work of the kind I have anywhere seen in Europe.

KIU-KIANG (FOREIGN SETTLEMENT).

KIU-KIANG is the second open port on the Yangtsze, 445 miles above Shanghai. This port was selected as a suitable place for foreign trade, because of its close proximity to the Po-Yang Lake, and to the vast system of water communication which branches from this point into the interior. But as the lake is closed against steam traffic, and as Kiu-kiang stands fifteen miles above the confluence of the lake with the Yangtsze, it has never taken a leading commercial position.

In 1868, the total value of its trade was estimated at £3,344,355, while in 1872 that amount had fallen to £2,940,210. Were it permissible to navigate the Po-Yang Lake with any other but native craft, the returns would probably be greatly increased, although its position above the junction of the two streams, instead of below them, would tend to neutralize the effect of so advantageous a concession.

The Taiping rebels were in Kiu-kiang in 1853, and their progress left behind it a ruined and depopulated city. It was not until the port was opened to foreign trade (in 1861), and the presence of a small foreign community had inspired feelings of confidence and security, that the natives flocked back to rebuild the town. It is walled round, and adjoins the lower extremity of the foreign quarter ; and this, as will be seen from No. 24, runs parallel to the bank of the river, yet still far enough from the verge to leave room for a broad carriage-way in front of the houses.

The strength of the current during summer, and the threatened destruction of the Bund, have made it necessary to support the bank with an elaborate facing of hard-wood stakes. This structure, however, is usually partially destroyed by the rise of the river from year to year, and is a constant source of anxiety and solicitude to the foreign municipal committee.

VOL. III, PLATE XIV

STREET GROUPS, KIU-KIANG.

HOW many out of the total industrial population of China pursue their occupations in the public streets, and may truly be described as "journeymen tradesmen," is a point on which no estimate can be formed. But in every large city these sort of people are to be counted by the thousand, and though in our own towns we should class them as tinkers or costermongers, this nomenclature would by no means comprehend the accomplished handicraftsmen whom we fall in with at every street corner in China, men far too poor ever to aspire to the dignity of a settled shop, seeking their employment in the public highways, and by wandering from door to door. Our venerable friend Ahong, on the extreme left of No. 25, has spent his days in the streets of Kiu-kiang. He knows what hardship is, and can tell strange stories of the rebels, who for a time disturbed the even flow of the trade there. Ahong is a maker of soup, and so was his father before him. Born of a "bouillon"-producing family, he early became a graduate in the mysteries of the small kitchen which he carries about on his rounds, meeting his regular customers at the stated hours, in certain parts of the town. He is pictured here as he receives, with an air of native *sang-froid*, the polite acknowledgments of a purchaser who has sat down to discuss a bowlful of his savoury broth. It would be well for our poor in England if we could import a regiment of such cooks as these men, who can produce wholesome and nutritious food out of the scantiest materials, and at a very moderate cost. Old Ahong will regale a patron with a bowl of his best for a halfpenny.

The gentleman in the centre of the picture is a public scribe, and is here seen writing a letter at the dictation of a lady. But his epistolary services, if those were all he had to depend upon, would not pay him; for the people, most of them, can conduct their correspondence for themselves. He therefore combines the avocations of a fortune-teller and physician with that of a penman, laying claim as an oculist to special skill, in professing himself able to cure seventy-one disorders of the human eye. His successes are said to be confined solely to this organ. On his table is opened a long list of the diseases with which he professes to deal. This catalogue he consults from time to time to refresh his memory as to the scope of his professional powers. As a soothsayer, he foretels the effects of the letters which his customers desire him to write, whether their contents pertain to law, or love, or commerce. He will also select the lucky day for a wedding, and raise, if required, the curtain of the future, so as to afford his dupe a sunny glimpse into the regions of the unknown. He is a crafty old rogue, and trades on human credulity with astounding success. His table, chair, and apparatus are of the most portable kind; and these he folds up at night and carries away with him under his arm. The figure behind him is one of the begging pests of Kiu-kiang

Next to this group we observe the itinerant barber, a man who performs a variety of professional operations on the organs of sense. He is not a surgeon, as was the case of old in Europe, but he must possess a delicate acquaintance with each of the "gateways of knowledge" situated in the human head. To shave the sconce and leave the usual disc of hair at the back supporting the tail is the rudest of his achievements. Besides this, he has to trim the eyebrows, cheeks, and chin, to remove refractory hairs from the nostrils and the ears, and to tickle the tympanum so as to open a free highway for the enchanting noises of the Flowery Land. The rolling eyes of his customers are cleansed and dressed after a process that it makes one's blood run cold to contemplate.

The little cabinet upon which this gentleman seats his clients contains four drawers. The upper one holds his earnings, the next receives his tiny instruments, and in the third perhaps a dozen razors are to be found, whereof each in its day has reaped acres of Celestial pates. The lowest drawer contains his towels, combs, and brushes, while on his left he has a water-basin, with a small furnace of charcoal beneath. Tradition tells us that the staff he carries as a sign of his order was presented by an ancient emperor to a distinguished member of the profession, as a reward for the skill with which, when a mosquito had settled upon the Imperial countenance, he cut the insect with a swoop of his razor in twain, leaving its legs and half the body, unconscious of the disaster, still planted on the bridge of the potentate's nose.

The two remaining figures on the right represent a wood-turner and his customer. The latter is examining the make and finish of a wooden ladle.

I might have gone on to fill volumes with such groups as these, for the representatives of almost every trade are to be found in the thoroughfares of China. In my concluding volume I shall hope to continue this phase of native life, giving some important additions from the metropolis, Peking.

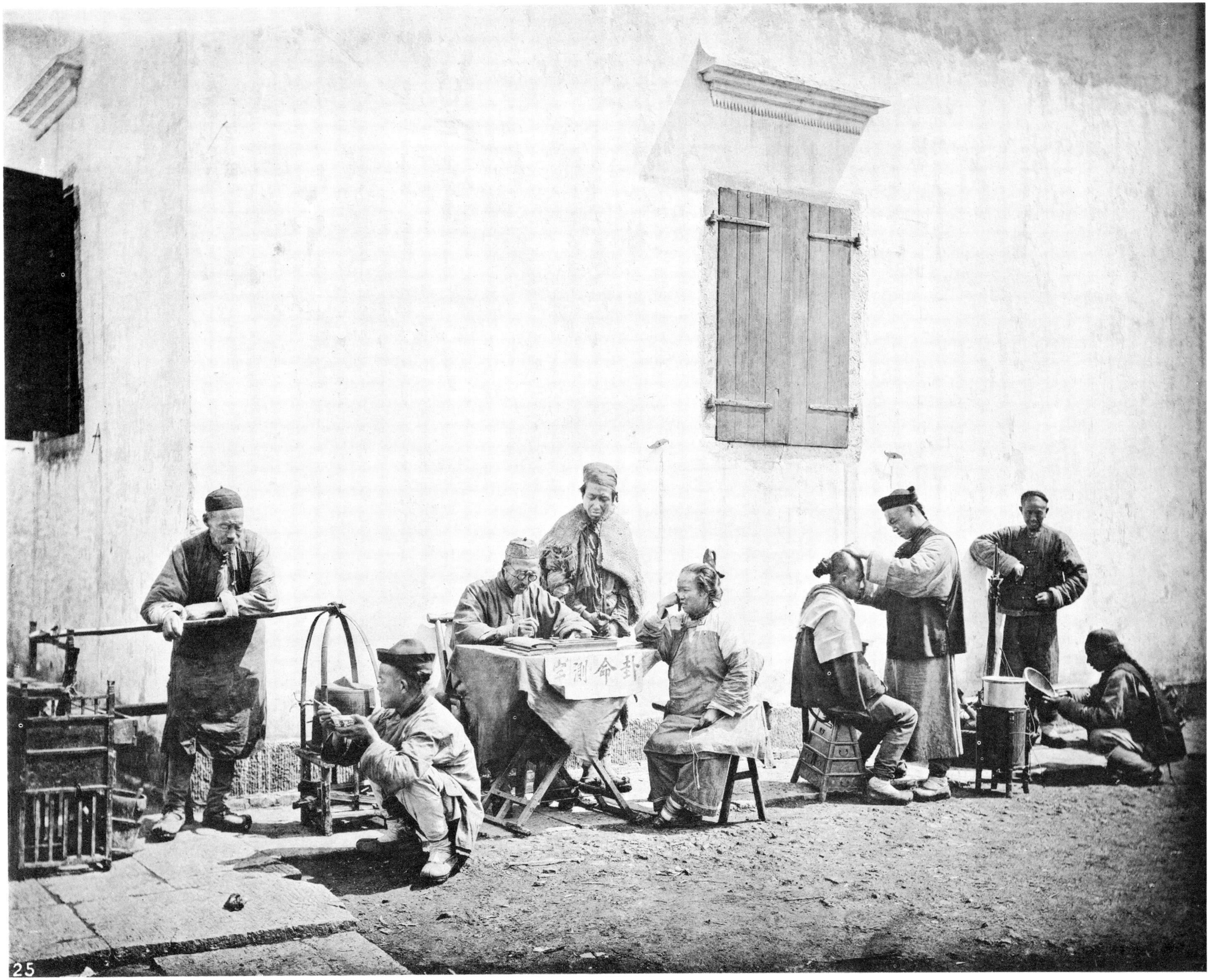

Vol. III, Plate XIV

KIU-KIANG WHARF.

THE buildings in the background of No. 26 comprise the house and offices of Messrs. Russell and Co., a firm whose splendid steamers have contributed greatly to develope the traffic on the Yangtsze. In the foreground we see a portion of a floating gangway used by the steamers to disembark passengers and cargo. On the landing stage, two Chinese assistants are super-intending the discharge of foreign manufactures in bales. These bales are slung between two coolies, and carried on a bamboo pole; the number passed into the warehouse is checked after a system which it may not be uninteresting to describe: there is a small strip of bamboo to correspond with every bale, and this the bearers, as they traverse the gangway, hand to a trustworthy native assistant. He, in his turn, delivers the total number of his strips to be entered in the books.

SAWYERS AT WORK.

THE Chinese contrivance for supporting a block of wood while they cut it up is a very simple and ingenious one. Like most of the appliances which that people have invented, it effectually performs the work for which it was originally designed; but it wears such a primitive look that we might reasonably expect, had we lived in that land 2,000 years ago, we should have found the same type of men doing the same description of work with the same appliances and in the same methodical fashion. This is among the most startling characteristics of China, and one viewed by a foreigner with continual surprise, accustomed as the latter is to Western progress, and inspired with an insane desire for novelty, as the Chinese themselves might describe him. These men of China, at some distant period of the past, must have had people of inventive genius among them who devised their present simple mechanical appliances, each one, in its own sphere, adapted to do a certain kind of work in a way which left nothing to be desired by succeeding generations. There is something in all this which might have attractions for Mr. Ruskin. The natives at the present time would rebel against the introduction of steam for the achievement of any result which can be brought about in the old way, and by the nimble hands of their working millions. I know a case where an entire village community of silk-spinners threatened to strike because their chief employer proposed to add a few extra reels and spindles to the ancient machine. I asked the master, who was a Cantonese, why he did not introduce the foreign method of reeling. "Ah," said he, "I have had enough of that. I once tried to effect a very slight alteration in the old machine, intending to introduce foreign apparatus in the end; but I was nearly ruined by the attempt." I suppose, in this way, inventive genius and its efforts at improvement must have been suppressed; and so the Chinese, having at an early time brought everything to comparative perfection, have rested since from generation to generation, content to go on, in filial piety, doing as their forefathers did. Perhaps they have found more true happiness in their simple ways than our civilized millions of people can realize in the glorious nineteenth century.

Our own sawyers and saw-pits are being numbered with the things of the past, and engines whose saws fly through a goodly tree in a few seconds have taken their place. Thus the furniture of our houses is now-a-days half constructed by steam. How different is this from the practice which still prevails in China! There, the carpenter

Vol. III, Plate XV

goes to work in front of his shop on a rough-hewn tree propped above a tripod, of which the tree forms one of the legs (see No. 27). The same man dresses the wood when he has sawn it up, and fashions it into chairs and tables, unless in busy towns, where the labour is more divided. Their largest saws have simple double handles passed through the two extremities of the blades. They are also cross-cut, and set just as ours are. There are besides a variety of saws gradually diminishing in size till they are reduced to the breadth of a watch-spring. These finer instruments are used for cutting out the most delicate ornaments in wood.

THE RIBBON LOOM.

THE ribbon loom is made chiefly of bamboo. Of this material all its inner frames are constructed, and those for holding the warp, as well as the transverse ones which support the woof, are all of them formed from the smallest stems of the same plant. Bamboo is also employed for fashioning the series of treadles which are worked by the foot, like the pedals of an organ. In employing this little machine, head, feet, and hands are all called into active operation, and the result produced is the most beautiful silk ribbon, richly embroidered with a variety of choicely-coloured flowers. This loom has in its construction the elements of the more complex one used by the Chinese in the manufacture of their ornamental silken fabrics—a machine so perfect as to enable a skilled workman to weave any pattern or picture that may be desired.

The ruins represented in No. 29 are at a place called Tai-ping-koong, ten miles from Kiu-kiang, in the hill country behind that town. A highly-tilled plain of rich alluvial soil intervenes between the hills and the town, studded with prosperous-looking farms, and shaded with willow-trees on every side. Not an available acre of land to be found here but what was laid under sedulous cultivation. At the time of my visit, the young rice just showed its green blades above the irrigated fields, splendid crops of peas and beans were in flower, the terraced sides of the hills were planted with vegetables, while the heights above were covered with pine and shrubs to supply fuel for winter. Most of the people I saw in this district were comfortably, and a few of them richly dressed, while all wore on their sleek faces a satisfied air of quiet prosperity and content. Indeed, this portion of the Kiangsi Province called up something of that ideal China which the story-books of our childhood suggest to us. From the hills, the plain wore the semblance of a vast landscape garden; there was many a green knoll, crowned with fine old trees, while rustic bridges spanned a multitude of willow-shaded streams.

The two towers shown in this picture are unlike anything I have met with elsewhere in China. They are said to be the ruins of a Buddhist monastery, one of the greatest which has ever been founded in the Celestial Empire. Judging from the mounds which mark its foundations, this sanctuary must have covered an extensive area. I found among a number of interesting blocks of sculptured stones which had been used in building a small modern temple in the rear, one or two representing the backs of foreign books as they appear in the shelves of a library. Possibly this may point to Ricci's mission to that part of the province about the year 1590, on which occasion the famous Jesuit missionary is reported to have enjoyed great popularity among the inhabitants of that locality.

I also visited the tomb of the celebrated sage, Chu-fu-tze. There is nothing striking or remarkable about its appearance. The hill, however, in which the sage rests commands an extensive view of the plain, and the lakes or lagoons by which it is partially covered.

VOL. III, PLATE XVI

HANKOW.

HANKOW is the highest point up the Yangtsze river at which foreign merchants are allowed at present to reside. It holds a most important position at the angle formed by the junction of the Han with the Yangtsze. The former, in ancient times, was known as the Mien river; and it was not until the last decade of the fifteenth century that it created its present channel, and those advantages of site to which Hankow in a great measure owes its prosperity. Previous to this change in the course of the Han, the town of Hanyang monopolized the trade, and is said to have been a flourishing port in the remote period treated of in the native " History of the Three States." Hankow, under the Ming rule, rose to be the commercial centre of the Empire, and indeed its prosperity during the centuries which followed steadily increased, meeting with its first severe check at the hands of the Taipings who in 1855, sacked and burned the town.

Wu-chang-fu, the capital of Hupeh, Hanyang, and Hankow, all stand in close proximity on a vast plain, with nothing except the confluent rivers to divide them from one another. Above Hanyang there is a low range of hills. Standing on a summit I had a wonderful panorama before me. Wu-chang was to be seen on the south bank of the Great River, and beneath my feet were the closely-packed houses and narrow alleys of the town of Hanyang; while beyond, across the Han, and separated by the tortuous windings of this important tributary, I could discern the crowded dwellings of Hankow, and further on the imposing buildings where the foreign settlers reside (see No. 30). The area covered by these three towns is probably the most densely-populated space in the Empire, the native population of Hankow alone having been estimated in 1872 at 600,000. In striking contrast to these populous towns is the country surrounding them, a district thinly scattered over with tiny hamlets and solitary peasant homes. The fact is that the alluvial plains are usually flooded in summer, and farmers are discouraged from settling there, as they run the risk of losing their labour and their capital. Many of the huts are built on artificial mounds. Descending to the Han, I found a busy and interesting scene. The narrow river was so crowded with native trading craft of all descriptions and sizes, that only a narrow channel for the passage of boats could be obtained. A small fleet of vessels from Szechuan had been built of undressed planks of pine, and had been simply put together for the down river voyage to Hankow, there to be broken up when their cargoes had been disposed of, and sold for firewood.

The chief exports of Hankow are tea, tobacco, silk, and oil.

HANKOW (FOREIGN SETTLEMENT).

HANKOW, as I have already indicated, stands on the left bank of the Yangtsze, and is separated from Hanyang by the Han, at the point where that stream falls into the Great River.

The foreign settlement there has a frontage to the Yangtsze, but the plot of ground on which it has been built is unfortunately lower than that occupied by the native town. Why this site should have been selected it is impossible to tell. The mistake is one which the natives themselves would never have committed, and it has entailed great suffering during times of flood. But the Chinese, with characteristic impartiality, raised little objection when the foreigners fixed upon the site. All they did was to demand an exorbitant price, though they ultimately consented to sell the land in lots, costing 2,500 taels apiece. During the time of my visit in 1871, the inner walls of the rooms in the lower flats of the foreign houses still retained the water marks caused by the floods in the preceding year. This flood had covered the Bund to a depth of about seven feet, when throughout the settlement boats were the only means of communication. The kitchens, or outhouses, had either been destroyed or rendered useless, so that native barges had to be hired for the accommodation of the servants, and for cooking. Boats were punted into the halls, and inner staircases were transformed into jetties ; dining-rooms became swimming baths; furniture fell to pieces ; the boundary walls of the property settled down into the mud ; and, in some instances, the houses themselves sank on their foundations, and threatened altogether to tumble down. Poultry and cattle had to be sent to the hills, or stowed in the upper bedrooms, till the flood should abate, while natives to the number of 40,000 sought refuge on the Hanyang Hill. But it was in the districts above the Tung-ting Lake that the suffering and disaster occasioned by the inundations attained their greatest proportions. There whole towns were flooded out, and crops were destroyed and washed away. " At I-chang more than half the houses are submerged to their very roofs. Kwei-chow is more than half in ruins." " Wan-hsien has suffered little ; but the suburbs, which were at least five times as extensive as the town itself, have been swept away ;" and so on, run the notices of disaster in the Customs Report of 1870. Besides all this, a disaffected portion of the suffering population of Hupeh rose in rebellion, and were reported to have formed a project for advancing against Hankow.

The Chinese built a great wall, at a cost of £80,000, from the Han to the Yangtsze, which sweeps round the back of the settlement. This wall was intended as a protection against organized raids from the banditti of the plain. It has proved most effective as a breakwater, and it gets the credit of saving the settlement from being swept into the Yangtsze by the flooded stream from the Han.

The river bank in front of the Bund was faced with stone, at a great cost, to a depth of sixty feet. But soon after the opening of the port in 1861 funds were freely lavished by the foreign merchants in carrying out such works as would add to the security and adornment of a place which seemed likely to become the greatest emporium in China. Costly and elegant residences were erected, and Hankow has thus been rendered one of the finest foreign settlements in the Flowery Land. These early expectations of a vast trade have never been fully realized, and land and house property, in 1871, had greatly fallen in value. Were I-chang to be opened to foreign trade—a step which has been strongly advocated for a long time—much of the present trade of Hankow would probably be monopolized by the new port. Native competition has had its share in taking part of the import trade out of the hands of foreign agents, inasmuch as the Chinese merchants have found that they can effect a saving by visiting Shanghai in the river steamers, and making their purchases direct from the home markets for themselves. This is a disadvantage which will increase rather than diminish as our trade with China expands ; and it may reasonably be expected, in process of time, that the Chinese will have their own establishments in Manchester and London.

The British concession at Hankow has a river frontage of 800 yards, with a great depth inshore. To the westward of this, additional land is taken up by the houses of the agents for the Steam Navigation Companies ; while on the east there is the unoccupied French settlement, which boasts a Consulate, imposing on the outside but apparently falling into decay internally.

The number of foreign residents, including missionaries, is about a hundred.

The trade under foreign flags, in 1871, was valued at £14,000,000. Hankow is the centre of the districts which produce Congou teas.

Vol. III, Plate XVI

THE WU-CHANG TOWER.

W U-CHANG Tower, one of the most remarkable objects in this part of the Upper Yangtsze, stands upon the extremity of a low range of hills which bisect the city of that name, and which terminate abruptly just below the town on the left bank of the river. A corresponding range, already noticed, rises on the opposite bank above the town of Hanyang.

As to the tower, it was built originally in the early half of the sixth century, when the Chin dynasty was on the throne, and the site then selected was the house of a wine-seller named Hsing. The tower was demolished by the Taipings, and barely three years have elapsed since it was completely restored. It now rests on a platform of solid masonry, rising boldly from the bank of the river, and the sole relic of the original structure is an ancient monument to be seen in front of the tower, upon which, if we are to believe the legend, the saintly founder alighted from the sky to partake there of a spiritual repast, and wake the echoes with a melody on his flute. It was in the year B.C. 202, or thereabouts, that this important incident occurred, and we are told that the sage, whose name was Fli Wei, managed his aërial flight on the back of a stork. Storks may still be found, but there are no musical sages to use them now. In Plate XVII., No. 32, a picture of this tower is to be seen, but it was not without difficulty that I obtained it. I found the court in front of the edifice filled with the customary crowd of idlers who loiter in the precincts of the temples—beggars, fortune-tellers, hawkers, city roughs, and street boys. I was therefore compelled to retire within the city wall, in order to avoid the throng. The gate was then shut to, but still the mob managed to scale the ramparts, perfectly civil, indeed, but intensely curious to watch my operations, some doubtless imagining that I intended to open fire on the town, as they saw my camera pointed through the ramparts. The weather was against me as well, for a high wind, charged with clouds of sand, was blowing up stream, and stirring up so great a tempest that the only native boats to be seen as we crossed the river were the well-equipped craft which bore " The Great Peace-Save Life Boats" inscribed in huge black characters on their sides.

I now propose to conclude the present volume with a short narrative of my voyage to the gorges of the Upper Yangtsze.

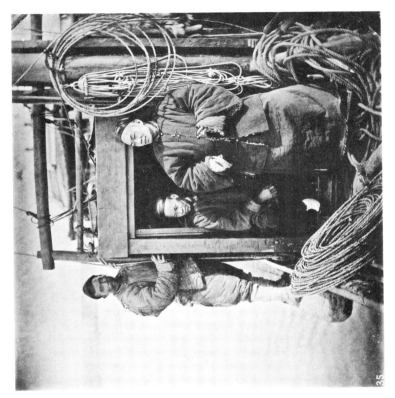

FROM HANKOW TO THE WU-SHAN GORGE, UPPER YANGTSZE.

URING the journey which I now propose to describe I was so fortunate as to have two American gentlemen for my companions. At Hankow we hired two native boats to convey us as far as I-Chang. In the smaller of these two craft our Chinese interpreter, the cook, and "the boys," or native attendants, were accommodated; the larger one was for ourselves. This arrangement proved in some respects a good one: we were not over-crowded, and we escaped the noxious odours of Chinese cookery; but, on the other hand, grievous delays arose, for the boats were of unequal sailing powers, and their crews were inclined to exert themselves as little as possible.

Of three of the illustrations on Plate XVII. No. 33 represents our boat's crew at breakfast; No. 34, the interior of our cabin; No. 35, our interpreter "Chang."

On the 20th January, 1871, with British and American flags flying, our expedition quitted Hankow; but we soon lowered our needless colours, and settled down to the tedious process of poleing the boats past the native craft, which lined the bank in thousands.

When night set in we cast anchor at the foot of Ta-tuen-shan, ten miles above Hankow. Our boat was divided by bulkheads into three compartments: the after one for the accommodation of the skipper, Wang, and his wife; the next formed our sleeping bunk; and the forward one, furnished with a stove, was converted into a sort of sitting-room. We passed an intensely cold night, for the wind blew through every crevice into the cabin, and we were forced next morning to make a liberal application of paper and paste to prevent a repetition of the inconvenience. Our sleep was further disturbed by a violent altercation between Wang and his spouse; the latter, seemingly a hot-tempered woman, and a true Tartar, having overruled her more youthful husband's wish to go and purchase provisions ashore. These people can hardly be said to go to bed,—they wear their beds around them. Their clothes are padded with cotton to such an extent, that, during the day, they look like animated bolsters. They never change their clothes, oh no! not until the winter is over; and then they part with the liveliest company in the world. The boatmen are a miserably poor lot; nine of them sleep in a compartment of the hold about five and a half feet square, and disagreeable indeed is the odour from that hold in the morning, for the boatmen keep the hatches carefully closed and smoke themselves to sleep with tobacco or opium, according to their means and choice. To get the poor fellows up early was a very difficult task; one by one they crawled out to face the cold north wind; and then came the time when their energy was most displayed. To their tiny enemies, which had to run to cover in the intricacies of their patched and padded coats, no quarter was given; and, this business concluded, they would commonly quarrel with their captain, Wang, or else among themselves; and at last, at about seven or eight o'clock, all hands would turn to and heave the anchor up, hoisting it by a capstan of simple make. As we advanced we were favoured with a slight wind, the sails were then spread, and the men squatted about the deck to enjoy their pipes, and the cheering prospect of a fair breeze, and no work to be done. The Yangtsze was now about a mile broad, and its waters were of a dark chocolate hue. The banks were low, furrowed or terraced with high-water marks left by the floods. These clay walls have a dark and tragic history, if one could but decipher it. Fragments of projecting wood here and there crop out from the clay,—the broken remnants, it may be, of some homestead, deposited with the *débris* of a long-forgotten flood. It is slow travelling in these China boats; the old stage-coach had the speed of lightning in comparison with them. During the early part of the voyage we suffered greatly from cold, as the coal we had with us would not burn, and the back draught from the sail filled the cabin with smoke.

A fair run brought us, at eleven o'clock, to "Farmer's Bend," by far the most unsatisfactory part of the Yangtsze, for here the river makes a *détour* of about twenty-two miles to the north and west, returning so nearly to the same point that a straight canal half a mile long would join the two extremities of the curve. The wind died away at sunset, and we anchored for the night at Pai-tsu, forty-six miles above Hankow. Next morning we were up early, but could effect no start till seven o'clock; for Wang was in his bed aft, and his crew were forward, stowed snugly in the hold. An interesting dialogue therefore ensued. The skipper pointed out to his men the propriety of their turning to; and they, in reply, insisted that it was a captain's duty to be himself the first at his post. On this, our second day, in West Reach, we passed a long sand-spit not shown on the Admiralty chart, and next morning we sighted the Pan-thi rock, which rises in mid stream about a quarter of a mile distant from the left bank. As this rock is submerged in summer, it would be dangerous for a steamer to venture too near the bank. At this place the river was about two miles wide, and at the end of the reach is the entrance to the lake stream, which debouches from the mouth of the Tung-Ting Lake. Very beautiful scenery is to be found in this district of the Yangtsze. The banks at the season of our visit presented a bold and striking front to the vast expanse of water, while in the vapoury distance we could descry a line of white sails, those of a fleet of trading junks, as if pictured in the clouds, travelling far away into space, and leaving only small portions of the hindmost vessels discoverable by the naked eye. Beyond the Tung-Ting Lake the Yangtsze is known to the natives simply as the Ta-Kiang or Great River, and up to the point of confluence of the two streams a steamer of six feet draught would find no difficulty, even at this season, when the waters are at their lowest, in ascending the river. Any one experienced in river navigation would usually find the channels and shoals where they might most naturally be expected; and the greatest difficulty, as I imagine, would be experienced during the summer months, when the banks are submerged, and no objects suitable for bearings are to be seen. At that period there are no trees nor landmarks of any kind to be met with in many of the long and difficult reaches, so that a steamer would run a great risk of grounding on the stiff clay banks, unless guided by a system of buoys. All the shoals consist of soft alluvial deposits; and, as I believe, when the Upper Yangtsze shall have been thrown open to steam traffic, it will be found necessary to make frequent surveys of the river, as the shoals and channels continually shift. Such a survey, even if made at low water in one season, would only lead to disaster were it relied upon the following year. We have had a day of snow, and there being no wind the men were compelled to track the boat up stream with a bamboo line affixed to the mast. After this, for some days' time, the routine of sailing and tracking was only equalled in monotony by the sameness of the scenery around. There was an endless flow of still and silent water, and level plains on either bank, without a single object of interest to break the even line. At length, on the 27th, we landed at a pretty rustic hamlet, beautiful in its quiet repose, and where everything seemed to have gone to rest for the winter. This village stretched along the crest of an embankment, and was backed by skeleton trees, whose snow-clad branches stood out coldly against a leaden sky. The sloping banks, too, were covered with snow, while the red light of reed fires gleamed from the open doorways, and sparkled in the oyster-shell windows.[1] There was no one astir, not a foot-print had marred the icy mantle in which the soil was wrapped; only on a level patch the leaves of a winter crop shot up in rows, and formed a pale green pattern on a snow-white ground. Our interpreter Chang was, I regret to say, of little service; for no member of our party understood his dialect thoroughly, and I found my own Hainan men, who spoke the Kwang-tung dialect and Malay fluently, of much greater use. Chang, however, had influence with the boatmen, who looked up to him on account of his literary attainment; he was useful as a master of ceremonies in the presence of native officials, and he also kept a careful journal. He esteemed himself our protector, and it was truly gratifying to notice how he courted the society of the officials to whom we had credentials, and before whom our interpreter exhibited us, at the same time introducing to their notice our foreign wine and our cigars —commodities with which he had been laudably sedulous to make himself acquainted beforehand. There he is, presented to the reader in No. 35, just after he had been droning, in an obscure corner of the cabin, over a whole classical commentary. The figure to the left is one of the boatmen, while a Ningpo boy is looking from the cabin door; the characters are faithfully rendered, and are engaged in the several occupations with which half their time was engrossed. The boat was under weigh in mid-stream when I executed this picture. We next halted at Shang-chai-wan, a small town, where we were able to purchase some excellent coal. It was about mid-day, but the boatmen, who had gone ashore with their captain, showed no inclination to return, although a steady breeze was blowing up the river at the time. At four o'clock, therefore, two of us ascended to search for the missing Wang, and quickly found him enjoying the nectar of a wine-shop close at hand. We did not venture into the town, as a great mob had collected around us. Foreigners were a rare sight to them, and my

---

[1] Oyster shells, reduced in thickness until they become semi-transparent, are still used in many parts of China as a substitute for glass. The shells are framed in small squares in the windows of the houses.

friend put them in good humour by purchasing a stock of cakes from an old man, which he distributed among the children in the crowd. The old man looked as if he had dressed himself in an ancient bed quilt, and glazed it waterproof by a surface coating of dirt. Our writer Chang announced that he was suffering from a severe cold, and sent one of the crew ashore to purchase a bottle of wine. It was instructive to notice the way in which he gave the order: while still inside the cabin he carefully counted the cash which his purse contained; and then, stepping out, handed it to the man with an air of perfect trust, remarking as he did so, "I do not know its contents; take what you require, and replace the balance." It contained in reality about sixpence.

On the 29th we had a visit from two Hunan custom-house officials; we also noted two cotton-laden junks ashore, at a place where the stream was apparently running with a five-knot current. Next day we found the banks dotted with huts made of pine-branches and millet-stalks; they reminded me of the pine-raft huts which I had seen below the Tung-Ting Lake, bound down to Hankow, but which I omitted to notice in the proper place. These rafts are of enormous size, and not unfrequently carry a small village on their decks. These villages are lifted on to the bank at Hankow, and there the wood is piled up for sale. About noon on the 31st, at She-show-hien, we passed a dangerous sand-spit, shooting out from the low land opposite the town. Here we bought two fish, one like a salmon, and the other of a kind which Captain Blakistow has already described. This fish has a long sword above its wide and toothless mouth, and it is said to employ that weapon for dislodging its finny prey from the mud, the wide mouth being at the same time brought into use as a trap. Its length, from the extremity of the sword to the tip of the tail, was four feet two inches, the sword being fourteen inches long. The belly was white, the tail and fins white and red. The back and head were slate-colour. She-show-hien, a town in itself of little commercial importance, formed one of the strongholds of the Taipings, by whom it was left partly in ruins. The place is surrounded by the first important hill-ranges we have seen since we had quitted Hankow.

We reached the great trading mart, Sha-si, about three hundred miles above Hankow, at one o'clock on Feb. 2nd. Here the river is one and a-half miles broad, and presents a splendid unobstructed channel. The town is on the left bank, in one of the finest reaches of the Yangtsze, and the lower river steamers would find an ample depth of water for anchoring close in-shore. An eligible site for a foreign settlement, beyond reach of the floods, and clear of the native population, might be found on a hill on the right bank, on the opposite side to the town. There is also another site lower in position, and below the city, which would probably be more advantageous for the purposes of trade. It was difficult to buy coal here, although we knew that it existed in great quantities in Hunan. Mines are, indeed, to be met with at Tsang-yang-hien, a few miles above Sha-si, and the coal there is good in quality; but hitherto it has been little in demand. Coal is also worked at Pa-tong-hien and Wu-shan-hien in the gorges above I-Chang; but except where made into fuel, which they cast in moulds, it is only sparingly in use.

We were now entering the mountain region of the Upper Yangtsze, and we could see in the distance the dim outline of what Blakistow calls the "Mountains of the Seven Gates," which rise about three thousand feet above the bed of the stream. The river at this point is from four to five miles broad, its bottom is hard and pebbly, and dangerous shoals abound.

As it was now getting dark, the men were advised to anchor; but they persisted in pushing on, and at last in mid-stream they ran the boat aground. They had to work for half an hour to get her off again, and then she drifted back to the old spot, and came eventually to anchor. Wang informed us that we must keep strict watch here, for we were in the midst of a region of pirates. We kept watch all night accordingly, and it was my lot to go first on duty. I spent the time in writing letters, with my revolver close at hand. Once, thinking that I could hear whispering and a hand upon the window, I grasped my pistol, and made up my mind to have a dear struggle for life. Listening, I heard the heavy breathing of the men piled in a sleeping mass in the forehold, and unconscious that a scene of bloodshed might the next moment ensue; then there was a noise in the cabin; and at last appeared my companion to relieve me on the watch. He had himself been the author of my unfounded alarm.

Feb. 4th.—Passed a rocky point, where men were fishing with otters. These animals, which appeared quite tame and tractable, were attached to the boats by long cords. They dived readily if gently pushed by their proprietors, and coming up when they had made a capture, freely yielded their prey to the fishermen. The towns and villages which bordered the river in this portion of the provinces of Hupeh and Hunan wore an air of solid prosperity, which contrasted favourably with the regions below. The same was observable in the well-tilled soil and in the general aspect of the people. The dogs are of a breed which differs from any I have seen elsewhere. They are short-haired, and carry long pointed ears, like the hunting dogs of Southern Formosa.

Feb. 5th brought us in sight of I-Chang Pagoda. Here the hills on the right bank fall in a series of bold cliffs into the river, and above rise the mountains in a chaos of cloud-piercing peaks and crags. Among other objects we noticed a monastery perched on a pinnacle of rock 1,200 feet above us, and overlooking a precipice 600 feet in depth. This sanctuary perhaps approached as nearly to heaven as it was possible for human hands to convey it. At I-Chang we witnessed a naval review. About a dozen boats, such as that shown in No. 39, made up the Imperial fleet, and I was much impressed with the strangeness of the scene, for behind these puny war-boats the deep blue ranges of I-Chang upreared their lofty masses, and shut us in all round with an amphitheatre of hills. The boats were moored in double line, and each was gay with flags and streamers of brilliant and beautiful hues. Their artillery practice was, however, defective; the firing being very irregular, and the guns, some of them, unwilling to be discharged at all. Indeed, when the sham fight was all over, we could still hear the guns going off at intervals during the night. We visited one of these fighting craft, and among other things which we found on board were rifle-stands supporting wooden rifles, placed, as it would seem, in conspicuous places to strike terror into the hearts of an enemy.

The town of I-Chang sweeps in a crescent shape round a bend on the left bank of the river, and is divided into two halves by a canal. The one half occupies high land, while the other is on lower ground, and comprises a large suburb, which suffered severely in the floods of 1870, but has since that time been rebuilt.

There are two or three unoccupied sites at I-Chang which are adapted for a foreign settlement. Building materials are also to be had in great variety and abundance. As to the steam navigation of the river up to this point, I have no hesitation in saying that small boats of light draught could reach I-Chang without difficulty, even when the waters are at their lowest, while during summer the steamers which now ply on the Lower Yangtsze would meet no obstacles greater than those they have already to surmount between Shanghai and Hankow.

We left our Hankow boats at I-Chang to await our return from the gorges, and hired a suitable rapid boat to carry us to Kwei-chow-fu, in Szechuan. Our new crew consisted of twenty-four wiry-looking fellows, men accustomed to the dangers of the gorges, and to the poor fare and hard work to be encountered there.

We left this inland port on the 7th Feb., and in a few hours afterwards had entered the mouth of I-Chang Gorge, fourteen miles above the city. This rocky defile presents a spectacle in imposing contrast to the level plains through which we had been journeying for so many hundred miles. The mountains here vary in height from 500 to 2,500 feet, and the Great River flows through a narrow cleft, in some places not more than a hundred yards across. The channel is everywhere deep and clear, gloomily overshadowed by the rocky walls which frown in gigantic precipices on both sides of the stream, and not unfrequently darkened with still greater intensity by a lowering sky. Rude fisher-huts, perched here and there upon the lofty cliffs, afford the only evidence of the presence of man. A few miles further on we came upon several houses of a better class, surrounded by patches of orchard ground. The inhabitants here obtain a livelihood by selling the produce of their gardens to the passing boats. To these more civilized dwellings there succeeded abodes of a most primitive type—cave hovels, closed in front with a bamboo partition, and fitted with doorways of the same material (see Plate XVIII. No. 36). These cabins were erected in the most inaccessible positions beneath overhanging cliffs, and their smoke-begrimed interiors reminded me of the ancient cave dwellings which sheltered our forefathers at Wemyss Bay in Scotland. It is in just such desolate spots as these that the frugality and industry of the Chinese race are most conspicuously exhibited. A number of the hardy natives live by fishing, while others are engaged in the stone-quarries close by; and wherever it is at all possible, the thin soil on the face of the rocks is scraped and planted, and vegetables, tended with ceaseless care, grow up there and mature. This is indeed taking bread out of a stone. It is here that the stone used for building and for embankments lower down the river is found in greatest abundance; and I was interested to note how, by the action of the water on the rocks, the softer fugitive particles had been washed away, leaving strange grottoes and caverns with grotesque columns to support the superincumbent masses.

A snowfall on the 8th mantled the mountain tops in white, but in the gorge took the shape of a refreshing shower, and brought out the bright hues of the plum-blossom, in an orchard hard by where we had made fast for the night. At this spot the river gave no soundings with ten fathoms of line. It was now the first night of the Chinese New Year, and the boatmen accordingly apprised us of their intention to spend the afternoon at the village of Kwang-loong-Miau, on the right bank of the river. This hamlet is surrounded with pine, and backed by a mountain 2,000 feet in height. A number of our crew proceeded to a temple to make

sacrifice, and later in the evening I was called upon to adjust a dispute. Chang protested that his honourable name had been sullied by the drunken behaviour of the boatmen; I, however, discovered quickly that our venerated interpreter was himself not without sin, being, indeed, unable to stand erect. The crew spent the night in drinking, gambling, and opium-smoking, rioting noisily, and firing crackers from time to time. In the morning the skipper sacrificed a cock to the river goddess and cast some wine upon the waters. After the libation he himself partook of the beverage with a liberality that made a deep impression on the thirsty boatmen, to whom he finally relinquished the well-nigh emptied flask. Two or three miles above the village we encountered the first rapid; and here, at a small hamlet, we lost much time in engaging additional hands, at holiday rates, to tow us up the stream. This task they accomplished by fixing a strong bamboo tug-line to the masthead, while a second rope was made fast to a rock at the top of the rapid, and hauled in on deck, so that we might be kept in position, if the towing line gave way. The water here was flowing at the rate of about seven knots, and the rapid, which was a dangerous one, had but a single narrow channel, surrounded above and below by jagged spikes of rock, which showed above water at that season of the year. I gather from the narratives of Captain Blakistow and Mr. Swinhoe that when the river has risen, there is no rapid at this point at all, and no special danger to be encountered. It would, however, be of the greatest importance to ascertain, by actual careful survey, the exact positions of these rocks, for a steamer might be easily impaled on any one of them during the period when they are submerged. Numbers of them could be removed by blasting when the waters are low; and this may be said of many other rocks in various parts of the gorges. The river is usually at its lowest during the month of February; and in July and August the floods attain their greatest height. At that time in the gorges, the waters apparently rise full seventy feet above their lowest level, the increase being of course greatest where the passage is most contracted. The drum seen in front of No. 34 is an instrument which can be heard above the roar of the rapid and yell of the trackers, and its sounds are supposed to nerve the men to greater exertion. In this instance the trackers, fifty in number, each with his bamboo loop slung over the shoulders and attached to the towing-line, were crawling forward inch by inch, hands and feet firmly planted in the rocks, on the bank, till at length they launched the labouring boat into the smooth waters above. The Lu-kan Gorge, which we entered on the afternoon of the 9th, presented a scene yet grander than any which we had hitherto encountered. Here, the mountains were more than 3,000 feet high, and sheer precipices of 1,000 feet rose up from the very margin of the water (see Plate XXIII. No. 50). Many of the rocks at this place contain strange vertical borings formed apparently with a sort of natural sand drill. Small hard pebbles, imprisoned in recesses of soft rock, have, with the aid of particles of sand and water, in time pierced these deep vertical shafts, and the attrition of the water upon the face of the rocks at last brings the tunnelled apertures to light. The second rapid occurs at Shan-tow-pien. Here we found two wrecks; and these made up in all nine wrecks of native craft, which we had noticed since we quitted I-Chang. The owner of one of these shattered boats, a very aged man, was living in a small cabin which he had made out of spars and matting; and there he had been waiting for a week. He seemed extremely wretched, and we volunteered

49

our help, but he made signs to us to go away.   Next morning, we ascended a smaller rapid (see No. 37), just below the great rapid of Tsing-tan, at the mouth of the Mi-tan Gorge.   As the Tsing-tan Rapid would present the greatest obstacle to steamers, I have made it the subject of two plates, (Plate XXI. No. 48 and Plate XXII. No. 49).   In the first of these we have a general view of the entrance to the pass, and of the position of the village of Tsing-tan. The rapid is just below the village, and above the point at which our boat is seen under sail.   The small boat, with two men on board, is one of the life boats always in attendance below the rapid.   It is customary for the Chinese traders to unship their cargoes below, and have them transported overland to the smooth water above ; there they reload their vessels ; and this precaution they take, not because the channel is too shallow, but in order that the boats may have less weight on them when ascending or descending the rapids.   No. 49 is an instantaneous photograph of the rapid, taken from the village above.   It was obtained, I may add, under the most trying circumstances ; for the villagers, who had never seen any such devilry as manufacturing pictures without a pencil, had thought fit to pelt me with missiles, and I narrowly escaped a stroke from an oar, as I took refuge in my boat.   In vain Chang reasoned with the mob ; we quietly secured the photograph, pocketed the insult and decamped.   My two companions were all the while in their boat on the other side, preparing for the ascent of the stream.   No doubt some of these villagers had heard the popular fiction that mystic pictures such as mine were made out of the eyes of Chinese babes.   This rapid is one of the grandest spectacles in the whole panorama of the Upper Yangtsze.   The water presents a smooth surface as it emerges from the pass.   Suddenly it seems to bend like a polished cylinder of glass, falls eight or ten feet, and then, curving upwards in a glorious crest of foam, it surges away in wild tumult down the river.   At this season sundry sunken rocks enhance the perils of shooting this rapid.   On our way down we persuaded Chang to come into the boat with us ; but as the vessel plunged and groaned in an agony of straining timbers, he became perfectly sick with panic fear.   The inhabitants of Tsing-tan all make a living in some way out of the rapid.   A few are pilots, the rest trackers, and besides all this there are many wrecks which help them to get along.   We had here to hire fifty trackers, to aid in towing our boat up stream.   The speed of this rapid was estimated at about eight knots, but I see no reason why the kind of steamer which Blakistow has suggested should not navigate this, and indeed, any of the rapids on the Yangtsze, the steam power to be detached, and made available either for towing the vessel up or for retarding her in swift and hazardous descents.   Were the river open to steam navigation and foreign trade, daring and scientific skill would be forthcoming to accomplish the end in view.

We made fast for the night at the small town of Kwei, in Hupeh.   This is built on sloping ground beneath the cliffs, on the left bank of the river.   It was puzzling to imagine on what the people can subsist.   There were no cultivated lands, no boats, nor signs of any sort of trade ; the only being we encountered was a solitary beggar, and he was anxious to depart from Kwei.   There are a number of coal mines near Patung, and in the rocks where the coal-beds are found the limestone strata have been thrown up from the stream in nearly perpendicular walls.   The coal is slid down from the pit's mouth to a dépôt close to the water's edge, along grooves cut for that purpose on the face of the rock.   The exact appearance of the entrance to one of these mines will be gathered from Plate XIX. No. 42.

50

Vol. III, Plate XXIII

The workings are usually sunk obliquely, for a very short distance, into the rock, and are abandoned in places where to our own miners the real work would have barely begun. They sink no perpendicular shafts, nor do their mines require any system of ventilation. The miners, of whom a group are shown in Plate XX., No. 44, work daily from seven A.M. to four P.M., and their wages average 300 cash a day, or about seven shillings a man per week. They use a small oil lamp fixed to the head, similar to that which our miners employed before the Davy lamp was invented. Others of the villagers work at the mines; some are coalporters, and carry their burdens in creels fastened to their backs, after the plan shown in No. 46. At this sort of work the men can earn two hundred cash a day. The young children manufacture fuel. This fuel is made by mixing the coal, which here is of inferior quality, with water, then casting it in moulds and drying it in the sun. The process is shown in No. 43, while in No. 45 we see the fuel ready for exportation. Each block weighs $1\frac{1}{3}$ lbs. and it is sold at the pit's mouth for about five shillings a ton. The Chinese still work their coal in a very imperfect manner, and they use it very sparingly for fuel, even in those provinces where it might be most abundantly obtained. Baron von Richthofen has assured us there is plenty of coal in Hupeh and Hunan, and that the coal field of Szechuan is also of enormous area. He further adds that at the present rate of consumption the world could be supplied from Southern Shasi alone for several thousand years, and yet, in some of the places referred to, it is not uncommon to find the Chinese storing up wood and millet stalks for their firing in winter, while coal in untold quantities lies ready for use in the soil just under their feet. These vast coal-fields will constitute the basis of China's future greatness, when steam shall have been called in to aid her in the development of her inland mineral resources. Wu-shan Gorge, which we entered on the morning of the 18th, is more than twenty miles in length. The river here was perfectly placid, and the view which met our gaze at the mouth of the gorge was perhaps the finest of the kind that we had encountered. The mountains rose in confused masses to a great altitude, while the most distant peak at the extremity of the reach resembled a cut sapphire, its snow lines sparkling in the sun like the gleams of light on the facets of a gem. The other cliffs and precipices gradually deepened in hue until they reached the bold lights and shadows of the rocky foreground. (See No. 51.)

The officers of a gunboat stationed at the boundary which parts Hupeh from Szechuan warned us to beware of pirates, and they had good reason for so doing. The same night, at about ten o'clock, an intense darkness having fallen upon the gorge, we were roused by the whispering of a boat's crew alongside us. Hailing them we got no answer, and we therefore next fired high, in the direction whence the sound proceeded; our fire was responded to by a flash and report from another direction. After this we kept watch during the entire night, and were again roused at about two o'clock to challenge a boat's crew that was noiselessly stealing down upon our quarters. A second time we were forced to fire, and the sharp ping of the rifle ball on the rocks had the effect of deterring further advances from our invisible foe. The disturbers of our repose must have been thoroughly acquainted with this part of the gorge, for even by day it is somewhat dark there, and at night-time is of such pitchy blackness that no trading boat would then venture to move from its rock-bound moorings.

On the 14th, as we were tracking up a small rapid, we were obliged to cut the bamboo line adrift, for the

51

boat had been caught in an eddy by a sudden gust of wind, and was on the point of heeling over. Freed from the tension of the tracking rope, she righted herself and spun away down the rapid till she settled on the right bank about half a mile below the scene of the accident. The breadth of the river now parted us from our men, and it was with great difficulty, and at an exorbitant rate, that we were at last enabled to hire a boat to bring them all across.

We reached Wu-shan-hien, in Szechuan, at about three o'clock, and we terminated our journey at this point, distant over 1,200 statute miles from Shanghai. It had been our intention to ascend the short pass which still separated us from Kwei-chow-fu, but we were detained by a storm of sand and wind, against which we could make no headway with our craft. In Wu-shan Gorge there are a number of caves, and we were told that one of them is used as a prison. This prison cavern was pointed out high up in the face of a precipice. It can only be reached by chains which are hung down over the rock. In another cave, nearly as inaccessible, we found an aged hermit, who had been living there alone on herbs and meditation for many years past.

I quit this part of my subject with some reluctance, leaving the incidents of our downward voyage untold for fear lest my readers may already have grown weary of my narrative.

VOLUME IV

VOL. IV

LIST OF ILLUSTRATIONS.

LIST OF ILLUSTRATIONS.

THE GOVERNMENT OF CHINA.

HE Government of China may be divided into central, provincial, and extra-provincial. The first division comprises the holders of high office in Peking; the second the governors of the eighteen provinces in which China proper is comprehended, and of the three provinces of the district loosely termed Manchuria, which stretches north-eastward of Peking. In the third class we may place the officials resident in those vast regions known as Inner and Outer Mongolia, in the country between Mongolia and Thibet, and lastly in Thibet itself.

Every Manchu mandarin of high standing has military as well as civil rank. The Manchu army, which conquered China in 1644, was divided originally into four corps, distinguished by the white, red, blue, and yellow banners under which they respectively fought. Four bordered banners of the same colours were subsequently added, and, in course of time, eight similar corps of Mongols, and eight of Chinese who had sided with the invader were established.

The chief commands of these (which it must be observed are of a mixed civil and military organization, where all are liable to bear arms, but by no means all are paid as soldiers) are shared among high officers of the three nationalities, the Manchu on the whole being the predominating class. Prince Kung is general of one banner, Wen-siang of another, Paou-keun and Cheng-lin of the third and fourth. Each of these officials, however, is also the head of some principal department in the central administration. As for the Great Council, it is an excrescence on the original establishment, but still it is the chief among the courts, for it confers upon its members the highest rank attainable in the civil service. The Grand Secretariat is made up of four chief and two assistant chancellors or secretaries, these posts being shared in equal proportion between the Chinese, the Mongols, and the Manchus. Wen-siang is an assistant Grand Secretary, but it is only lately that he has been appointed to that post. Membership of the Secretariat, as will be seen elsewhere, does not render residence at the capital obligatory, indeed distinguished provincial governors are often raised to that dignity, only so, however, when vacancies occur. Next in degree to this office, and of far more practical importance, are six boards representing as many departments in the administration. These are the Board of Civil Service; the Board of Finance; the Board of Rites, Obligations, and Observances (including public institutions and state worship); the Board of War, having charge both of the military and naval services; the Board of Criminal Jurisdiction; and, lastly, the Board of Public Works. Each of these six boards has two chief officers, or, as we should style them, Presidents, at its head, one of them is always a Manchu, and the other a Chinese. The ministers of the Tsungle Yamen possess a fair proportion of these appointments. Thus Paou-keun is the Manchu President, and Tung-sean the Chinese one over the Board of Finance. Shen-kwe-fen is the Chinese President over the Board of War. Maou-cheng-he (properly the Chinese President over the Board of Works) is acting for an absentee on the Board of Civil Office; while Chung-lun, now eighty years of age, is the Manchu President of the Board of Works, and at the same time President over a court by us termed the Colonial Office, though really having charge not of tributaries like Corea and Cochin China, but of dependencies such as Mongolia and Thibet. The ministers Wen-siang, Paou-keun, and Shen-kwe-fen enjoy, however, a position even higher than any of the above roll, for, like Prince Kung, they are all of them members of the Great Council. This Council, in which the real power of the central government may be said to reside, has been already described as an excrescence upon the regular establishment. In point of fact it was introduced shortly after the foundation of the dynasty, and is composed of Manchus selected not on the recommendation of the departments of state, but by the emperor's own choice. The number of its members has never been a fixed one. At this moment, Prince Kung included, it contains no more than five. The fifth is the emperor's private tutor, while the other four, as has already been stated, are all members of the Tsungle Yamen. It will thus be perceived that what is really the central government is thoroughly identified with the administration of Foreign Affairs.

In the provinces the civil and military establishments are more distinct than at first sight they might appear to be in the capital. A province usually has a governor at the head of its affairs; but there are some exceptions to this custom. Thus we find in two instances a Governor General, or Viceroy, but the title translated as governor is borne by an official who has two, or, in one case, three provinces under his rule, and governors below him to conduct the affairs of each province.

Thus Li-hung-chang is Governor-General of Peichihli, the province in which Peking lies. Tseng-quo-fan (who is but lately dead) was Governor-General of Kiang-su, Ngan-kwui and Kiang-si, while Jui-lin is Governor-General of Kwang-tung and Kwang-si. Of the officers just referred to the first is a Chinese, and is an assistant Grand Secretary; the second also a Chinese, and the third, of Manchu blood, are both Grand Secretaries. The Governors-General and Governors have each a small body of troops at their disposal, but they do not command the naval or military forces of the provinces. In particular places, generally the provincial capitals, as well as in the maritime and inland frontier provinces, permanent Manchu garrisons, under Manchu officers of very high rank, are established. In Canton, Chang-fang, brother-in-law to the Princess Kung, commands the Manchu garrison, whereas the Chinese forces of the province are under a separate general officer, after whom comes a series of subordinates, with ranks as numerous as those of our own army if we count from ensign to major-general. These officials all draw pay, but the troops or constabulary assigned to them exist principally on paper.

The civil functionaries play a part that is much more real. A province is divided into a number of districts, each about the size of a small English county, and officered by magistrates and assistant magistrates, with the occasional aid of the literati and people of character and substance. A group of districts forms a department, and this is ruled by a prefect, or sub-prefect. A number of these departments again makes up a circuit, of which there may be two, three, four, or five in a province. There are again under-intendants, but the working officers are the prefects and magistrates, the bulk of the work falling more especially on the latter. Add to the above list a commissioner of finance, who is also a sort of dean of the civil establishment, one of criminal justice, one of the commissariat, and one of the salt revenue (the latter with a large staff to help him), and you have, without pretension to minute accuracy, a fair *résumé* of the machinery by which the government of China and its dependencies is supposed to be carried on.

The Board of Foreign Affairs holds its meetings in the Tsungle Yamen, which corresponds to our English Foreign Office. This new department of Chinese administration sprang out of the close and important treaty relations now existing between China and Western nations. Its creation was one among the train of events which followed the ratification of the treaty of Tientsin, in 1858. Up to that time all foreign diplomatic correspondence had been conducted through the Colonial Office to which I have already alluded, and, in consequence of this circumstance, the great powers were practically placed on a level with native dependencies. An able writer in the *New York Herald* claims for Mr. W. Reed, at that time American minister to China, the credit of having been the first to protest against the indignity offered to his nation by classing it with such lands as Corea and Lewchew. Be that as it may, the establishment of the Tsungle Yamen, in 1861, was an important and startling concession on the part of the Chinese, more especially when we consider that its members are ministers of the highest rank in the Empire, and as it implied a permanent recognition of the independent sovereignty and equality of the treaty powers. Prince Kung presides over this council, and is ably supported by the following members :—

Wen-siang, a Manchu, born at Mukden in 1817. He ranks next to Prince Kung on the Board of Foreign Affairs, and has held the position since 1861. He is also a member of the Grand Council, President of the Board of Civil Service, and member of the Imperial Cabinet (plurality of offices is, therefore, by no means disapproved of in China). His rare intellectual powers (Sir F. Bruce pronounced him one of the strongest minds he had ever encountered), coupled with his long experience in the functions of high office, cause Wen-siang to be looked upon as the most influential statesman in China. Formerly he was esteemed exceptionally liberal in his views, but of late years he has discovered symptoms of a reactionary tendency. His portrait is given in No. 2.

Paou-keun (No. 5), a Manchu, and member of the Grand Council, is one of the Presidents of the Board of Finance. He is now sixty-five years of age.

Cheng-lin (No. 4) is the youngest member of the Foreign Board, being not yet more than forty-five. Three years ago he, occupied for a short time, the post of superintendent of trade, vacated by Chung-hau during his mission to France.

Shen-kwe-fen (left figure in group, Plate 1), President of the Board of War, and member of the Grand Council, is a Chinese, fifty-six years of age. He was lately governor of the province of Shensi, where he distinguished himself by an effort to suppress the growth of opium.

Tung-sean, Chinese President of the Board of Finance, is a celebrated scholar, and the author of numerous works, notably one of an historical and topographical character. His last publication (a treatise in forty-eight volumes) on the Hydrography of Northern China, was just issuing from the press when I left Peking. Tung-sean (central figure in group, Plate 1), is sixty-one years of age.

Maou-cheng-he, a Chinese, is fifty-six years of age, and President of the Board of Works. Formerly he held the position of First Vice-President of the College of Censors (right figure in group, Plate I.)

Vol. IV, Plate I

LI-HUNG-CHANG.

I-HUNG-CHANG stands foremost among the viceroys of the eighteen provinces of China as the man who exerts, probably, the greatest influence on the progress and destinies of the Empire. Foreigners generally know him best as the associate of Tseng-quo-fan, and Colonel Gordon, in dealing to the Taiping rebels their final blow; but more recently he has established the Nanking Arsenal, the first of the kind in China, and has, besides this, been familiarizing the Chinese soldiery with foreign discipline and drill. To his influence also, direct as well as indirect, the country owes the comparative security which, for the present, she enjoys; and the other indications to be found of growing progress in the unremitting labours of her various arsenals and training schools, as well as in her fleet of steam gun-boats and iron-clads, which, built by native skill, and launched from native dockyards, manned, and officered, too, by native crews, are lending security to trade both on the rivers and along the coast.

These home-built vessels have been armed with modern weapons of the finest make, and are ready at all times to defend the interests of their flag in the China Sea.

On land, advance in the same direction is no less apparent, troops trained in vast numbers in the modern arts of war, and armed with the best-known weapons, have already done good work in suppressing rebellion, and in extending the influence of the central government. According to the latest accounts they have cleared Chinese territory of the Mahometan insurgents, who, until recently, held some important strongholds in the Empire.

It is commonly, and let me add erroneously, supposed in England that little or no progress is being made in China. All eyes are turned towards Japan. There it has become the fashion to discover the pet example of Eastern advancement. Out of the darkness of semi-barbarism, Japan has shot up, planet-like, in search of a wider orbit and a brighter sun. While China, seemingly only faithful to the gravitating influences of ancient tradition, is, too, undergoing a gradual process of transition and development. Yet she esteems the philosophy of her sages as highly as in former days, and maintains her belief in the old institutions which have supported her in proud isolation and independence for so many centuries. For all that, and notwithstanding the obstacles to progress presented by her Feng-shui, or Geomancy, from sheer necessity, and the instinct of self-preservation, she is drifting slowly towards our Western ways, adopting our sciences, educating her sons at our universities, remodelling important branches of her administration, and making concessions to meet the friendly requirements of closer foreign intercourse. Nor is this all. Her merchants can now boast of their Steam Navigation Companies, and, a fact perhaps less gratifying to us, they are so thoroughly masters of what they have undertaken in this direction, as to be competing successfully with foreign companies in the carrying trade on the coast and rivers of their country. In process of time the same remark will apply to every branch of their trade and industry. China will then be able to supply not only the staple material grown on her own soil, but skilled labour and machinery to produce the fabrics which she is now obliged to import, and upon which our own trade mainly depends. Her plains are teeming with millions of poor, patient labourers, ready to turn their hands to any industry that will furnish them with the simple necessaries of life, men capable of being trained to engage in the highest branches of skilled labour. Her mountains abound in metals and minerals, and her vast coal-fields are stored up to kindle the fires of a coming age of steam and iron. Western nations have woke the old dragon from her sleep of ages, and now she stands at bay, armed with iron claws and fangs of foreign steel.

It may be a long time yet before she will take her place among the powerful nations of the earth, but the civilizing agencies which now operate on the Central Flowery Land all tend to further the accomplishment of an end which, in the Chinese interest, is so much to be desired. The tide of civilization, too, which now annually carries labourers by their tens of thousands towards other shores, is not without its influence on the parent country. For abroad the Chinaman is quick to learn, so quick and so successful, indeed, as to make him a formidable rival to the artizans and operatives of the West, and he invariably returns to his native town taking home with him the know-ledge as well as the capital which he has acquired abroad.

Vol. IV, Plate II

I need no excuse for introducing details regarding the life of a man such as Li-hung-chang, who occupies the most prominent position in China, and thus exerts a powerful influence on the well-being of nearly one-third of the human race.

Li-hung-chang (see No. 3), the second of five sons, was born two years after the accession of the Emperor Tau-kwang, in the province of Ngan-whui. His father was an obscure literary man, who, notwithstanding poor circumstances, yet managed to give his children a liberal education. Young Li, the subject of these notes, succeeded in passing the different degrees at the Government examinations, and in 1848, being then twenty-six years of age, became a member of the Han-lin College. When the rebels invaded his native province he raised a local regiment, and placed himself and his troops at the disposal of the Viceroy of the two Kiang. Li joined Tseng-quo-fan, under whom he was advanced to the rank of Taotai, and subsequently to the command of a division of Tseng's Grand Army in Cheh-kiang.

In 1861, the first year of the Emperor Tung-che, he was recommended by Tseng-quo-fan to be acting-Footai of Kiangsu, and then, by the aid of Colonel Gordon, with his Ever-victorious Army, he cleared the province of rebels. On the fall of Soochow he (it is said, but opinion is divided on the subject) ordered all the rebel wangs (Kings) to be beheaded, in defiance of his guarantee that their lives should be spared; the condition on which the city was given up. I have been informed by an officer, who was present at the time, that the massacre of Soochow was not an act of treachery on the part of Li, the order came from another and a higher quarter. Li-hung-chang was, however, greatly incensed, when, the day after the capitulation, the rebel kings visited him wearing their rebel robes, and the long hair which was a badge of rebellion. He must have assented to the massacre, and the central government approved the bloody and treacherous deed, and confirmed Li-hung-chang in the office of Footai. In addition to this the Emperor conferred on him the "Yellow Jacket," one of the highest rewards bestowed in China for eminent military services, and also gave him the title of Fai-tsze-shaou-paon, or Inner Guardian of the Throne. Li-hung-chang now removed to Soochow, and as the rebels had destroyed the residence of the former Footai there, established himself in the palace of the "Chung Wang" (or "Faithful King"), a splendid edifice which had been erected by this rebel chief. Here he remained till Nanking had fallen in 1864, and he was then ordered to proceed to that city as Viceroy of the Two Kiang. He was at the same time created a noble of the third class, and decorated with the double-eyed peacock's feather for conspicuous services. In 1866, Tseng-quo-fan and Li-hung-chang changed places, the latter proceeding against the Neinfei rebels, whom he succeeded in clearing from the north. In 1867 he was appointed Viceroy of Hupeh and Hunan, and from there he was dispatched with an army against the Mahometan rebels, who for some years back had set up the standard of revolt in the western provinces of the Empire. After the Tientsin massacre, Li was replaced by his elder brother in the government of Hupeh and Hunan, and appointed Viceroy of Peichihli. His proper title is now Li-chang-tang, for he was raised to the rank of a second noble about three years ago. He is now the greatest son of Han, and in appearance the finest specimen of his race which it has been my lot to come across. He stands six feet high, his bearing is erect and noble, and his complexion exceedingly fair, while dark, penetrating eyes, and a mouth shaded by a dark brown moustache, betoken inflexible determination.

At the risk of being deemed impertinent, I may add, for the information of readers who have not had the good fortune to come in contact with educated Chinese, that Li-hung-chang possesses the cultivated polish and graceful courtesy which are invariably the attributes of a gentleman. But these, indeed, are qualities he shares in common with all mandarins of rank.

Although thoroughly Chinese by sympathy and education, Li-hung-chang has an intense admiration for our sciences, and for the inventive faculties displayed by the races of the West. He is also ever ready to admit the superiority of our arts and appliances, and eager to advocate their practical introduction into China.

VOL. IV, PLATE III
CHEFOO.

N my last volume I left the reader to find his way back to Shanghai from the rocky gorges of the Upper Yangtsze, and in order to beguile the time which he may be supposed to spend in the monotony of a downward voyage, I have introduced to his notice the high magnates of the Empire, some of whom, although exercising so wide an influence over the greatest people of Eastern Asia, are wholly unknown to European fame. It takes about three days to go from Shanghai to Chefoo, the passage being not unfrequently a rough one, for this part of the northern coast is subject to breezy and boisterous weather. The harbour of Chefoo offers safe anchorage for the largest vessels, and its port—on the northern side of the Shun-tung promontory, and known to the natives as the town of "Yentai"—is the only one open to foreign trade all along the coast, from the river Yangtsze as far as the Peiho. I gather from the Official Customs Report for 1872 that the trade of Chefoo, ever since the port was opened to foreign commerce, has been making steady progress, and more especially in the exportation of silk. Thus the Pongee silk, for which the place has now become noted, has regularly increased in quantity as a leading article of export, 650 piculs of this commodity having been shipped in 1868 and 1,175 piculs in 1872. In like manner the wild raw silk has risen from six piculs in 1868 to 977 in 1872, and yellow silk from 289 in 1868 to 301 in 1872, while foreign imports, although they do not show so marked an advance, are still in steady demand. The duties collected during 1872 amounted in the gross to 330,972 tls. Of this sum British trade contributed considerably over one-third; and from these facts it will be seen that Chefoo, like all the other treaty ports of China, is a place of great importance to our own home trade. The spot is also a favourite resort for Shanghai foreign residents during the hottest months of summer, for cool breezes and sea-bathing may here be enjoyed in one of the finest bays on the coast of China; and close to the sloping sandy beach there is a foreign hotel, conducted on a scale suited to the requirements of the wealthy Shanghai merchants and officials who flock to this welcome sanitarium when jaded with toil and exhausted with the fierce midsummer heats.

The town of Chefoo, or rather the foreign settlement there, is not very picturesque in itself, and (see No. 6) I agree with Mr. Williamson in his opinion that the site, in so far as trading facilities and the comfort of foreign residents are concerned, has been badly chosen, being "exposed to the full blast of the north-west wind."[1] I had my own bitter experience of that north-west wind. When I executed the illustration which I introduce to my readers I was standing in eighteen inches of snow drift. The thermometer being very low, I should say near zero Fahrenheit, I had engaged a group of coolies to hold my dark room down, for the wind threatened every moment to hurl it off its legs. When washing the plate free from cyanide of potassium the water froze on its surface, and hung in icicles around its edges, so that in order to save the picture I was forced to take it to a neighbouring native house, and there to thaw the ice above a fire.

The climate of Shun-tung to some extent resembles that of the more northern countries of Europe, although during two months of summer the maximum of heat is higher, while during winter the temperature is frequently very low. Nevertheless the seasons are so well defined as to enable the farmer not only to raise the fruits and cereals grown in warmer climes, but also to produce those common to colder latitudes, such as pears, apples, wheat, barley, and so forth. Some parts of the province are exceedingly fertile, and yield to the tillage of the labourer three or four crops a year.

The province of Shun-tung is about equal in area to Great Britain and Ireland, but it is not yet well known to foreigners, although the classic land of China. Here the labours of the great Yu were in part performed; Confucius was born in Shun-tung in 550 B.C.,[2] and so also was Mencius, 179 years afterwards. Thus the one of these celebrities was cotemporary with Pythagoras, and the other with Plato. It is also interesting to note that Shâkyamuni Gâutama Buddha, the great reformer of Brahmanism and the founder of the Buddhist faith, is supposed to have died just seven years before the birth of Confucius. "It is now generally agreed upon by European scholars that the year 543 B.C. is most probably that in which Shâkyamuni Gâutama Buddha died."[3] We thus find two men flourishing at about the same epoch, whose religious and moral teachings have exercised for so many centuries a most powerful influence upon the Chinese.

The father of Confucius is said to have ruled over Yen-chow-foo, and the direct descendants of Confucius and Mencius are still to be encountered in the province of Shun-tung.

Taking steamer again to Tien-tsin, a short run across the Gulf of Peichihli brought us to the mouth of Peiho, where I visited the famous Taku forts, which command the entrance of the river. These mud strongholds have been often and well described. During the time of my visit the guns within their ramparts were badly mounted, and the

---

[1] Journeys in North China. Rev. A. Williamson. Vol. i. p. 89.   [2] The Chinese Davis, p. 222.   [3] "Three Lectures on Buddhism." E. J. Eitel, p. 9.

foreigner in charge of the steamer-signal-staff informed me that the native artillery practice was extremely defective. Since then, however, a battery of Krupp guns has replaced the old smooth-bores, the forts have been properly garrisoned, and undergone thorough repair. This information I have received on the best authority, otherwise I should feel inclined to discredit it, for at the time of my visit, forts, batteries, and garrisons presented a miserable makeshift appearance. Doubtless at that conjuncture there was a very sufficient reason for the disorganized condition of these important defences of the river by which we approach the capital. The fact is a great flood had laid waste the lower portions of the province between Taku and Tien-tsin, and the starved-out inhabitants, clamorous for food and shelter, had flocked in overwhelming numbers to Tien-tsin. Hence the presence of an efficient military force at that city was essential to secure public safety. The scene which presented itself as we steamed up the river can never be effaced from my recollection. The country was under water, and the native trading craft were sailing in direct lines for Tien-tsin, over fields and gardens and the ruins of homesteads. The villages and farm-houses, built mainly out of mud and millet stalks, had settled down into damp, dank mounds, and their occupants, with their furniture and cattle lashed to stakes, were to be seen perched on the fallen roofs of their houses, fishing with assiduity and success. Fish indeed were caught in such abundance as to sustain thousands, who would otherwise have perished from starvation. As we neared Tien-tsin we passed a vast burial ground, where men were engaged mooring the coffins to trees and posts, while many corpses were drifting away towards the sea.

The central government exerted itself to mitigate the sufferings of the people by a supply of food, clothing, and shelter, and, much to the credit of the Chinese, private contributions for the same humane object flowed in from the coast and from different parts of the Empire. This is one of the benefits conferred by rapid steam communication along the coast. It is a matter of regret that, while we note with satisfaction the unmistakable signs of progress in China, more especially in those parts which have been brought face to face with the civilizing influences of Western intercourse, we at the same time cannot avoid remarking the equally manifest symptoms of decay which too frequently present themselves in the interior of the country. There we find bad roads, bridges and embankments broken and abandoned, and a poverty-stricken population. Much of this state of affairs is attributable to the niggardliness and rapacity of the officials. It would probably be a sounder policy on the part of the central and local governments of the Empire if attention were earnestly directed to improving the old trade routes of the country, by repairing and strengthening the river embankments, so as to secure the people from the misery of constantly recurring inundations. If, in short, by honesty and fair dealing, the people could be inspired with a conviction that their government and social condition were matters worth defending. As it is, the authorities are assiduously studying the modern tactics of warfare, and arming a poorly-paid soldiery with the deadliest weapons. During last year the flood in Peichihli was repeated, notwithstanding the fact that a large sum of money had been granted by the central government for the survey and repair of the river embankments. The task was inefficiently performed, and, as might have been foreseen, the horrors of the inundation occurred once more. It almost seems that the embankments of the streams in North China have fallen into such a bad state as to defy the skill of native engineers.

TIEN-TSIN.

TIEN-TSIN is the capital of the prefecture of that name, which extends along the coast in a south-east direction, as far as the Shun-tung promontory, and comprises one inferior department and six districts. The city lies at the junction of the Grand Canal with the Peiho river, and next to Peking is the most considerable in the province of Peichihli. Previous to 1782 it was nothing more than a military station for the protection of the river traffic, but at that time it was raised to the status of a prefectural city. Its present estimated population is about 400,000, of whom perhaps one-half reside within the walls.

No. 7 represents a group of Tien-tsin labourers, as I found them engaged in removing the *débris* from the Chapel of the Sisters of Mercy, who had been massacred on this spot in the preceding year. Of the chapel itself nothing had been left standing except the bare walls (see No. 8); but I need hardly offer further remarks on this subject, as doubtless the harrowing details of the bloody event are still fresh in my readers' recollection. As we look from this point up the reach of the Peiho we see the ruins of the Roman Catholic Cathedral, by far the most striking object in Tien-tsin, and I could not help thinking at the time that, from what I know of the Chinese character, this noble structure must have been a dreadful eyesore to the natives, towering as it did high above any of their most sacred buildings, and drawing down evil influences from the sky. Just above the chapel we encountered an interesting specimen of a floating bridge, a section of which had to be drawn up to allow my boat to pass through.

There is at Tien-tsin a small foreign settlement of well-built houses, but many of these residences had suffered from the floods. Thus the gardens which surrounded them were under water. The English Club, and the Joss-house in which the treaty of Tien-tsin was signed, could only be reached by boat. The solitary hotel in the settlement, called the Aster House, well-nigh conceals its modest proportions beneath a huge signboard inscribed with its name. This hotel had been built of mud, and now a window on one side had fallen out, and a wall on the other had fallen in. I had a look at the accommodation of this unpromising interior, and also held some conversation with its proprietor, an Englishman. I found him lamenting the wreck of his property, of which only two apartments remained. In one there was a good billiard table, and in the other a bar. Two of the bedrooms had dissolved, and could be seen in solution through the broken wall, with sundry limbs of furniture sticking up to mark its resting-place. The stables at the rear had taken a header into the water, and the place which had known them in dry weather was dimly seen through a cloud of mosquitoes, which were the pests of the settlement. There is at Tien-tsin a manufactory of gunpowder on the foreign model, where a number of foreigners are constantly employed.

Vol. IV, Plate III

THE KWO-TSZE-KEEN, OR NATIONAL UNIVERSITY, PEKING.

WEST of the Yung-ho-kung, the great Lamasary, where a living Buddha rules, stands the college attached to the Confucian temple and known as the Kwo-tsze-keen. In this building, prior to the reign of Kien-lung, the ancient classics were expounded. But that monarch determined to imitate a much more ancient structure, and accordingly built the edifice known as the Pi-yung-kung, or Hall of the Classics, which we can here discern through the archway in Plate No. 9. The building is a square, and its three remaining sides correspond with that shown in the photograph. Its upper roof rests on a series of carved wooden brackets; pillars of wood also support the lower one, and the whole is crowned with a gilded copper ball. The base is marble, and the edifice is approached by four bridges of the same material, spanning a marble-walled moat, surrounded with white marble balustrades. The hall stands in the centre of a court, and on the right and left of it, in long open verandahs, there are about 200 tablets of upright stone. On these tablets the complete text of the nine classics has been engraved, an idea repeated from the Han and Tang dynasties, "each of which had a series of monuments engraved with the classics in the same way."[1]

In front there is a yellow porcelain triple archway, or pai-lau, having the inner portion of its arches built of white marble. It was through the centre of this structure that the picture here presented was taken.

---

[1] "Journeys in Mongolia, &c.," Rev. A. Williamson, *seq.* by Rev. J. Edkins, vol. ii.

Vol. IV, Plate IV

PEKING OBSERVATORY.

ATHER LE COMTE visited the Peking Observatory in 1688, just after the death of Father Verbiest, under whose directions the new instruments had been constructed there. Le Comte seems to have formed but a poor estimate of the ancient Chinese instruments, which had been already removed and stored in an obscure hall, in a court below the wall. He describes them as buried in dust and oblivion, but he only saw them "through a window close set with iron bars."

Among those rejected instruments was the one I have here shown, and which has since been set up at one end of the court. I have no doubt had this devoted missionary seen it, even in its present condition, he would have arrived at a much higher appreciation of the beauty and comparative finish of its workmanship.

The old Chinese astronomical instruments, although constructed with an amazing degree of skill and exactness, would now be perfectly useless; for the mode of taking astronomical observations at that time was widely different from the system in use at present, besides which the circles are inaccurately divided.

The instruments, constructed under the superintendence of Father Verbiest, do not show so marked a superiority over those of the Chinese astronomers as I had expected. They are undoubtedly finer and more accurate; but they too were constructed by Chinese artificers, and Le Comte says of them, " I would rather trust to a quadrant made by one of our good workmen in Paris, whose radius should be but one foot and a-half, than to that of six feet, which is at this tower." The divisions of the circles, though more accurate than those of the old instruments, are still defective.

I have in my possession a Chinese narrative wherein Verbiest describes the rude appliances with which he had to work, and my only surprise is that he should ever have been able to construct instruments such as those which I have pictured in No. 10. We are shown in the volume referred to, how the castings of the great circles appeared in the rough; how they were sawn into shape; and how finally they were turned upon a horizontal lathe made like an ordinary Chinese flour mill, with a donkey to drive it. It pictures, in addition, the mode in which the celestial globe was turned. This globe was simply laid into its frame, upon an axis having one extremity fitted with a handle, like that of a large circular grindstone. Motion was next imparted to the globe from this handle, and from the feet of an operator treading upon the upper surface of the metal sphere, while the hand of an operator was used to steady the turning tool in order to dress the metal, and render it perfectly globose and true on its axis. All the appliances are of the same primitive sort. The dividing of the circles must have been done by hand in some open shed; whereas in Europe, at the present time, we find it necessary, when an important circle is to be divided, to have the dividing engine built upon a rock and enclosed in a chamber where the temperature is kept uniform until the process of dividing the circle has been completed. By this device we avoid contractions and expansions of the metal circle, which would otherwise mar the perfect accuracy of the divisions.

The globe is described by Le Comte as follows—"*A Celestial Globe.* This in my opinion is the fairest and best fashioned of all the instruments. The globe itself is brazen, exactly round and smooth; the stars well made, and in their true places, and all the circles of a proportionate breadth and thickness. It is besides so well hung that the least touch moves it, and though it is above 2,000 lbs. weight the least child may elevate it to any degree." This globe, seen on the left of the illustration (No. 10), is still in a perfect state of preservation, although it has been exposed in the open air without covering for full two centuries. The stars on this celestial globe are all raised brass, and distinguished according to their magnitude, for the convenience of feeling on a dark night. The old Chinese method of division is abandoned on these instruments, the circle being divided into 360°, and each degree into sixty minutes, as in Europe.

Armillary sphere on the terrace of the Observatory at Peking, No. 10. This is also one of the instruments made under the directions of Father Verbiest. The circles are divided, both in their exterior and interior, by cross lines into 360°, and each degree into 60 minutes, and the latter into portions of 10 seconds each by small pins.

I am greatly indebted to Mr. A. Wylie for valuable information regarding the Observatory and other places of interest in Peking.

10

PEKING OBSERVATORY.

PEKING consists of two cities: one the Tartar or Manchu city, with the Imperial palace in its centre; the other, the Chinese, containing the altars of heaven and earth, where the State worship is carried on.

The Tartar city is enclosed by massive walls, nearly in the form of a square, each side measuring about three miles and a-half. These walls are pierced with nine gates; three on the south side and two on each of the others.

The Tartar city is supposed to contain nothing except the Imperial palace, the abodes of the nobles, and the barracks for the accommodation of the bannermen, already described, who form the body-guard of the Emperor. Several causes, however, have contributed to alter this the original state of things; the most prominent of which are, the long residence of these bannermen in the capital; their familiar intercourse with the less warlike Chinese; their proud disdain for trades or handicrafts of every sort; and the inadequate support which the government allowances can supply. Many of the old families of the Manchu bannermen have thus become impoverished, and the lands allotted to them at the time of the conquest have been sold, and have passed to Chinese proprietors; so that now there is a considerable Chinese population to be found within the Tartar city.

The Chinese city adjoins the southern wall of the Tartar city. It is also walled, in the form of a parallelogram, and covers an area five miles long by three broad. Access to this division of the metropolis is gained through seven gateways; two on the north, one eastward, one westward, and three others on the southern side.

The Chinese town is thinly populated, and a great portion of the enclosed area is under cultivation. Mr. Edkins estimates the entire census of Peking at something over a million, whereas, he says, the Chinese set it down at two millions and a-half.

Having ascended one of the well-built slopes of stone which conduct to the summit of the city walls, I found myself traversing a paved surface thirty feet in width, and commanding a view of the capital from an elevation of about fifty-five feet.

The prospect from the walls is by no means a striking one; the eye ranges over a multitude of low roofs, and brick walls enclosing the pleasure grounds of the rich, with shrubs and trees overhanging them; or over the mud hovels of a multitude of poor, proud, bannermen, divided by broad thoroughfares in well defined lines, and cut across also by narrow lanes of communication to the walled-in dwellings.

When one gazes upon a Chinese city, such as Peking, one cannot help being struck by its labyrinth of walls. You must first mount the ramparts to see them, and, this done, you may descry beneath your feet countless lanes hedged in with high brick walls, where every dwelling of any pretensions is shut in round about by brick enclosures all its own. Thus each family seems fortified against vulgar or offensive intrusion.

The houses are so arranged that the inner family dwelling is isolated in a sort of sacred seclusion. The only approach is by a small outer doorway, through a dead wall, leading into a court and outer chamber, beyond which a stranger may not intrude. Next to this succeeds a reception room for guests, and further in are the apartments devoted solely to the family circle.

I cannot help holding it to be a defect in the national character, which renders such formidable barriers necessary. Moreover, when I looked towards the centre of the city, my eyes caught the light reflected by the yellow roofs of the Imperial palace, and I found the idea of family isolation carried out in the strong walls and moat which encompass the grounds of the "sacred purple capitol," within which the Emperor and his family reside, and his eunuchized retainers are condemned to dwell in splendid misery. In addition to the palace of the Emperor and the abodes of the Princes, a few stately temples rear their heads close by, and break the monotony of the prospect.

Near to the palace, and on the east side of the Tartar city, rising a considerable height above the battlements, the Observatory is to be seen. This Observatory was erected during the Yuen or Mongol dynasty, towards the

end of the thirteenth century, Ko-show-king, one of the most renowned astronomers in Chinese history, being chief of the astronomical board at the time. The instrument shown at No. 11, constructed under his directions, now stands below the wall at the east end of the court. It is of huge dimensions, cast in solid bronze, and is of the most beautiful workmanship. The stand of this piece of mechanism has a mythological significance, and its design is of remarkable artistic excellence. Four of the dragons, which play such an important part in Chinese geomancy, are there seen chained to the earth, and upholding the spheres. The perfect modelling and solidity of the metal proves that the art of casting was well understood in those days.

A substantial metal horizon, crossed at right angles by a double ring for an azimuth circle, forms the outer framework. The upper surface of this horizon is divided into twelve equal parts, marked respectively by the cyclical characters, " tsze, chow, yin, maou, chin, szi, woo, wei, shin, yu, seih, hae," being the names applied to the twelve hours into which the Chinese divide their day and night.

Round the outside of the ring these twelve characters appear again, paired with eight characters of the denary cycle, and four of the " book of changes," designating the points of the compass, thus, " jin-tsze, kwei-chow, kan-yin, kea-maou, yih-chin, seuen-sze, ping-woo, ting-wei, kwan-shin, kang-yu, sin-seih, keen-hae."

The inside of the ring bears the names of the twelve states into which China was anciently divided : every part of the empire being supposed to be under the influence of a particular quarter of the heavens.

An equatorial circle is fixed inside this frame, within which a movable series of rings turns on two pivots at the poles of the azimuth circle. The latter consists of an equatorial circle, and a double ring ecliptic, an equinoctial colure, and a double ring solstitial colure. The equator is divided into twenty-eight unequal portions, marked by the names of so many constellations of unknown antiquity. These are, " keo, kang, te, fang," &c. &c.

The determinant points of each of these constellations are used for so many meridian lines, from which all distances are measured, just as we use the vernal equinox for right ascension.

The ecliptic is divided into twenty-four equal parts, into which the year is portioned out. Inside this, again, there is a double revolving meridian, with a double axis ; and in it a tube is fixed, turning on a centre, for taking sights.

All these circles are also divided into $365\frac{1}{4}°$ corresponding to the days of the year, and each degree is subdivided into a hundred equal parts ; for at that time the centenary division prevailed for everything less than degrees, and was only abandoned on the arrival of the Jesuit missionaries in the seventeenth century.

At the corners of the base, and outside the dragons, are four miniature rocks in bronze, with the respective inscriptions, " keen shan, north-west or celestial mountain ; kwan shan, south-west or terrestrial mountain ; seuen shan, or south-east mountain ; kan shan, north-east mountain."

These are probably symbolical in reference to an old tradition.

NOTE.—Owing to the difficulty of procuring the Chinese cyclical and other characters in England, I have given the sounds of the characters in English.

CHINESE HOUSES.

N O exhaustive or thoroughly satisfactory description of the domestic architecture of the Chinese house has, so far as I am aware, ever yet been given. A principal reason for this omission is the lack of anything like complete acquaintance with the subject. The fact is, the country is in itself a vast one, and its domestic architecture, though remarkably similar throughout, yet presents wide divergences of construction, designed to meet the varying requirements of climate and position.

A second difficulty arises from the strong dislike entertained by the people against admitting strangers into the inner courts of their dwellings; for these they hold to be sacred and inviolate. To such an extent, indeed, has this idea of privacy and family isolation been carried, that Chinese homes have for ages been constructed, on all occasions, after a model which seems to aim at perfect family seclusion from relatives even, and friends, no less than from strangers.

I cannot venture to describe here all that I have myself observed with respect to the architectural styles adopted in different provinces of the Empire. I must limit myself to a few general remarks, such as bear more especially upon the illustrations numbered 12, 13, and 14.

I enjoyed exceptional advantages for gleaning information about the inner life of the Chinese wealthy classes, and the arrangements of their households, inasmuch as I never let slip an opportunity of volunteering to take family portraits, in order that while thus engaged I might obtain for myself such groups and interiors as those which I have here represented.

The dwelling to which I am about to introduce the reader is that of Mr. Yang, a gentleman enormously rich, and holding an official rank in Peking. His abode, like all others of its kind, is walled around, and can be entered only by a plain doorway through a high brick wall which skirts an obscure alley. Within the door were two silk lanterns, dangling from supports above, and daubed with the name and titles of Yang. About six feet from the lintel was a movable partition designed to conceal the inner court, as well as for purposes of geomancy. Having entered the first court within the wall, I was brought to a stand-still by the porter and his huge dog, a shaggy brute, who fiercely showed his fangs. The porter conveyed my card to Mr. Yang, and the latter thereupon came to the threshold of an inner court to meet me, and conducted me through a quaint, narrow passage, overgrown with a grape-vine, into a sort of Chinese paradise. In this paradise was a miniature lotus lake, spanned by a marble bridge. A small marble pagoda embowered in vines and fruit-trees, rose on the one side, while on the other an artificial rockery had been constructed, and ferns and flowers were growing out of its mossy crevices. Passing along a marble-paved pathway, roofed over, and open in front, to this half-garden, half-quadrangle, I came next to the reception-hall. It is the interior of the reception-hall which is shown in No. 13, and I must own that never during my wanderings in China had I fallen in with anything more quaint and pretty than the view from this apartment into the second smaller court, to be seen in No. 14. Symmetry, as nearly perfect as possible, had been observed in the design of this establishment, as well as in its details; and the interior of the reception room will convey a very just impression of this feature in Chinese dwellings. One exception only to this rule of severe symmetry was to be discovered, and that was the central window, whose frame had been filled with irregular forms, and glazed with sheets of European glass. This last circumstance was due to the excessive predilection for foreign appliances entertained by Mr. Yang, of which we shall have more to relate further on. The other windows were regular in design, and were covered with white paper, as in most houses of this class. This paper, one might suppose, would have the advantage of preventing the curious from seeing what is going on inside. But such is not really the case, for the ladies, who are so strictly secluded in China, have devised a means of seeing through it, while they themselves remain unseen, and thus they make themselves acquainted with the appearance and manners of the guests of their lord. Their plan is to steal up noiselessly to the window, and applying the moist tips of their tongues to the paper, the soft substance yields silently to the little weapon, and thus a hole is made through which a bright eye surveys the interior of the forbidden chamber, and a quick ear drinks in the delicious tones of the prohibited conversation.

The seat of honour in the reception-hall has its place beneath the central window, facing the highly-carved and ornate pillared entrance; while the seats for the use of those inferior in social rank are ranged right and left along the sides of the apartment. Above the window an inscription, always to be found in a similar position, conveys some words of welcome or classical phrase. In the present instance it ran thus :—" The hall of joyful fragrance."

My friend furnished a choice repast, of which grapes formed one of the chief attractions. Here, indeed, as in many other parts of China, I was treated with the greatest courtesy and kindness. I had occasion to repeat my visits in fulfilment of a promise I gave Mr. Yang, to show him how to make for himself certain photographic chemicals with materials which he could procure in Peking.

No. 12 will convey an idea of the kind of buildings which divide one court from another, and also of the grotesque elegance of their ornamentation. It will show, too, how well the design has been suited to the exigences of a climate such as that which prevails at Peking, where the summer heat recalls the tropics, and the winter reminds us of Iceland. The heavy roofs of tiles reflect the heat and keep out the cold, while the verandah can be thrown entirely open, or kept closely shut; thus provision is made against the two extremes of temperature. The walls are built of grey bricks; the beams, joists, pillars, and panels being constructed out of hard wood, and thickly varnished to improve their appearance, as well as to prevent decay, and the inroads of destructive insects. The pierced ornamental brackets, equal in their strength to solid material, impart the additional charms of grace and lightness to the whole design.

Here, however, I cannot venture on a more detailed account of Chinese houses. I may have scope for this and other subjects of no less interest, should I decide on publishing a full narrative of my travels. The group in No. 12 represents my friend, his son, and a party of the ladies and younger children of his household.

His love of foreign machinery led him to erect a steam pump in one of the courts in the ladies' quarter. For this purpose some of the marble slabs were removed; the pump was then sunk till it met the water, and there this strange, rusty monument still stood. Once and for all had its owner succeeded in starting the steam-engine; and seemingly he could not stop it again in time, for the pump, which had worked nobly, flooded the quadrangle, and the overflow had not subsided up to the time of my visit.

A narrow, dark passage led to another part of the ladies' quarter, a chamber containing a splendidly-carved square bedstead made of hard, black wood, furnished with varnished wooden pillows, and draped with richly-embroidered silken curtains. The roof of this apartment was panelled and covered with a ceiling of cloth, stretched flat and whitewashed. Here, on a long table of carved black wood, was arranged an array of chemical and electrical apparatus, interspersed with ancient Chinese relics, classical books, and copies of one or two of our modern scientific treatises, which missionaries had translated into Chinese. Indeed, on this table were brought face to face the two principles that are now struggling for the mastery in China, and among the nations of the East. In the old relics and older books could be discovered the deep-rooted veneration for the wisdom of by-gone ages, and in the modern scientific appliances the elements of that living progress which is day by day affecting the destinies of the civilized world.

My friend Yang was groping in darkness with many of those things, although he had an intense desire to grasp their proper uses. He had made many mistakes. Thus, in an adjoining court or poultry yard, he had set up a saw-mill, a planing machine, and a steam-engine on wheels. As to the mill, he said that it was a wonderful contrivance, for which he had, at great trouble, procured a quantity of wood, but he added with regret that the machine had only been in use one day, in which space of time it had got through a surprising amount of work; having, in fact, sawn up everything he could think of to feed it with. The contrivance had, however, proved too much for the Pekingese. Alarmed by the hissing and throbs of the engine, and by the whirr of the saw, the citizens procured ladders, and scaled the walls in such numbers that the house-top was a black mass of chattering spectators. Besides all this, a number of the fowls, shocked and disheartened at the sad turn which affairs had taken, died off in a fright, or else poisoned themselves by drinking photographic water, tainted with cyanide of potassium.

Vol. IV, Plate VII

FEMALE COIFFURE.

IN China, as in other countries, we find dress obedient to the shifts of capricious fashion. Yet by no means slavishly so, as is the case among ourselves. The principal changes known to the Chinese may be reduced to the casting aside of winter costume, and the putting on the summer dress. The style of dress worn during these two seasons is much alike, frequently all that is done is to render the summer coat a warmer one by padding it with cotton for winter wear, or else it is lined, sometimes with sables, sometimes with inferior sorts of fur. In these last cases the fur is turned inside, and the silk which, with us, would serve as a lining, forms, with the Chinese, the outside surface of the garment. Besides the above variations, there is also a special style of dress to be used on marriage; and one of another kind is the only costume permitted at funerals. The full robes of a Chinese lady or gentleman of the better classes are highly picturesque, and remarkable also for the richness and beauty of their materials. The costume, besides this, is ample, graceful, and well adapted to the requirements of any climate, light in summer, and warm enough in winter to do away with the necessity for the artificial heat of an in-door fireplace.

Le Comte, who was in China about two centuries ago, thus describes the dress of Chinese ladies, and his account is a fitting description of the costumes in vogue among them even at the present day. "The ladies wear, as men do, a long satin or cloth vest, red, blue, or green, according to their peculiar fancy; the elder sort habit themselves in black or purple; they wear, besides that, a kind of surtout, the sleeves whereof are extremely wide, and trail upon the ground, when they have no occasion to hold them up. But that which distinguishes them from all the women in the world, and does, in a manner, make a particular species of them, is the littleness of their feet."

Le Comte names only three colours as being fashionable for dresses, but the hues adopted by the Chinese ladies now-a-days are infinite in their variety and shade; I may add that delicate and quiet tints are most in favour. Red is used as a bridal dress; blue is slight mourning; and a white spotless robe denotes the deepest sorrow.

Plate No. 15 shows another variety of dressing the hair common among the ladies at Swatow, while Nos. 16, 17, 18, and 20 represent the coiffure of married Manchu or Tartar matrons. Of this last head-dress, which differs widely from anything Chinese, Nos. 16 and 17 show respectively the full front and the full back views, so perfectly as to enable any of my fair readers to try the experiment with their own tresses if they so please. The basis of the device consists of a flat strip of wood, ivory, or precious metal about a foot in length. Half of the real hair of the wearer is gathered up and twisted in broad bands round this support, which is then laid across the back of the head. I confess myself unable to explain the mysterious mode in which the tresses have been twisted, but careful study of the illustrations will, I doubt not, reward any lady who may desire to dress her hair "à la Manchu." The style is simple and graceful, and must have been designed, one would almost think, to represent horns, enabling the wearer to hold her own against her antagonistic husband. It might be called the trigonometrical chignon, for, it will be observed, that if we produce two lines from the point of the chin to the tips of the chignon, an equilateral triangle is obtained, whose three sides support the axiom, "Things which are equal to the same thing are equal to each other;" and my fair reader is quite at liberty to deduce, as a just consequence, that a lady is quite equal to her lord. Joking apart, I would seriously advise the ladies of our land to try this chignon, as it would be a decided improvement upon those now in vogue, and should their husbands or brothers be devoted to artistic or literary pursuits, the basis could easily be procured in the shape of a limner's brush, a ruler, or a paper-knife, while the flowers and other ornamental accessories would be readily found where ladies always obtain them.

The old dame presented to the reader in No. 19, shows still another style of head-dress, one worn by Mongol women during the winter months. The cap is of fur. We might, at a first glance, suppose that we see here the lady's own hair, devoid of the bonnet we are used to in some elevated positions. The whole is, however, in reality the bonnet, or hat, of the wearer, who has an eye to comfort as well as to adornment. The jewels or ornaments which are indispensable to the gentler sex of every clime, are, in this instance, fixed principally to the lobes of the ears. The face, with its high cheek bones, is one thoroughly characteristic of the Mongol race.

VIEW OF THE CENTRAL STREET IN THE CHINESE QUARTER OF PEKING.

THIS view (No. 21) is taken from the city wall of Peking, close to the Ching-yang-men, or central gate, between the Chinese and Tartar quarters. It is in a direct line with the centre of the palace, and is the route which the Emperor traverses on his way to the Altar of Heaven.

In the foreground we see a white marble bridge which spans a kind of city moat.

This street, like all the thoroughfares in the Tartar city, is a very wide one, and is a place of great concourse and traffic.

The lofty triple roof of the Temple of Heaven appears in the distance. The brick wall on the left is a portion of the great building which has its counterpart over every gate in Peking. These edifices were originally intended for storing ammunition, but the one shown here served for many years as a depository for the engraved wooden blocks employed in printing books. Formerly it contained the complete blocks for the collection of the Buddhist Scriptures, numbering over six thousand volumes, but these have been recently removed to a Buddhist temple in the north-east angle of the city.

Wheeled vehicles are forbidden to cross the centre of the bridge, this being reserved for the sole use of the Emperor. It is, however, a favourite resort for beggars—one among many such—and is known, therefore, to the European residents in Peking as the Beggars' Bridge. Here we may see these beggars gambling in groups, or stretched upon the pavement to expose their sores and nakedness to the public gaze. Many of these unfortunate and homeless beings are annually cut off by the keen frosts of early winter, and are found dead on the Imperial Bridge.

There are a great number of stalls scattered along the principal streets, some of which are built like the old booths of the High Street of Edinburgh. In the centre of each street a raised causeway has been made, broad enough to accommodate two carts abreast, and intended for the carriage traffic. Between this raised causeway and the shops on either side of the road run broad spaces taken up with booths, tents, and stalls so closely packed as only to leave a narrow footpath close to the shops on the one side, and a chasm of deep mud pools on the other. From these pools material is taken for plastering and repairing the raised causeway. Most of these pools are stagnant and extremely polluted.

One of my most disagreeable experiences during my visit to Peking was a ride along the road whilst the mud from these putrid pools was being ladled on to the highway to lay the dust. The dust, indeed, was laid, but fumes like those of the decomposing dead were raised in its stead. It would have been still worse had I, as some natives have done, lost my footing in a dark night, and been drowned in the mire. The verge of this slough teems with interesting life.

Those who traffic in the stalls find many eager customers to buy their costly wares. I have seen one of these little booths, no better than that of some London costermonger, laden with over a thousand taels worth of jewels. The booths attract the attention of pedestrians. One finds in them all sorts of commodities for sale, and here and there are closely-packed crowds listening to the clever harangue of some auctioneer, who, with rare and ready wit, is extemporising rhyme in praise of cast-off silks, satins, or furs. In one I recollect a Mahometan butcher was plying

Vol. IV, Plate IX

21

his trade : the smiling follower of the prophet, encircled by carcases of sheep, ghastly heads, and entrails, stood behind a small wooden counter, knife in hand, giving a tender cut to a blooming slave girl, whose swarthy face was radiant with smiles, and whose cheeks were adorned with patches of rose-coloured paint.   At another counter in this butcher's booth, a care-worn mother, with a nursing child in her arms, was fondling some miserable bones, and pleading with a greasy assistant for a bargain ; but, frightful to behold, in the shade of the booth, my attention was riveted by a pair of gleaming blood-shot eyes, not indeed those of some ghastly head spitted on a meat-hook, but the hungry orbs of a street beggar, stark naked but for a thick coating of mud with which his body was smeared.   A group of Peking street Arabs were tormenting this wretched being, until at last I saw him seize the ringleader, and daub him over with a ball of moist mud which he carried as a weapon.

Adjoining this booth there was the tent of a dramatic reader, or story-teller, entertaining a well-dressed audience, seated before a long table on two rows of forms.   At my approach he laid down his lute, and had a sly thrust at the loitering foreigner, which convulsed his hearers with laughter.

Close by this was a cook's shed, with a series of brick ovens and fire-places in front.   From these a powerful savour of roasting meats arose.   Above a reeking caldron, puddings, spread on a clean board, were temptingly displayed.   A group of boys and beggars were gathered in front to enjoy the pleasures of contemplation.   The presiding genius of this *cuisine*, as he stuffed his puddings with their savoury contents, each time announced the fact in a shrill voice to the neighbourhood.   His assistant was engaged with his left hand in kneading dough, while with his right hand he twirled his rolling-pin on the board, so as to attract the notice of his customers.   The agonized shriek of the master, and the twirling of the pin by the servant combined to maintain a constant stir and apparent bustle, which told upon purchasers.   I presented a small boy with two cash.   This gift enabled him at once to realize his fondest hopes.   He invested in a reeking pudding, and, after a brief but affectionate look, devoured it with a relish that was truly gratifying.

The footpaths, close to the shops, exhibit a scene of great interest.   One has frequently to follow along a narrow space left by a number of coal-laden camels, whose drivers are refreshing themselves at the nearest tea-shop, or else to make a *détour* to avoid damaging the wares which some shop-keeper has spread out upon the ground.   Occasionally we brush past the cloth-covered sedan of some high mandarin, whose bearers and followers are shouting that the way must be cleared for the approach of The Great.   After this, perhaps, a Tartar lady is encountered, rich in her jewels and her silken attire.   Her face, we can see, is carefully enamelled, and her lower lip is finished with a ravishing spot of vermilion, and behind follow her slave women, who add their own charms to their lord's seraglio, and who bear their mistress's purchases and the ills of their lot with equally stolid indifference.

The liveried servants, or Yamen runners, hurry past in their conical extinguisher hats and red feathers, wearing in their faces an expression of sneaking contempt for the foreigner.

Handicraftsmen ply their trades on every vacant space ; and well-dressed merchants bustle to and fro, each intent on business of his own ; whilst at every hundred steps at least an equal number of natives pass, who possess no distinctive characteristics, and of whom all that a foreigner can say is that they resemble their neighbours.

THE BELL TOWER, PEKING.

ELLS appear to have been used in China from the earliest times. It is reported in the Shoo-king, or "Classic Historical Documents," that during the reign of Chung-kang, 2159 B.C., every year, in the first month of spring,[1] "the herald with his wooden-tongued bell goes along the roads proclaiming," and at the present day in China we still meet the counterpart of this ancient prototype striking his bell with its wooden tongue or mallet. We can thus invest the office of town-crier or bell-man, whose occupation in England is now all but gone, with a splendid classic antiquity.

During my stay in Peking, I accompanied one of our attachés to a shop in "Curiosity Street," where I saw a small bell, reputed to be the most ancient in the empire. It partook to some extent of the modern bell shape, but besides having an inscription in the most antique Chinese characters, it was adorned externally with a series of knobs so arranged that a sort of gamut was produced by striking each in succession with a mallet. It is thus possible that the herald of antiquity may have proclaimed the orders of his imperial master in rhyme, and charmed the ears of the people with a harmonious accompaniment on his single bell.

The Bell Tower of the illustration (No. 22) is situated about a quarter of a mile beyond the Hou-Men, or north gate of the capital, and contains one of the five great bells cast when Yung-lo of the Ming dynasty occupied the imperial throne. Each of these bells weighs about fifty-three tons, and its proportions, according to Verbiest, are, width 13 feet, circumference 40 feet, and height 12 feet. One bell is in the palace beside the Tai-ho-tien; another, cast with the entire text of a Buddhist liturgical work on its outer face, now hangs at a temple outside the north-west gate of Peking; a third is here, while a fourth lies half buried in an obscure lane near this tower, and there is a fifth in some other temple. These bells are slightly conical and dome-shaped at the upper end. The fourth one was rejected on account of a flaw, but the others are as perfect examples of the art of casting great masses of metal as we could produce in Europe at the present day, and the like indeed may be said of the astronomical instruments belonging to the same period, and which I have already described. The Tower bell has a rich mellow tone, which can easily be distinguished, when the watches are struck at midnight, all over Peking.

THE DRUM TOWER.

HE Drum Tower of Peking stands a little to the south of the Bell Tower, and is also a structure dating from the beginning of the fifteenth century. When first erected it contained (so Mr. Edkins assures me) a clepsydra for determining the time. A clepsydra of this sort consisted of four cisterns, together with a little automaton time-beater, and I saw at Peking the remains of an ancient instrument in one of the halls of the old Observatory. It is difficult to say where the Chinese obtained their water-clocks. Sextus Empiricus[2] says "that the Chaldeans divided the zodiac into twelve parts, which they supposed to be equal, by allowing water to run out of a small orifice during the whole revolution of a star, and then dividing the fluid into twelve equal parts;" whereas Beckmann[3] asserts "that this ingenious machine, which we know at present under the name of a water-clock, was invented in the 17th century;" and he was evidently unaware that water-clocks were in use in Peking during the 15th century. The Tower now contains a drum such as is commonly to be found in all Chinese cities, for marking the time, sounding alarms of fire, and similar purposes. Drums also were anciently employed in China in connection with state ceremonials. One eight feet long is noticed as existing during the Chow dynasty, that is, about 2,500 years ago; the probable date also assigned by scholars to the ancient stone drums of the Confucian Temple, Peking.

---

[1] The Shoo-King, III. iv. 3, Jas. Legge, D. D. [2] Inventions, Beckmann p. 82.
[3] History of Inventions, Beckmann, page 83.

A PEKINGESE SHOP.

IN describing a Peking street, I purposely omitted the picturesque appearance of the shop fronts, of which No. 24 affords a very good type. There are many which are much more elaborate and imposing in appearance than this one, and many more which are in every respect inferior. The foundation and flooring of the shop are of granite, and the walls, to a height of about three feet, consist of the same material, while the upper portions of these latter are built of well-fired bricks. The shops of Peking differ in many respects from those in the cities of southern China. The former, as will be seen from the present example, are closed in front with ornamental partitions of hard wood, having narrow arched doorways. Above these doorways are blinds, or sunshades, which can be raised and spread out horizontally in front of the shops. The balustrade above presents always some Chinese design, very pretty, both in its open lattice-work and in the huge characters which denote the name and occupation of the tradesman. We gather, from the large gilt characters above, that cotton and Manchester goods are imported, and, from the sign-boards below, that silk, satin, and other fabrics may also be bought here; while the pedestal in front supports the announcement that the great foot measure is alone used in this establishment.

A LIVING TOMB.

WHEREVER the Buddhist faith prevails it is deemed a work of great merit to erect a new temple, or to restore an old one, and more especially so if the accomplishment of these objects involves acts of self-denial or penance. In Siam, where the Buddhism is of a type purer than in China, the rich make it their custom to rear new temples and monasteries, in order that the soul of the builder after death may transmigrate into some being of a still higher and holier mould. In China few new monasteries or temples are now-a-days erected, those already in existence being more than sufficient for the wants of the priest-ridden population. Here, therefore, the Buddhist devotee is forced to confine himself to renewing or restoring the old edifices.

I remember falling in with a Bonze, in a lane in Peking, who was wandering from door to door raising contributions to repair a shrine. This wretched being sought to awaken the slothful souls of the citizens to charitable acts by beating a gong. He was a ghastly object to behold, for he had passed an iron skewer through his cheeks and tongue, and strode the streets in mute agony, with blood-besprinkled robe and a face of death-like pallor. Le Comte narrates some stories of the deception practised in his time by these Bonzes. "Two Bonzes, seeing one day in a rich farmer's yard two or three large ducks, fell on their faces before the door, and sighed and wept grievously. The good woman, seeing them out of her chamber window, came down to see what was the occasion of their tears. We know, said they, that the souls of our fathers are transmigrated into these creatures, and we are in fear lest you should kill them. It is true, said the good woman, we did intend to sell them, but since they are your fathers, I promise you we will keep them." The good men so wrought upon the feelings of the woman that she finally presented them with the ducks, and that very evening they enjoyed a feast on their degraded fathers. In another passage he tells of a Bonze who stood erect in a sedan, "the inside of which was like a harrow, full of nails," and these nails set so close to his body that he could not stir without wounding his flesh. Two men carried this devotee from house to house, and everywhere he assured the citizens that he had been shut up in that chair for the good of their souls, and was resolved never to quit his confinement till they should have bought up all the nails, to the number of 2,000 or thereabouts. I told him that he was very unhappy to torment himself thus in this world for no good, and counselled him therefore to come out of his prison, to go to the temple of the true God to be instructed in heavenly truths. He answered calmly and courteously, "that he was much obliged for the good advice, and would be much more obliged if I would buy a dozen of his nails." This mode of doing penance is still in vogue in China.

The subject of the illustration (No. 24) is a small tower in front of a monastery in the outskirts of Peking. This tower has been built over a living Buddhist priest, whose only means of communication with the outer world is through the four small windows. When I saw him he had been shut up for many months, and intended so to remain for years if necessary, until he had collected funds enough from the charitably disposed to repair the ruined monastery in the rear. His sole occupation appeared to be tolling a bell at regular intervals, by means of the cord to be seen issuing from the aperture in front.

CHINESE MEDICAL MEN.

THE practice of medicine in China dates from a very early period. We find the Emperor Woo-ting, who reigned 1300 B.C., noticing the effect of medicine upon a patient, and counselling Yue, one of his ministers, in the following words: "Be you like medicine, which, if it do not distress the patient, will not cure the sickness." (Shoo King, Book VIII. 1, 3.) [James Legge, D.D.]

This idea of causing a patient inconvenience by exciting a pain or irritation in one part of the body, in order to cure a malady in some other part, still obtains in China. It is customary, for example, if a person suffers from a severe headache, to pinch the back of the neck till it becomes black and blue; and the irritation caused by this process sometimes effects a cure.

Dr. Dudgeon, in a series of interesting papers, which appeared in the "Chinese Recorder," in 1870, gives an account of the ancient and modern practice of therapeutics prevailing in China.

During the reign of the great Kubli Khan a college was founded in Peking for the instruction of medical students. This institution comprised thirteen departments, where the following branches of study were taught:—Diseases of men, or the doctrine of the pulse in relation to adult males; miscellaneous diseases; diseases of children; wind diseases; female diseases; eye diseases; diseases of the mouth, teeth and throat; dislocation; wounds; ulcers and swellings; acupuncture; charms or prayers, which we may call spiritual medicine; and, lastly, pressure and friction. This medical course, however, in our day actually consists of the first, third, sixth and seventh of the above-enumerated branches, with the addition of the practice of surgery, a science not included in the foregoing list. After all, however, the medical art in the Celestial Empire is bound up to a remarkable extent with the Chinese scheme of physics, expounded by Sir J. Davis; who shows that the planets Saturn, Jupiter, Mars, Venus, and Mercury are supposed to rule the five viscera, the elements, the colours, and the tastes.

In the college of the Yuen dynasty acupuncture was taught by means of a model human figure, cast in bronze, and punctured with holes over the blood-vessels. On examination-days this figure was covered with a layer of paper, and the professional skill of the students was determined by the accuracy with which they hit the position of the pin-holes in the figure beneath.

The Chinese doctrine of the pulse is characterized by Sir J. Davis as a "mere mass of solemn quackery," while Le Comte says, when treating of the same subject, that in this respect they have something extraordinary, nay, even wonderful. He, however, adds the caution that "a man should always mistrust them," because, in order to preserve their reputation, "they make use of all means imaginable to get themselves secretly instructed concerning the patient's condition before they pay him a visit."

It is possible that the great Kubli, who gave a kind reception to the missionaries sent out by Innocent IV., and whose history has been recorded by Marco Polo, was induced, by the foreigners who visited his capital, to establish this college of medicine. Although the institution has been neglected for centuries, and though the metal figure has fallen into disuse, there appears at the present time to be a brighter future in store for the science of medicine, and, indeed, for every other branch of knowledge. This is indicated by the recent foundation of a chair of anatomy in the Peking College, and the appointment of an English professor to fill it. In addition to this circumstance the medical missionaries (such as Drs. Lockhart, Dudgeon, Maxwell, and many others) have laboured effectually to extend knowledge among the native practitioners who have assisted them in their exertions.

Notwithstanding all this, there still remains an army of quack doctors, tens of thousands strong, holding their ground against foreign innovations, and prepared to cure or kill their deluded patients by the arts of geomancy, or by potent pills. These pills frequently contain a little of almost everything, and their compounders trust to the principle of elective affinity, by which the disease will elect its own remedy from the heterogeneous compound. Empirics such as these are to be found all over the country, and their small yellow posters disfigure the walls of all the great cities. Even the meanest street-barber professes a certain curative skill. Turning up the eyelids of his patients, in order to cleanse and dress them, he removes the lubricating mucus, and thus gives rise to a class of eye-diseases common among the Chinese. He is also frequently seen pummelling the back of his patient with his fists in order to cure or prevent rheumatism. Many of the Chinese city quacks compound their medicines at the street corners, under the public gaze; and there they deliver eloquent harangues to their customers on the virtues of their pills and plasters.

While at Peking I sent for a dentist, who brought with him a case of ivory fangs, and offered to fix in a feline-looking incisor for about one shilling. It was to be attached by wires to the neighbouring teeth. I declined the ornament, but paid him a fee for his advice.

The subject of the illustration, No. 26, is a travelling chiropodist, operating upon a corn, and dressing the toe-nails of a customer; while a second patient waits placidly until his own turn arrives, smoking the pipe of peace from a broken window.

STREET AMUSEMENTS AND OCCUPATIONS, PEKING.

IN all Chinese cities there are to be found a great variety of itinerant showmen, jugglers, fortune-tellers, play-actors, and peep-show men. Besides these we have ballad-singers, and a host of story-tellers and public readers, who frequent the tea-shops and favourite haunts of the leisure-loving Chinese. There are still other places of public resort, where the citizen may spend his leisure in gambling or opium smoking, or where he may go to feast with his friends to the accompaniment of lute and guitar, and the shrill piping voices of painted female musicians. Some of these lady performers must appear supremely enchanting to the male frequenters of their musical dens, viewed as they are through the illusive vapour of hot wine, the fumes of opium, and the flare of smoky lamps. Seen from a little distance, these damsels, many of them, look simple and pretty, but a nearer glimpse is much less satisfactory, as they are daubed with enamel and dressed like dolls in the most tawdry tinsel. They appear, indeed, to have heads which resemble those of cleverly-made clay figures, and capable of being lifted out of the fine silk and satin robes in which they are set. This reminds me that the natives of Tientsin make painted images out of clay more life-like than any which I have ever seen elsewhere. Each image is a perfect work of art, and the artist is about as poorly paid as if he were an ordinary tiller of the soil.

Puppet-shows, exactly like our street Punch and Judy, are common in China. The motion is imparted to the puppets by introducing the fore-finger into the head, and the thumb and second finger into the sleeves of the figure, while the heads, too, can be adroitly changed, in order to bring a number of different characters on the scene, and to suit the requirements of the play.

There is another sort of puppet-show, a night one, to be met with at fairs and festive gatherings. In an exhibition of this kind the shadows of the puppets are thrown upon a white screen by means of a lamp behind.

The peep-show also (see No. 27) enjoys a large share of public favour. It is fitted with a series of lenses in front, through which the 'eye of the spectator beholds the wonders of the world. Foreign pictures share the attractions with Chinese representations and moveable figures, the showman delivering a running commentary on

Vol. IV, Plate XI

the mysterious scenes as he introduces them, and dexterously manipulates the whole by means of a series of cords. Some of the subjects are of the most indecent character.

The stand, and indeed the whole apparatus, is extremely light and ingenious. The stand is made up of a series of iron rods, linked together, so that they may at once be folded up beneath the box; and this done, the showman will shoulder the whole, and march off to some new field.

The figure of the showman, here represented, gives a perfect specimen of the winter dress of a Pekingese labourer. It is made out of coarse cotton cloth, and is lined with sheepskin, or padded with cotton wool. The smallest figure is that of a young Tartar or Manchu girl, and depicts one sort of shoe worn by Manchu women, who never compress their feet. The third figure is that of a poor Manchu bannerman in his regulation sheepskin coat.

DEALERS IN ANCIENT BRONZES, &c.

LIKE all foreigners who visit Peking, I had been but one night in the metropolis when I found myself waited upon by half a dozen dealers in curiosities, introduced to my notice by a servant whom I had engaged at Tientsin.

These curiosity-mongers spread out before me sundry specimens of old china, and a variety of articles such as those shown in No. 28, and for all these they demanded the most extortionate prices. However they seemed by no means anxious to sell their goods. I had been warned beforehand to be careful in my dealings with these gentlemen, but after all I was more than once taken in. It is customary for dealers of this sort to effect an arrangement with a foreigner's servants, undertaking to share with them the profits of a sale, so that they must, of necessity, charge high prices in order to make the thing pay. These vendors of "articles de vertu" come from three streets in the Chinese city. One is occupied by booksellers, another by picture dealers, and a third consists of old curiosity shops. They are most interesting shops to visit, not only on account of their miscellaneous stores, but also because the shop-keepers carry on their business in their own most peculiar style. Thus, if you enter one of their shops, the proprietor treats you with the utmost degree of unconcern, smoking his pipe without interruption, and retaining his seat behind the counter. You may try to put him off his guard by looking at every article except the one which you want, and by inquiring, in an off-hand sort of way, the price of the piece of goods on which you have set your heart; but your dissimulation is all in vain, for the vendor seems to know instinctively what it is you are seeking, and asks treble the fair value of his wares; and then tells you, with an air of supreme indifference, that this thing has been sought after by some of the first collectors of Peking, and that he has now a very good offer for it. You make a bid, and he simply resumes his pipe with a shake of the head, and allows you to depart in peace. But the placid face of the rascal, and the atmosphere of intense respectability generated by his careful dress, his polite but careless mien, and his well-ordered establishment, bring you back again the next day. You find the place and the man just as you left them; but somehow the rare object of your affection has grown in your estimation. You buy it at the seller's own price, and carry it away, feeling grateful to the polished rogue by whom you most probably have been done.

A lady, for many years connected with one of the Protestant missions in Peking, after having, for some time, lost sight of two or three ordinary foreign-made plates, discovered one of them, when passing through the Ia-sha-lan, exposed for sale in a shop. On inquiry, she was informed that it was a rare gem in its way, a specimen of ancient porcelain ware, and to be bought for six taels, or £1 15s. of our own currency.

There are shops of course in this street, as in all others, of the highest respectability, where a foreigner, conversant with the language, can purchase articles at their fair market value. Indeed, taken as a whole, and judging from my own experience, I believe that, in upright dealing, the shop-keepers in Chinese cities are not inferior to those of Europe. I cannot say that they are as honest and truthful, on principle, as the traders in Christian lands; but they deal fairly because they find it pays. This applies with greater force to the Chinese commercial classes, and will be borne out by the experience of our own merchants, who have colossal interests at stake in China.

Plate No. 29 is a type of a Pekingese costermonger, one of the lower orders. This man carries his shop on his shoulders; and we see him here informing the dwellers in a narrow lane that he has brought to their doors the choicest grapes of the season. When he succeeds in getting a customer, the latter accosts him, armed with a stick resembling a yard measure, but in reality a portable lever weighing-machine, and with this he secures his fair weight of the fruit. This rod is in common use all over the land, so that light weights are but little known there.

CHINESE BRONZES.

THE art of making vases of bronze, of gold, and of silver, was practised by the Chinese at a very early period, and is said to have been lost in modern times, as both the metal used, and the workmanship of the most ancient vases and tripods are esteemed superior to anything which the artificers of the present day can produce. There are, and indeed there always have been in China, native collectors of objects of antiquity, some of whom have left valuable works, copiously illustrated with careful drawings of ancient bronzes, and facsimiles of the primitive characters cut or cast upon their outer surfaces, which enable the modern antiquary at once to identify the specimens of different periods. Thus we have an ancient Chinese work entitled the Pŏ-koo-too, which extends to sixteen large volumes, and contains several hundred plates of sacred vases, &c. &c. of the Shang Chow and Han dynasties.[1] Chinese scholars are, I believe, divided in opinion regarding the genuineness of the ancient inscriptions on these vases. The accession of the first emperor of the Shang dynasty carries us back to 1760 B.C., and during his reign many of the finest sacrificial vases and tripods were produced.

The ambitious Hwang-ti, the builder of the Great Wall, in his attempt to establish a new era, and unwilling that the ancients should afford a model for his new government, ordered that all memorials of antiquity should be destroyed, and that all documents should be consigned to the flames. Notwithstanding the characteristic determination with which he carried out his plans of destruction, the members of the *literati* frustrated his endeavours by concealing copies of the ancient classics, and burying the sacrificial vases and tripods, many of which exist in China to the present day.

The high vase standing in the centre of the upper row (No. 30) is of great antiquity, while the others grouped around are more or less modern, and are such as are used in Chinese Buddhist shrines. A comparison of the design and workmanship of the ancient and modern bronzes here presented to the reader will bear out what I have said above.

ANCIENT CHINESE PORCELAIN WARE.

THE finest China porcelain is supplied from a district east of the Poyang Lake from " The celebrated manufactories of Kingteh-chin, named after an emperor of the Sung dynasty, in whose reign, A. D. 1004, they were established."[2] This mart still supplies all the fine porcelain produced in the country, and upwards of a million workmen are said to be employed in its manufacture. Many of the articles made are also painted in the district, while others are left plain, and are subsequently painted and glazed in the districts to which they are exported. " The central vase presented in the upper row (No. 31)

---

[1] See Thoms' " Ancient Chinese Vases," Journal Royal Asiatic Soc., vol. i.
[2] " Middle Kingdom," vol. ii. p. 92, Williams.

Vol. IV, Plate XII

affords an excellent example of landscape painting during the early part of the present dynasty, probably of the reign of Kanghi (A. D. 1662-1722). The next vase to the right, set on a stand of wood, is probably the finest example in the collection, exhibiting flowers of the characteristic blue colour of the Ming dynasty on a pure white ground. The period is indicated by the six characters at the top, Ta Ming chia ching nien chih, *i. e.* 'Made during the chia ching reign of the great Ming dynasty,' A. D. 1522-1566. A vase of the same character and period occupies the centre of the lower row and is ornamented with the five-clawed imperial dragon surrounded by a pattern of curved lines representing the waves of the sea. To the left is a curious and elaborately ornamented vase: the bowl is perforated work, through the interstices of which is visible an inner concentric bowl covered with delicate painting of the Kienlung (1736-1795) period. The other specimens have their dates inscribed on the under surface in the seal character. The covered tankard with curved handle, in the lower row, shows the influence of Western art during the Kienlung period. To the extreme right of this there is a model of a dagoba commonly erected over graves or relics in Buddhist temples."[1]

---

[1] Note by Dr. Bushell, Peking.

MANCHU LADIES AND A MANCHU MARRIAGE.

THE Manchu or Tartar lady may, on the whole, be said to approach more nearly than her Chinese sister to our Western notions of female beauty and grace. The former enjoys greater freedom, and her feet, which are never compressed, appear to be naturally small and well-formed. Their rich dresses, too, are always elegant, but their faces, alas! they paint to imitate the natural peach bloom of health which heightens the beauty of our English belles. Although these Tartar ladies are probably less secluded than the Chinese, yet these coatings of paint serve like veils to conceal their true complexion from the outer world, and we may, perhaps, say of them in the language of Moore :—

> " Oh! what a pure and sacred thing
> Is beauty, curtain'd from the sight
> Of the gross world, illumining
> One only mansion with her light."

In Manchu families, when a son has reached the age of fourteen or sixteen years, his mother selects him a partner, and the latter will be brought into the family, and entirely subjected to her new parent's rule; so that should the young bride have a hard-hearted mother-in-law, she may look forward to spending the first years of married life in a state of abject slavery, and is even liable to be beaten by her mother-in-law, and husband too, if she neglect to discharge her duties as general domestic drudge. It is therefore always deemed fortunate by the girl's friends if the mother of the bridegroom be already dead.

The sons of the rich are married at an earlier age than are those of the poor, but no Manchu maiden can be betrothed until she is fourteen years of age. Usually some elderly woman is employed as a go-between to arrange a marriage, and four primary rules exist (though they are by no means regularly followed) to guide the matron. First, the lady must be amiable. Secondly, she must be a woman of few words. Thirdly, she must be of industrious habits, and lastly, she must neither want a limb nor an eye, and, indeed, she ought to be moderately good-looking. The matter is discussed by the aged go-between and her employer over a cup of tea, and the former then describes in detail the accomplishments and prospects of her son. When an eligible girl has at length been found, a geomancer is called in to fix a lucky day for an interview with the young lady, and an examination of her work. On this occasion she is trotted out before her future mother-in-law and carefully inspected. If found suitable, the geomancer is again consulted, and he settles a lucky day for receiving the presents and the betrothed. He is guided in his reckonings by the names of the contracting parties, and by the dates of their births. He also determines whether they are suited to each other. On the morning of betrothal the young lady is informed of her fate, and is dressed in a simple red cotton or silk robe borrowed or bought, according to her station in life. She is then placed sitting upon the Kang, or bed, there to await the bestowal of gifts from her future lord. The suitor's mother next places a bracelet upon the left wrist of the bride elect, and a lady friend binds another bracelet on the right wrist, and they, as they bestow the presents, wish her long life and happiness. After this formal betrothal, the lucky day is fixed for the marriage, and until the consummation of that joyous event the lady is supposed to seclude herself from public gaze. Her trousseau begins with the making of shoes, for of these she must possess from seven to thirty pairs, many of them richly embroidered.   Her father or brothers look after furniture, which probably consists of three tables, four wardrobes, four trunks, four boxes, two looking-glasses, two brass wash-basins and stand, cloths, rails, chairs, and footstools.   Teapots, cups, kettles, dressing-case, and an imposing array of boxes for odds and ends, flower-vases and trays, and a glass globe for gold fish, are also essential to complete the collection.

The dress varies according to rank.   A month before marriage another set of presents is despatched by the bridegroom to his bride.   These commonly are four pigs, four sheep, four geese, and four jars of wine, besides twenty loaves of bread; also a number of changes of dress, with ornaments for the hair made from the feathers of the kingfisher, together with about one pound of silver called "pin-money."   Materials for bedding, two mattresses and two coverlets, are included in the list.   These commodities are carried in procession through the streets by hired bearers, headed by one or two domestics.   A woman who has had sons and daughters is always selected to make up the material for bedding—a duty which widows or childless women are never permitted to fulfil.

Ten days before the marriage invitations are issued.   These are printed on sheets of red paper about a foot long and half a foot broad, and enclosed in envelopes of the same gigantic proportions.

On the day before marriage the bride's plenishing is carried through the streets in procession to the house of the bridegroom's father, the escort being composed of bearers to the number of eight, or some multiple of eight up to 120, which figure denotes the highest rank.   Ten official gentlemen are invited to accompany these goods, and to add to the pomp and display.   When the bride enters her sedan, she must turn her face in a certain direction, and when she quits it she must look in a certain other direction.   The bride's sedan is covered with crimson cloth.   Her veil is also crimson, and richly embroidered.   Midnight marriages are most fashionable among the Manchus.

Many other tedious details too numerous to mention follow, and are the essential accompaniments of the dreary monotony of a Manchu marriage, in this respect more irksome and painful than the prolonged ceremonial of a Manchu funeral, and fully as uncertain to terminate in peace.   The most sensible thing the assembled guests do is when they take leave of the married couple by drinking to their united happiness in a parting glass of wine.   The newly-married pair sit down to a repast, but the lady quits the table, and her lord is supposed to breakfast alone, a form very soon over.

On the ninth day after marriage the wife wakes up to industry, and makes a pair of nether garments for her husband; and this practice she adopts because the character for "treasury" in Chinese has the same sound as that which denotes "trousers."

33

35

32

34

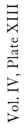

THE CONFUCIAN TABLET IN THE GREAT HALL
OF THE SAGE, PEKING.

THE broad paved approach to the Hall of Confucius is shaded with avenues of venerable cypress trees, and forms one of the most imposing scenes in Peking. Having ascended a double flight of white marble steps, divided into two by a sloping marble slab, upon which the imperial dragon stands in high relief, you reach a broad marble terrace in front of the hall. Within, the lofty roof is supported by solid teak pillars fifty feet in height, and the tablet of the great sage faces you as you enter the hall. In front of this tablet there is a simple altar surmounted by a bronze censer, and flanked by bronze candelabra. The tablet itself consists of the plain strip of wood, which is shown in the centre of No. .36, and is inscribed with these words in Manchu and Chinese, "The soul of the most holy ancestral teacher Confucius." There are also the tablets of his four chief disciples ranged on each side of his own. The inscription above is in large letters of gold, and runs thus, "The teacher and example of ten thousand generations." This hall contains in less prominent positions the tablets of twenty-two other followers of Confucius as well.

Sacrifices are offered at the vernal and autumnal equinoxes in honour of the tablet of the great sage; oxen and sheep are then slain, and the carcases stripped of their skins are placed upon stands in front of his tablet. It is the spirit of the sage supposed to reside in the tablet that is thus honoured.

There is a temple devoted to the worship of Confucius in every Chinese city. One of these halls, the finest I have seen, was at Foochow; but they are to be met with, indeed, over the length and breadth of the land, each adorned with tablets inscribed with the names of the sage and his most distinguished disciples.

LE-SHEN-LAN AND HIS PUPILS.

LE-SHEN-LAN is professor of mathematics in the Imperial College, Peking, and is now about sixty years of age. In his youth he studied thoroughly the native mathematics, reading the Jesuit translations, and the works of native authors as well. More than twenty years ago he visited Shanghai, and there made the acquaintance of the English missionaries. He remained for many years, translating works on mathematics and natural philosophy. Had it not been for the valuable aid afforded by Englishmen connected with the various Protestant missions, China could not have boasted such a mathematician as Le-shen-lan, a man who has reaped the advantage of Wylie's translation of Euclid's Elements, or rather his completion of the work which Ricci had begun when he translated the first six books about two centuries before; of the Taé-soó-hëŏ, a treatise on algebra; and of the Taé-wê-tseïh-shïh-keïh, or the Elements of Analytical Geometry, Differential and Integral Calculus, and other similar works.

Some five or six years since, Le-shen-lan was recommended to the notice of the Emperor, and appointed to fill the post of professor of mathematics in the Peking College. He has compiled several small works on mathematics, for the most part original investigations, and appears to have a mind thoroughly adapted for mathematical study, being a minute and close reasoner, and accurate and rapid in calculation.

He is presented to the reader, surrounded by his pupils, in No. 37.

A PEKINGESE PAI-LAU.

THIS Pai-lau, or Chinese honorary portal, is erected at the gate of the Ta-ka-tien temple which the Emperor visits when he prays for rain. Structures of this sort are very numerous in Peking. Many of them span the widest thoroughfares, and, when freshly painted, break the monotony of the scene with their bright colours and imposing proportions. A man may obtain permission to erect a Pai-lau in honour of himself or children; many erect one in honour of deceased parents; or a widow who has not ceased to mourn for many years for the loss of a loved husband may perpetuate the memory, not of her dear husband, but of her own virtues, by erecting such a monument, and receives from the Emperor an honorary name to be inscribed over the centre of the structure. Anciently, Le Comte tells us, these triple gates were to be met with crossing the trade routes of the interior, when they were inscribed with directions for the traveller regarding the route to be followed, and the distance to different towns.

MANCHU FUNERALS, PEKING.

THE Manchus, like the Chinese, deem it their duty when they are advanced in years to make provision for their own decease. Accordingly they themselves determine what kind of coffin shall carry their remains to the grave, and will have one, if they can afford it, made of Szechuan wood, costing sometimes as much as three hundred pounds of our money.

The aged owner takes a great interest in the varnishing and finishing of this his last resting-place; and he also takes care to purchase his own grave-clothes. These are, with the rich, of red silk, lined with light blue and thickly wadded, having a mattress also, and a pillow, to accompany them; and in the case of a mandarin, a suit of his finest official robes, which will be placed over his body, in what is euphemistically termed his "longevity case." This sort of phraseology is adopted because the people do not admit the idea of death; the close of one's days is simply the passage from life to life, from one world into another, or from one state of existence into a different one. When the hour of dissolution approaches, the body is laid upon a stretcher which the undertaker supplies, and surrounded with a pall of black satin, and then the dying person is dressed in his most costly robes. They have a belief that if the body were to be dressed after decease instead of before that event, the soul would pass naked into the next world, whereas, if decked out while life is still present they suppose that it will carry the robes and rank of the wearer along with it in its flight. Nor do they in Peking allow a person to die upon his bed, lest the spirit should haunt it afterwards. If a female, her ornaments of gold are worn in the hair, but her bracelets are laid by her side and never put on, for fear that Yen-wang-yen, the prince of hell, should use them as shackles to bind her in the other world. For the same reason a mandarin never wears his necklace.

Pillows in use with the Manchus in the north of China are generally filled with small millet husks, but those for the dead are stuffed with paper, each small husk being supposed to represent a period of time, which for many ages would prevent the entrance of the spirit into another body; on the top is a cover on which a quotation from the classics has been woven. This aids the spirit's flight to the southern heaven, and for the same purpose the ancestral tablets and idols are covered, and neglected for the space of one hundred days. A pearl wrapped in red paper is placed between the lips of the corpse, or with the poor, a little tea instead. This is held to act as a charm against decomposition for ever. They never use worsted or furs in dressing the dead, lest the spirit should transmigrate into the sheep or animal to which the fur coat belonged. If it be a parent who has died, the children kneel and howl in a discord of distress, then undoing their hair, and cutting off about two inches of it, they place the shreds, if it be a mother, in her right hand, if a father, then in his left. The geomancer next foretells the day on which the spirit will quit the house, and places a paper surmounted by a small mirror on the breast of the corpse. On the day foretold, some sounds are heard which indicate that the spirit is about to depart. Then the geomancer is again called in and determines the day of burial, and the position of the grave. The day must fall on one of the odd numbers, as the fifth or seventh of the month, and not the sixth or eighth. The mourners wear robes of white coarse cotton, white shoes, and white thread plaited into their hair. Musicians sit at the door on the day of burial and announce the arrival of a gentleman by beating a drum, or of a lady mourner by blowing a trumpet.

Guests frequently contribute to defray the funeral expenses of poor relations. Buddhist and Taoist priests preside and chant prayers. Heavy debts are thus at times contracted, for there is no limit in the north of China to the outlay on mortuary rites.

Paper model residences and furniture, horses, carriages, and servants of the same material are burned in front of the dwelling, the fire transforming them into the spirit residence and retinue of the deceased.

The funeral procession is elaborate and costly, the coffin may be borne by sixty-four men, and perhaps the canopy which covers it is of richly embroidered white satin.

The women of the household follow, wailing, in carts covered with white. The hired bannermen who take part in the procession are shown in No. 39. They are commonly beggars dressed up by the undertaker for the purpose. The funeral of the wife of a salt merchant in Peking was said to have cost £40,000.

When a bride dies they frequently burn her expensive trousseau for her use in the spirit world.

The banners and paraphernalia used by the Manchus are quite different from those in fashion amongst the Chinese. Each Manchu bannerman has a small allowance from government to meet his funeral expenses.

Three years is the customary period of mourning for a parent, and where the sons are mandarins they may not hold office until the period of mourning has elapsed. This is an exceedingly ancient custom in China. We are told in the "Shoo-king" that when Yaon died he was "mourned for as a parent for three years,"[1] and that his successor did not ascend the throne until the three years of mourning had expired.

---

[1] Shoo-king, bk. i., ch. iii., 13, J. Legge, D. D. I am indebted to Mrs. Edkins, wife of the Rev. Josh. Edkins of Peking, for the information regarding funerals and Manchu marriages.

CENOTAPH ERECTED TO THE BANJIN
LAMA OF THIBET.

THIS monument, which is probably the most magnificent in Peking, stands more than a mile beyond the north wall of the city, in the huge pile of buildings known as the Hwang-she. It is said that formerly it was the site of a royal palace, and its history goes back for nearly a thousand years. Last century it appears to have been used as a Thibetan Lama temple, and was then fitted up for the reception of the Banjin Lama towards the close of the reign of Kien-loong.

The Banjin is second only to the Dali Lama, and is also looked upon as a lesser incarnation of Buddha. As Thibet owes an allegiance to China, the Emperor conceived a jealousy of the friendly reception extended to the English by the Banjin, and therefore courteously invited his holiness to visit Peking. The latter is said to have been most unwilling to set out, pretending a dread of small-pox, or some less doubtful poison. Seeing, however, that the missive, though clothed in all the suavity of court etiquette, was far too peremptory to be disobeyed, he reluctantly started from Lassa on the 15th of July, 1779, and reached this temple early in the following year. His worst fears were realized. After being fêted as a divinity, and worshipped in person by the Emperor, he was in due time attacked with small-pox (so the story goes) and died in the chamber adjoining his reception hall, or, as the Chinese phrase it, his spirit changed its abode, and went to animate a body of tender years in Thibet. It has been strongly suspected that he was poisoned at the Emperor's suggestion.

The remarkable monument seen in this picture (No. 40) was erected at immense cost to commemorate the Lama's visit, and is built of white marble, after the Thibetan model. The bell-like cupola and the upper ornaments are of gold, and the whole is most elaborately carved with allegorical subjects ; the sides of the lower octagon portion represent, in relief, as many scenes in the mythical life of this divine personage, and four handsome turrets at the corners of the upper platform are inscribed with Sanscrit mystic prayers engraved in Chinese characters. The two side entablatures of the façade also bear sentences in the ancient Devanagari characters, and on the columns are inscriptions in Chinese. The erection is carefully preserved, and the steps inside the wooden gate are decorated with flowers. The body of the Lama was taken back to Thibet, but it is said that his clothes have been buried in this spot.

40

THE OPEN ALTAR OF HEAVEN AND THE TEMPLE OF HEAVEN, PEKING.

THREE miles to the south of the Imperial Palace, in the Chinese quarter of Peking, is an extensive park-like enclosure, containing the temple and the open altar of Heaven shown in Plates Nos. 41 and 42. In the enclosure here referred to are two altars, one to the north and the other to the south, protected by triple walls, of which the outermost is nearly three miles round. The northern altar, commonly designated the Temple of Heaven, is shown in No. 42, and is, as nearly as possible, a counterpart of the open or southern altar. Both are built of marble, and both have triple terraces, surrounded by marble balustrading. The north altar, however, supports in its centre a building with triple roofs, covered with light blue tiles, and symbolical of heaven (the altar in its original form had no such superstructure), while the south altar presents on its top a plain round marble platform open to heaven, where the Emperor offers sacrifice to Shanti, the Supreme Lord of Heaven and Earth, at the winter solstice, on December 21st. Such altars as these seem to be relics of an extremely ancient and primitive form of worship in China, when monotheism was probably the prevailing faith. Here, as Le Comte asserts, we possibly see the purer form of patriarchal worship practised by the Chinese before the advent of Confucius, and before the Buddhist missionaries had appeared. The ceremonials connected with this state worship, when the Emperor officiates as high-priest, are still followed out with the strictest minuteness of detail. Le Comte says, " Fohi, the first Emperor of China, carefully bred up seven sorts of creatures, which he used to sacrifice to the Supreme Spirit of Heaven and Earth, and at the present time special breeds of animals sacred to the temple are reared in the adjoining parks, and subjected to the scrutiny of the Emperor before they are offered in sacrifice. The bullocks are black, and are chosen with the greatest care, so as to be free from blemish ; no less pains being taken with the smaller animals. I visited the slaughter-house, where the victims are put to death and prepared. This building, which is reached through a cloister 700 feet long, had fallen out of repair, but I was assured that all would be set right in time for the winter solstice."

" The south altar," says Mr. Edkins, " is the most important of all the religious structures in China." He also gives very interesting details of its dimensions, as well as of the symbolic numbers of the stones which form the upper platform, of the terraces, the balustrades, and even of the flights of steps. Nine and multiples of nine make up, in every case, the most prominent combinations, for nine is the favourite number in Chinese philosophy. " The altar consists of a triple circular terrace 210 feet wide at the base, 150 in the middle, and 90 at the top. On these notice the multiples of three, $3 \times 3 = 9, 3 \times 5 = 15, 3 \times 7 = 21$, &c." The platform is laid with marble stones, forming nine concentric circles, the inner circle consisting of nine stones, cut so as to fit with close edges round the central stone, which is itself a perfect circle. Here the Emperor kneels and is encompassed, first by the circles of the terraces and surrounding walls, and then by the circle of the horizon. He thus seems to himself and his court to be in the centre of the universe," and so on, the same symbolism being carried on throughout the details of the altar.

The sacrifice at the time of the winter solstice takes place before daybreak ; three huge lanterns swing from high poles, casting their lurid light over the scene, while the air is filled with the smoke of burnt offerings, and the sound of music. For further details on this point, I refer my readers to the interesting account of the Temple of Heaven given by Mr. Edkins in the concluding chapters of Mr. Williamson's " Journeys in North China."

Vol. IV, Plate XVI

There are other altars devoted to the worship of Shanti, the Supreme Lord of Heaven and Earth. To one of these, which I visited in Foo-chow-foo, the local representatives of the Emperor annually repair to pray for rain. The altar in this instance conveys to my mind the most correct impression of what the Altar of Heaven really was in its most primitive form. Le Comte[1] tells us of a certain Emperor who offered sacrifice to God on the summit of a mountain; and here in Foochow we find a simple stone altar on the top of a hill in the city. This will explain the meaning of Nan-tan, or Southern Mount, the old Chinese name by which the southern altar of Peking is known. It is, indeed, nothing more than an artificial mound raised above the level plain upon which the city stands. A theory has been advanced that this altar may have been originally a burial mound, but I believe I am right in saying that there is no classical evidence to support the hypothesis. These old Chinese altars were in early times erected on mounds or mountains, just as Servius tells us the ancients set up altars intended for the celestial and superior divinities on substructures or mounds, and, as in the patriarchal times, altars were consecrated to God on mountain tops.

---

[1] "The Empire of China," page 322.

MANCHU SOLDIERS.

 HAVE already had a good deal to say in these pages about Chinese soldiers, and about the weapons which they use in modern times, but upon their military competitive examinations I have not yet touched. These examinations take place periodically in the chief cities of the Empire, and by their agency an incentive is held out to the soldier who, by his personal prowess and by his skill in the use of arms, may rise to the higher grades in the army. The Chinese, however, or rather the Manchus, notwithstanding the fact that the system which admits of promotion by prowess and skill is a good one, will have to remodel their military examinations, if they would maintain their ground against the nations that are growing up around them. The tests of bow and arrow and muscular power must become things of the past, and be replaced by tests of engineering knowledge, of the art of disciplining troops and marshalling them for the field of battle, and, indeed, of whatever we understand in Europe as the modern science of war. At present, in addition to exercise in the use of the old weapons, military candidates are required to write out a short treatise on Chinese military tactics.

Nos. 43 and 44 are fair types of the Manchu soldiers of the north of China. On September 18, 1871, I witnessed the review of an army of men such as these on the plain that stretches away northwards outside the An-ting gate of the Tartar city. Many of the troops assembled there were armed with bows and arrows, and many more with the old fuse matchlocks shown in No. 43, while in the belt a row of breech-loading cartridges was stored. The subject of No. 44 held military rank, and was also a dexterous marksman.

MONGOLS.

 HE Mongols here shown (No. 45) belong to the nomadic and pastoral races inhabiting the steppes of Mongolia. They visit Peking in great numbers during the winter months, and bring with them herds of cattle, quantities of frozen game, as well as the rich furs for which their country is famous. There is a Mongol market at the back of the British Legation, and there they congregate and pitch their tents. I found that this old lady's family had rented a Chinese dwelling, and, strange as it may seem, had stabled their mules in the dwelling-house proper, while they pitched their own tents in the courtyard outside. This is no uncommon practice with them, and shows how habit among these nomads has become a second nature. Dr. Williams gives us a correct description of the physical appearance of these Mongols. He says:—" The Mongol tribes generally are a stout, squat, swarthy, ill-favoured race of men, having high and broad shoulders, short broad noses, pointed and prominent chins, long teeth distant from each other, eyes black, elliptical, and unsteady, thick short necks extremely bony and nervous, muscular thighs, but short legs, with a stature nearly or quite equal to the European."

They seem now-a-days to have forgotten the art of war, and, indeed, to have changed their whole nature since the time of Genghis Khan.

COREANS.

COREA is one of the nations tributary to China, and although her king may be esteemed an independent sovereign, he yet sends an annual embassy of tribute-bearers to Peking. I happened to be in that capital in 1871 when that embassy arrived, and I was fortunate in obtaining a single picture (No. 46) of two of the officers. I was much struck with what I may term the European type of their countenances, and, judging from the ambassadors and their retainers whom I saw at the Corean quarter, the facial characteristics which I then remarked would seem to be common to their race. I was also favourably impressed with the spotless purity of their garments, which were almost entirely of white. The apartments in which they dwelt were also so scrupulously clean that one was reluctant to set down a dusty foot upon the white shining straw mats. The walls, too, were covered with paper tough in texture, and of the purest white. The gentlemen of the embassy seemed timid about holding intercourse with Europeans. On one occasion, I found an American ambassador there engaged in a discussion with the chief Corean minister. They could not understand each other's language, and for reasons of their own they had not employed a Chinese to interpret, so that the conversation was carried on in Chinese writing.

Judging from what we know of the pluck of the Coreans, the Japanese, if it be true that they are going to war with them, will have hot work before them. Chinese who have visited Corea describe the country and people in glowing terms. Its inhabitants are said to be skilful as tillers of the soil, as traders, and as workers in metal. The Corean swords are remarkable for their temper, and their guns and armour for dexterity in workmanship.

Williamson tells us that the Emperor of the Tang dynasty (A.D. 645) had hard fighting to expel the Coreans from the country east of Lian-ho district, which they had occupied for 260 years.

They still live in isolation, only holding fairs at fixed localities outside a definite barrier line, and they repel all attempts at closer trading relations even with their neighbours the Chinese. The soil of Corea is said to be productive, and her numerous mountain chains abound in mineral wealth.

YUEN-MING-YUEN.

THE imperial pleasure grounds lie about eight miles to the north-west of Peking, and Yuen-ming-Yuen is the name by which they are most commonly known, although belonging strictly to that part of them only which were walled in and kept sacred to the Emperor. Wan-show-shan is probably the hill which, with its surroundings, is the portion best known to foreigners. This summer retreat, with its palaces, lakes, and gardens, covers an area of twelve square miles, and was laid out by the Emperor Kunghi. It must, at one time, have been a most fascinating spot, and even as I saw it, in its ruins, and as the allied forces had laid it waste and left it, there was a charm about it all its own. The whole presents us with a Chinese landscape garden; white marble bridges span lakes bedecked with lotus flowers (see No. 47), where summer pavilions rise among the islets on every side. The hills, too, are crowned with temples and pagodas, and herds of deer and other sorts of game wander in the woods that shade many a ruined palace.

The marble bridge of the picture contains seventeen arches, and is the finest I have seen in China or, indeed, anywhere in the East; and I can picture to myself what the scene must have been when the lake was ablaze with the pink flowers of the lotus, and the air laden with their fragrance,

> " A perfume breathing round
> Like a pervading spirit ; "

while pleasure parties in their light canoes skimmed the surface of the lake, and lent the rich colours of their costumes to enliven the scene.

Father Ripa gives an interesting account of the Emperor's summer retreat as he saw it when he was attached to the court, about the beginning of the last century.

The hill descried in the distance is Wan-show-shan, and is surmounted by a temple built of white marble and porcelain. This temple, like the bridge, has been left almost uninjured, although two lions of white marble, and colossal in size, which stand at the base of the stone-work, have been destroyed by fire. There are many hills in this vast enclosure adorned with palatial retreats, and designed for the enjoyment of the Emperor and of the princes attached to his court. But the whole place remains as it was left by the allies. Nothing has been attempted in the way of restoration. Indeed, I suppose that the Chinese have had neither the spirit nor the funds to enter upon such an arduous undertaking, or that the place is left ruinous and desolate designedly as one means of keeping the hostility of the nation active, and as an ever-ready witness to the wanton barbarities to which foreigners will resort. Many of the educated Chinese have this feeling, and look upon our conduct as an act of heartless vandalism, and say that we might have brought pressure to bear upon their government in some way more worthy of our much vaunted civilization.

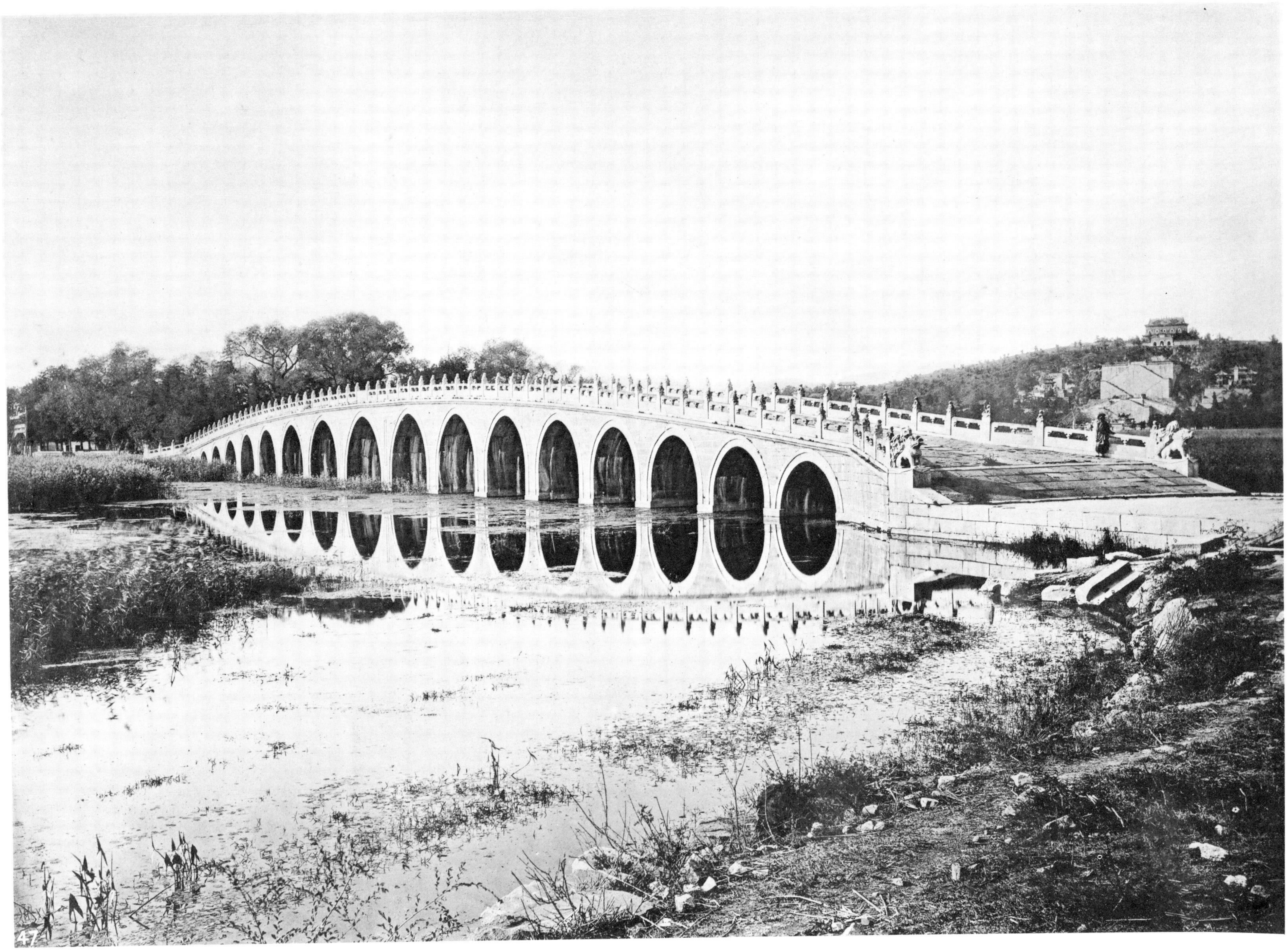

Vol. IV, Plate XVIII

BRONZE TEMPLE, WAN-SHOW-SHAN.

HIS picture, No. 48, presents to the reader one of the most interesting buildings in the grounds of the Imperial Summer Palace, standing at the foot of Wan-show-shan upon a basis of white marble, and constructed—doors, windows, pillars, roofs, and all—entirely of solid bronze. It is a very perfect example of Chinese temple architecture, showing, as it does, the most minute details of construction, and the skill with which the Chinese can work in metals, and adapt them to almost every use.

The picture is taken with the instrument facing the sun, or against the light, in order thus to obtain for the temple a bold and clear outline, and at the same time to give a soft, and unobtrusive pencilling to the objects of the distant landscape, and by this means heighten the pictorial effect.

During our visit to these Imperial pleasure grounds we put up at the monastery of the Sleeping Buddha, and I was so fortunate as to have for my companion one of the foreign residents, a gentleman well known in Peking, and a native member of the Chinese Civil Service, who was studying the photographic art. The imposing buildings of the monastery, the well-paved courtyards shaded with fine old trees, and adorned with an array of flowering plants in ornamental pots on porcelain stands, the rows of clean cloisters, the kindly disposed abbot and monks, these all contributed to make our visit agreeable as well as interesting. One of the priests told us that the establishment had not been very well supported for some years past. Indeed, the profitable occupation of this body of poor and devout-looking Buddhists all but departed when the Summer Palace was destroyed. They have lands, but not sufficient to support them. They also enjoy a small grant from the Imperial treasury, and they are occasionally called out to attend the marriage or burial ceremonies of members of the Imperial clan. But more marriages, and more funerals, and the more frequent visits of devotees to the shrine of the Sleeping Buddha were much needed to swell the revenues of the establishment. Theirs is a beautiful retreat, nestling in quiet seclusion beneath the brow of a richly wooded hill; and when I gazed upon it I felt as if I should have liked to try a few months of this perfectly retired life—an uneventful, dreamy existence, nourished on the fruits and vegetables of the earth, and almost an incarnation of the vegetable kingdom itself.

The surrounding hills were crowned with buildings of porcelain and marble; one of them, not far from the monastery, and buried in the recesses of a wood which covered the summit of a hill, must have been a princely edifice not many years ago. We reached its ruins along a path cut through a group of rocks wrapped in ivy and fern, and came at last upon a marble basin in one of the inner courts. This was still filled with clear cool water, and teemed with fish. Here, perhaps, the ladies of the establishment beguiled the hours in their dreary days of solitude. The adjoining apartments had once been lofty and imposing, but little of their former magnificence was now to be seen. Ivy had cast a mantle of green over the charred and battered walls, creeping in and out of the broken balustrades and wreathing many a marble ornament with its tender leaves.

48

Vol. IV, Plate XIX

STONE ANIMALS, MING TOMBS.

THE tombs of the Ming Emperors of China stand about thirty miles north of Peking, and in their general design resemble those of Nanking, which I have already described. They are, however, in their dimensions still more imposing than even the tomb of Hung-woo, the first sovereign of the dynasty.

In this valley of tombs, which is backed by a crescent-shaped range of hills, having a radius of from two to three miles, the mausolea of thirteen Ming sovereigns are to be found. The first interred there was Ching-tsoo (better known as Yung-lo), the third monarch of the dynasty, and who succeeded in driving his nephew from the throne.

I have chosen the illustrations for this subject from the tomb of Yung-lo partly on account of its historical interest and partly because it affords the finest example of these funereal monuments to be found in China. They are interesting besides because they show the durability of monumental and sacred architecture among the Chinese. There are in China no architectural remains which can boast of a very remote antiquity; the reason for this has never been clearly explained, some writers attributing it to political convulsions, and others to the constant use of materials less durable than stone. It seems strange therefore that they should have preserved their ancient classical books, written many of them on bamboo. In this perhaps we may see something of the practical common sense of the people. Their sages uttered imperishable truths and imparted wise councils, which have had an important influence in keeping the nation together; hence they perhaps set the less store upon useless stone edifices, which can do nothing except perpetuate an empty fame. Many of their sages and emperors esteeming no honour so great as to have their deeds handed down in living tradition through endless generations. The monument which has the greatest antiquity is the famous wall erected as a barrier against their nomadic foes.

The tomb of Yung-lo is approached first through an avenue of animals, sculptured out of white lime-stone, and then through a double row of stone warriors. The latter present much the same characteristics as those erected in front of the tomb of Yung-lo's father at Nanking, twenty-four years earlier; and art does not appear to have made much progress within that period of time. All the figures wear an expression of tranquil repose, thoroughly in keeping with their duty as the guardians of the dead. As to the animals there are two pairs of each kind, two of which are kneeling and two standing upright. Thus we first meet two pairs of lions; then two pairs of unicorns; these are followed by two pairs of camels, one of which is shown in the foreground. Two pairs of elephants succeed, and beyond these are two pairs of fabulous animals called "keaon," and still further on are the mail-clad warriors.

249

THE GREAT SACRIFICIAL HALL AT THE TOMB
OF THE EMPEROR YUNG-LO.

BEFORE the great Sacrificial Hall of Yung-lo is reached the visitor has to pass through an outer hall and a marble-paved court into the second or sacrificial quadrangle where imperial offerings are still made to the emperor of a former dynasty. The illustration here shewn (No. 50) was taken from the marble platform of the outer hall, and gives a front view of the Court and Hall of Sacrifice. This hall, in common with the majority of Chinese temples, faces the south; a rule which also obtains to a great extent among all the dwelling-houses in China, although many exceptions are to be met with in different parts of the country.

The Manchu emperors, though we thus find them sacrificing to the departed spirits of the Ming sovereigns, bestow but little attention upon the buildings at their tombs. Weeds grow in rank luxuriance over the marble pavements, on the steps, the balustrades, and the roofs. Notwithstanding all this, the substantial nature of the structure has defied the ravages of time.

The hall has a splendid interior, and the thirty-two teak pillars from Yunan, which support the lower roof, must have been kings of the forest. Each of these pillars is four feet span and thirty-two feet in height. The upper roof is again thirty-two feet above the lower one, and the hall measures seventy yards long by thirty broad. The sacrificial table, and the tablet of the Emperor Yung-lo, are similar to those of Confucius, shown in No. 34. The outer roof of this building is covered with yellow glazed tiles, and the eaves project ten feet outside the walls. Beyond the main edifice there is still another court, and to the north of that a well-built tunnel, thirty yards long, conducts through the burial mound to the doorway of the tomb; a second passage runs at right angles in the form of a T, and a flight of steps at the extremity of each arm leads to a terrace on the top of the tumulus. Arrived at the summit we find the tombstone inscribed with the posthumous title of Yung-lo— " The Tomb of Ching-tsoo-wen Whangti."

The trees in the courts and on the mound are cypress and oak.

50

ONE OF THE CITY GUARD, PEKING.

THE subject of this picture (No. 51) is an old Tartar bannerman, a humble member of the Manchu camp, who kept watch at the gate of the French hôtel by night; and although in the pay of the government, and allowed a salary sufficient for his own support, yet, by the time the amount reaches his hands through the official channel, it dwindles to about six shillings a month, and a regulation sheep-skin coat once a year. Old Wang, for I believe that was his name, was perhaps an unfortunate specimen of the soldiers of the standing army, the bold conquerors who once subjugated China. Wrapped in his sheep-skin coat, and in an underclothing of rags, he lay through the cold nights on the stone step of the outer gateway, and only roused himself at times to answer the call of his fellow-watchman near at hand. This call is supposed to be passed from watchman to watchman all round the city. Wang employed also a wooden clapper to let the inmates of the house know he was astir, and to scare away thieves. It is not uncommon, when a thief is discovered on the roof of a house in Peking, for the people within to open a door in the court below, and hold a good-natured parley with the intruder, telling him that it would be much more to his advantage if he were to go on to the next house. Often the ruffian will bid his friendly advisers a polite adieu, and, descending his bamboo ladder, will march off to have a trial in some other quarter. No. 52 is a picture of a literary agent, as we may call him. So great is the veneration of the Chinese for letters, that men such as our old friend here are employed to collect scraps of printed paper, which are afterwards burned before some shrine. This is, however, only one branch of the old man's business—he picks up rags and bones from the dust-heaps as well, and disposes of his miscellaneous collection to some dealer when the day's work is done. He can exist on very little, poor old fellow, and he has no expenses to speak of. He never removes his coat unless on a warm, sunny day, and then it is with an eye to business, for as he suns the garment, he coaxes out his tiny enemies and slays them.

Poor and miserable as he seems, he is not without a family and friends of his own, and his old age gains him respect.

THE PEKINGESE CAMEL.

AT certain seasons of the year, camels may be encountered in tens of thousands crossing the desert of Gobi, laden with brick tea, on their way to the Russian frontier. This brick tea, in the absence of metallic currency, forms the circulating medium in Mongolia, Siberia, and Thibet. When in the province of Peichihli I witnessed the departure of a train of 2,000 of these camels laden with brick tea to be sold in the Russian markets. These beasts are also employed in transporting coal, and other commodities, from one part of the province to another, and they are highly esteemed by the Mongols, as they can be easily managed, and can accomplish long journeys in arid regions with scant supplies of food and water. As many of my readers are aware, the camel is physically adapted for traversing the sandy plains of Asia, where they are found in the greatest numbers. The stomach is supplied with bladders which enable the animal to carry a store of fresh water, and in like manner the humps are furnished with a store of food in the shape of fatty matter which may be absorbed in case of need.

The Pekinese mule-litter is shown in No. 54. It is the usual conveyance adopted by the Chinese, if they wish for ease and comfort, when they visit localities outside the great wall. Two long shafts support the litter, and are harnessed at the ends to the backs of two mules. It was to this chair that I consigned myself on the occasion of my journey to the Great Wall. I had formed a high opinion of the sagacity and patience of Pekingese mules; but I was, if possible, still more favourably impressed with their docility after the experiences of the litter. The defile known as the Nankow Pass is extremely rugged, and the path runs sometimes over rough, precipitous, and dangerous hillsides, sometimes over jagged rocks and boulders; yet the mules planted their steps with care and precision, never stumbling, and only slightly incommoding the occupant of the litter. The shafts of this mule sedan, as may be observed on a close inspection, are long enough to act as springs, so as to do away with the hard jolting, which is a leading characteristic of the Peking cart.

THE NANKOW PASS.

WE enter the Nankow Pass at about thirty miles distance from Peking. This pass is a bold, rocky defile, separating China proper from the lands of the barbarians beyond. I visited the place, and the Great Wall also, in the company of Mr. Wylie, a gentleman who, some years ago, brought to light the remarkable Buddhist inscription found in the arch at Kew-Yung-Kwan. There is a small hamlet at the Chinese end of the pass. It is here that we see the first spur of the Great Wall, or rather an inner wall or fortress which, in ancient times, would form the final barrier to the invading hordes. When we enter the defile, we are struck with its rugged and picturesque appearance, and with the absence of any road save the little that remains of the old Mongol causeway, which must have been a splendid work in its time. But its time has long past, and the ordinary trade route now-a-days lies along what looks like the bed of a stream, and over boulders into which steps have either been cut or worn. There are, however, some few parts of the ancient road which are still in comparatively good order. Here we find blocks of porphyry, marble of various colours, and granite polished with the traffic of generations long gone by. As we penetrate the pass, limestone rocks crop out on every side; but it is not till we are within four miles of the Great Wall that we come upon the scene presented to the reader in No. 55. At this point the pass narrows down considerably, and makes a sharp bend. On a rocky peak to the left rises a picturesque little edifice, dedicated to Kwei-Sing, the god of literature; on the opposite side of the ravine is a small two-storied temple, approached by a steep staircase cut into the face of the rock. The lower story is consecrated to Kwan-te, the god of war, and the upper one is called the cave of Kwan-yin, the goddess of mercy. Inscriptions in Chinese, Thibetan, and Sanscrit characters are cut on the surface of the rock below.

One would imagine that the defile was all but impassable in some places which I have not pictured. Vain delusion! There is a constant traffic at the very worst parts. We look at them, and nothing whatever is to be seen save huge angular rocks jutting out of cairns, and patches of sand. We look again, and in a moment the scene is alive with donkey-men and muleteers who, leaping from rock to rock as they guide their sure-footed beasts through clefts and out of pit-falls, disappear at last among the stones; and so the traffic goes on from year to year, and no attempt is made to improve the route, or to help the weary trader on his journey.

ANCIENT BUDDHIST ARCH AT KEW-YUNG-KWAN,

NANKOW PASS.

 DOUBLE line of wall rises from the village of Kew-yung-kwan, and, running up the mountain side, unites with another wall that sweeps across the crest of the hill. This point is considered one of the most important in the Nankow Pass, and it is the spot where, it is said, Genghis Khan was successfully routed in his attempt to enter the north of China. There is at this village a very remarkable marble arch (see No. 56), erected apparently during the Yuen dynasty, and said to have originally carried a pagoda on its top. This pagoda was taken down shortly after the Ming Emperors got possession of the throne, and this was done to propitiate the Mongols, who were deterred by superstitious fears from passing beneath the shrine. The arch is remarkable on account of its octagonal form, and also for the strange figures from the Indian mythologies with which its surface is adorned. These ornaments very closely resemble many of the sculptures found on the ruined temples of Cambodia. I was at once struck with the similarity when I first saw the arch, and having since compared its entablatures with the photographs which I took in Cambodia in 1866, I find my original impressions confirmed.

It will be observed that the key-stone carries a mythological figure flanked with two others wearing crowns of a seven-headed snake, while the bodies of the snake flow into the ornamentation on either side. The date of the erection of this arch would be about 1345 A.D., at any rate, that is the date of an old inscription on its inner surface. Mr. Williamson mentions a fine arch and marble bridge near Kal-gan, ornamented with marble figures of monkeys, elephants, &c. These structures may prove to belong to the same period, and may point to some connection with Cambodia beyond what we can trace in the style of their ornaments. I have obtained further evidence regarding the knowledge possessed by the Chinese of the ancient Cambodians which throws light on the greatest period of their history, or more probably on the epoch when they had ceased to conquer, and were showing unmistakable marks of decline by raising great stone monuments to perpetuate their memory. But as this subject is somewhat foreign to my present work, I cannot introduce it here.

The interior of the arch is also elaborately sculptured, and two of the kings of the Devas in Buddhist mythology are to be seen on both its inner sides. As to the upper surfaces, these are covered with a great multitude of small images of Buddha carved in bas-relief. Between the two Deva kings is a Buddhist inscription in Sanscrit, with translations into the characters of five other languages, i.e. Thibetan, Mongol, Ouigour, Neu-chih, and Chinese. For a full notice of this inscription see Wylie's Translation, "Journal of the Royal Asiatic Society," vol. v. Part 1, pp. 14 seq.

THE GREAT WALL OF CHINA.

M Y readers doubtless share with me in feeling that no illustrated work on China would be worthy of its name if it did not contain a picture of some portion of the Great Wall. This wall is an object neither picturesque nor striking. Viewing it simply as a wall, we find its masonry often defective, and it is not so solid or honestly constructed as one at first sight would imagine. It is only in the best parts that it has been faced with stone, or rather, that it consists of two retaining walls of stone, and a mound of earth within. In other places it is faced with brick, and there are again some other parts, of the highest antiquity, as is supposed, where we find it to consist of an earthen mound alone. Not a few travellers regard this wall as the greatest monument of misdirected human labour to be met with in the whole world, and those who have no sympathy with the modern

56

57

Vol. IV, Plate XXIV

scientific theories regarding the great pyramids, would make these no exception to this view. But I think that the Chinese can claim something more for their wall than the Egyptians can for their pyramids. The wall was built to save the country from the raids of the nomadic northern hordes, and this object it actually attained, more especially when the country was under a stable government. Thus Genghis Khan himself was repulsed before the inner wall. The erection of the Great Wall, which has a length of 1,500 miles, was the last great work of the Emperor Tsin-she-hwang, B.C. 213. This monarch has been called the Napoleon of China, and he is said to have carried out other famous and probably more useful enterprises during his reign, erecting public buildings, cutting canals, and making roads, undertakings of a kind much needed in China at the present day. He too it is who has the memorable fame of having attempted to destroy all the ancient records of the Empire.

The Great Wall seems to me to express a national characteristic of the Chinese race. All along that people loved to dwell in their own land in seclusion, pursuing the industries and the arts of peace, and to them China has ever been the central flowery land. Within it everything worth having is concentrated, and outside of it, on narrow and unproductive soils, dwell scattered tribes of barbarians ever bent on predatory excursions into the paradise of the Celestial Empire. These outer barbarians, among which we ourselves are still secretly included, have always been an endless source of trouble, now beyond the wall on the north, now along the coast on the south and east, and at other times in the mountain regions to the west.

This view was taken from the north of the inner wall, at a place called Pata-ling. The inner wall stretches across the northern end of the Nankow Pass, and climbs in many places almost inaccessible steeps. It has been repaired at different periods, and was built originally about A.D. 542, when the Emperor Woo-ting of the Wei dynasty was on the throne. It is about 500 miles in length, and at its extremities joins on to the older outer wall. The granite and limestone with which it is faced abound in the rocks of the Pass. It is furnished with square watch-towers, at short distances apart, in the passes, and at longer distances in less accessible regions. In the background of the view (No. 56) we see one of the many inner spurs of this wall sweeping across the Pass. When emerging from the gateway seen on the right, one cannot fail to be impressed with the massiveness and apparent strength of the structure.

The height of the wall is over thirty feet, and it is about fourteen feet broad on the top.

To venture upon any further description of this ancient barrier would only be to repeat an oft-told story with which my reader is, perhaps, already well acquainted. I will conclude, therefore, by expressing the hope that the work will convey a faithful impression of the places over which my journeys extended, and of the people as I found them, so that my five years' labour may not have been in vain.